RESTRICTED ACCESS

Restricted Access

Media, Disability, and the
Politics of Participation

Elizabeth Ellcessor

NEW YORK UNIVERSITY PRESS

New York and London

NEW YORK UNIVERSITY PRESS
New York and London
www.nyupress.org

References to Internet websites (URLs) were accurate at the time of writing. Neither the author nor New York University Press is responsible for URLs that may have expired or changed since the manuscript was prepared.

ISBN: 978-1-4798-1380-3 (hardback)
ISBN: 978-1-4798-5343-4 (paperback)

For Library of Congress Cataloging-in-Publication data, please contact the Library of Congress.

New York University Press books are printed on acid-free paper, and their binding materials are chosen for strength and durability. We strive to use environmentally responsible suppliers and materials to the greatest extent possible in publishing our books.

Manufactured in the United States of America

10 9 8 7 6 5 4 3 2 1

Also available as an ebook

CONTENTS

ACKNOWLEDGMENTS

If access is a variable relationship between numerous material, social, and cultural factors, it is no surprise that a book about access would arise from particular relationships, circumstances, and confluences. Three such junctions are particularly rich for the development of this work.

First, I am indebted to many individuals who shaped and supported my Ph.D. research at the University of Wisconsin–Madison. Oddly, I remember the very moment that this project came to be, while discussing Lev Manovich's software studies classic, *The Language of New Media*, in a graduate seminar. In the distinctions between "form" and "content," I recognized the practices of accessible web development— taught to me in a professional context by Courtney O'Callaghan at the Feminist Majority Foundation/*Ms.* Magazine—and proceeded to investigate these elements theoretically, historically, and through the lens of disability. Mary Beltrán, Michael Curtin, Julie D'Acci, Greg Downey, Michele Hilmes, and Lisa Nakamura were each important influences and supporters. Ellen Samuels introduced me to the field of disability studies, which transformed my scholarship in ways for which I could not have prepared. My fellow graduate students also read, heard, questioned, and pushed this work; I am especially grateful to Megan Sapnar Ankerson, Germaine Halegoua, Lindsay Hogan, Derek Johnson, Danny Kimball, and Erin Copple Smith. Finally, above all, I benefited from the insightful comments and unfailing support of Jonathan Gray.

In the conduct of this research, I have found support and enjoyed collaboration with a range of individuals and organizations without whom this project could not have been completed. I am forever grateful to those bloggers, accessibility professionals, government officials, developers, and individuals with disabilities who participated in interviews and ongoing conversations about the nature of digital media and disability. Their expertise, experiences, and perspectives permeate this text. Archival and interview research for this book was supported by a grant from the National Science Foundation, which enabled a 2012 trip to Washington, D.C., for the conduct of interviews and research at the Library of Congress. Indiana University supported travel to the 2013 California State University–Northridge Technologies and People with Disabilities Conference, where I conducted many interviews and made many observations. A portion of these interviews were transcribed by Blake Hallinan and Julia Rizzo, who served as valuable sounding boards in making sense of such material. NYU Press series editors Karen Tongson and Henry Jenkins, and especially Alicia Nadkarni, have been tirelessly supportive of this project. The comments of NYU's anonymous reviewers improved this work immeasurably, and I am grateful for the reviewers' intellectual rigor, excitement, and generosity. Others who have read and commented upon portions of this work include Alison Kafer, Gerard Goggin, and many conference committees, panelists, and audiences in fields ranging from internet to gender studies.

A third confluence comes in the relationships with colleagues at Indiana University and beyond, which have sustained me in this research, this career, and this life. Barb Klinger, Stephanie DeBoer, and Ryan Powell have been expert guides, thoughtful readers, and good friends. The student-led Disability Studies Reading Group fostered many useful readings and conversations, and I am particularly grateful to Sami Schalk for bringing me into this community. All of the graduate students in my 2014 Digital Media Access seminar have earned a thanks in these pages; teaching this material, and seeing it through their eyes, pushed me into new, difficult, and fruitful directions. I am also endlessly grateful for the mentorship and friendship offered by Meryl Alper, Katie Ellis, Gerard Goggin, Bill Kirkpatrick, Mara Mills, and Jonathan Sterne as we develop a disability media studies.

The trajectory that marks this book has also left deep marks upon my life. In graduate school, I met my partner, Sean Duncan. Then, as now, he offered a keen eye, a curious mind, and a boisterous enthusiasm. I can imagine no better reader, no better friend, and no better supporter in my work as well as in all of the travails that make life challenging and rewarding. After our move to Indiana, our son, Hugo, was born. Though he cannot yet read, he is nonetheless a part of these pages—many of which were written in anticipation of his arrival, during his naps, and while he was playing with one of several amazing young women who cared for him in his first two years. Thus, it is to Sean and Hugo—and the life we are building together—that I dedicate these pages.

Introduction

Interrogating and Integrating Access

In January 2011, comedy duo Rhett and Link (Rhett James McLaughlin and Charles Lincoln "Link" Neal) released a YouTube video entitled "CAPTION FAIL: Lady Gaga Putt-Putt Rally." To produce this video, the duo wrote and performed a short sketch in which one told the other, over the telephone, about his plans for an upcoming Lady Gaga concert. They then uploaded the video to YouTube and, using YouTube's autocaption feature, downloaded the captions generated for the video. Using those captions as a new verbal script, Rhett and Link performed the sketch again, retaining the original blocking and emotional performances. They repeated this process a second time, performing a third version of the sketch based on captions of the captioned sketch. Finally, all three performances were played back to back, with the words being performed at any given time displayed at the bottom of the screen. The eponymous line—"I got tickets to the Lady Gaga putt-putt tournament and monster rally" (already a tongue twister!)—became "Advantages to the Lady Gaga puppet tenemos a drug right," which in turn transformed into "Advantages of the Lady Gaga puppets in a lot of Iraq."[1] The video functioned comedically both through the increasing surrealism of the scripts and through the unexpected meanings and juxtapositions created by the technological process.

Since the release of "Lady Gaga Putt-Putt Rally," which now has had more than 2.5 million views, the duo has released six additional "CAPTION FAIL" videos, in addition to producing numerous other videos, advertisements, and a television show for cable channel IFC. McLaughlin and Neal could easily be considered an example of the possibilities of online participatory cultures, which offer "low barriers to creative expression and civic engagement, strong support for creating and sharing one's creations, and some type of informal mentorship."[2] Viral videos, and the YouTube community, are commonly invoked examples of participatory culture, and McLaughlin and Neal's work fits into the zeitgeist of online sketch comedy.[3]

However, to look at this series and see only a case study in the potentials of online participatory culture is to overlook the very specific technological context for these videos. In the opening moments of the first "CAPTION FAIL" video, Rhett and Link briefly explained YouTube's autocaption feature, stating, "The whole process is automated. The computer listens to the video, and displays what it thinks it hears. So, the results are always off, and usually pretty hilarious."[4] They compared the video to playing a game of "Telephone" with the software, in which misunderstandings that came from this speech-to-text technology were captured and displayed. Speech-to-text technology has long been highly desirable in assistive technology for d/Deaf[5] and hard-of-hearing audiences, as the ability to automatically create captions in real time offers the possibility of greatly increasing access to a range of audiovisual materials. However, it is also an incredibly difficult software to develop, with even leading technologies such as Apple's personal assistant (Siri) and the dictation software Dragon Naturally Speaking regularly misunderstanding content.

These videos skewer autocaptioning and speak to the ways in which digital media technologies have not solved problems of access and inclusion for people with disabilities and may even have exacerbated them. YouTube's autocaptions could increase the quantity of captioned content on the site, offer more resources for d/Deaf and hearing-impaired viewers, and increase the potential for automatic translation of videos into other languages. In a 2009 press release, "Innovation in Accessibility," YouTube claimed to be "making video accessible everywhere (web, mobile, TV) and to everyone (other countries, languages, alternative access modes)."[6] Google's explanation of autocaptioning acknowledges that captions would be imperfect but asserted that they were "better than nothing."[7] From the point of view of viewers with auditory disabilities, however, as clearly demonstrated in the "CAPTION FAIL" videos, autocaptions may, in fact, have been worse than nothing.

The humor and technological failures of this video reveal how digital media cultures take for granted an able-bodied user position, potentially restricting access for users with a variety of disabilities. In the absence of captions, d/Deaf and hard-of-hearing viewers are limited in their ability to find and view audiovisual content. In the absence of audio-description, in which video images are described aurally, blind and visually impaired users are prevented from accessing the content of audiovisual material. In more mundane contexts, the lack of proper HTML attributes can render web forms impossible to use by people who rely upon screenreaders, input devices other than a point-and-click mouse, or other assistive technologies. This can interfere in all kinds of life activities, from online shopping to social networking.

In each of the cases described, one might say that technology not only fails to "fix" disability but in fact creates it, as these technological barriers function to exclude certain bodies from full participation. Not only do those who are easily identified as having a disability due to a specific medical condition or embodied state suffer from disabling technology, but so may technology create new disabilities. Feminist disability scholar Susan Wendell eloquently explains that the inability to walk several miles at a stretch is not considered a disabling impairment in much of Western society, whereas it could be seen as such in a different cultural context in which walking to and from, say, a distant well is an expected part of daily life.[8] Similarly, digital media create new interfaces, actions, and expectations for human bodies and may create disability both through the pressures exerted on bodies (fatness, carpal tunnel, eye strain)[9] and through the social pressures that increasingly construct the functional life to be the technologically competent life, rendering those who do not master these technologies effectively disabled in ways that would have been inconceivable thirty years ago. Perhaps as a result of these and similar exclusions, people with disabilities are less likely to be internet users than the U.S. population at large; as of 2010, only 54 percent of Americans with disabilities used the internet, as compared with 81 percent of able-bodied Americans.[10]

Such production of disability through cultural contexts and material conditions is illustrative of the social model of disability. Arising from activist contexts and forming a foundation of disability studies, the social model of disability argues that physical impairments are not the cause of disability, but a society that cannot accommodate physical difference produces disability as an experience of oppression. Unlike earlier understandings of disability as an individually embodied tragedy (the individual model), as a diagnosable physical condition (the medical model), or as a site of collective pity (the charity model), the social model asserts that "it is society which disables physically impaired people" and positions people with disabilities as an oppressed class.[11] Media technologies—like other material, institutional, and structural phenomena—can thus produce barriers that render forms of embodiment disabling and contribute to ideologies of ability that devalue deviations from a normative form of embodiment and subjectivity.

This book builds upon existing work on disability and online media by engaging with both critical disability studies and contemporary cultural studies of media not simply to produce new theoretical applications but to suggest ways in which these fields might fundamentally inform one another. It is no longer enough to discuss how media or technology are disabling, following the social model; it is time to delve into the ways in which the intersection of technologies, bodies, and cultures may both reproduce and trouble existing cultural norms and relations of power. Though disability is an understudied phenomenon within all sites of media studies, I do not adopt a disability studies framework merely to add another identity-based lens through which to approach the study of media. Instead, I argue that at the intersection of disability and cultural studies we can find new questions. Centering disability in the study of media ought to upend conventional wisdom, challenge traditional categories, and introduce previously invisible considerations. Through the endless diversity of disability, we may be forced to consider the endless variation of humanity at large; once we have done so, discussing "the audience," "the meaning," or even "the production" of media content or technological tools becomes unthinkable. Disability upends universalism, requiring new, robust means of studying a mediated world in which media's access, use, and meaning occur in diverse contexts and infinite variations.

Upending lingering universalism within studies of media is especially necessary at the current moment, characterized by the blurring of audience and producer, professional and amateur, gift and profit, freedom and control, individual and collective, online and off. Much current scholarship in media and cultural studies wrestles with what has been called participatory culture; in these online spaces, communities can form, creative work can be shared, individuals can oscillate between creating and consuming content, and media industries can engage with (or take advantage of) the increased interaction among audiences. Participatory culture offers an attractive vision of a mediated future in which increased access to cultural production, political participation, and social collaboration produces more just, egalitarian forms of culture.

The exclusion of people with disabilities from online media and attendant participatory cultures is particularly troubling given the potential of these spaces to foster engaged, active citizens of the world. Much has been written about the democratic potential of online cultures, whether as potential public spheres or civic cultures or through other relationships of public, private, state, and corporate interests. However, as the physical world has amply demonstrated, a public sphere founded upon exclusions is capable of gross oppressions.[12] This is why it is imperative to consider the place of access and inclusion in emergent media cultures, particularly those in which scholars celebrate the benefits of production, "produsage," collaboration, spreadability, interactivity, or the social.[13] These celebrations too often take access for granted, and thus cases in which access is absent reveal the fissures in new media theories. After all, if a so-called participatory culture only facilitates the participation of those who are already privileged, then its progressive potential is unrealized, if not transformed into a regressive affirmation of existing power structures.

Studying digital and participatory media in very specific contexts, such as that of disability in the United States, is crucial to ensuring that these media do not simply reproduce dominant ideologies, identities, and neoliberal economic and political structures. Such specific scholarship, whether demarcated by age, nation, sexuality, ability, use, or other markers, is necessary to the continued utility of theories of media participation because it destabilizes the unitary user, prevents flat or hierarchical conceptions of uses, and engages with the technological and industrial components of digital media sites, services, and devices. If "participatory culture is being co-created every day, by vloggers, marketers, artists, audiences, lawyers, designers, critics, educators," and others,[14] then the barriers to technological and cultural access, including barriers of disability, must be addressed so that such co-creation does not occur without the input—or against the interests—of less powerful populations. Particularly in relation to the political dimension of participation, participation's value, in relation to its political dimensions, lies in the ability of individuals to access and achieve desired goals and act in ways that may be publicly visible and thus influential.[15] This book shares in these attempts to preserve the progressive public values of participation and to consider participation's relationship to economic and political structures under neoliberalism through the study of specific contexts, users, and uses.

This book tells stories about digital media use by people with disabilities and contextualizes them with analyses of the surrounding technologies, policies, and cultures of digital media accessibility. I suggest that by reconsidering digital media and participatory cultures from the standpoint of disability, we may better see the omissions and exclusions in these often-celebrated spaces and their theorizations and come to understand access as fundamental to all studies of media. Throughout, my argument is threefold: First, access must be understood not in terms of availability, affordability, or choice but in terms of an individual's ability to engage meaningfully with a medium/technology and its content; second, a hegemonic user position is created by digital media technologies and their usages, and this user position is not neutral but perpetuates an able-bodied norm and contributes to inequalities of access; and third, studying access in the context of disability and digital media reveals the importance of an intersectional analysis of access for recognizing the neoliberal imperatives in contemporary social, economic, and political life and for opposing them through variable, coalitional politics and collaborative projects.

Thinking through Access

Colloquially, *access* is used to talk about a wide range of experiences. We may access our email, gain access to restricted areas or information, or win an all-access backstage pass. *Accessibility*, similarly, is regularly employed to refer to the *ease* of access, the user-friendliness of a system, or financial affordability. It is not uncommon to hear references to the increased accessibility of the internet, of digital media production tools, or of educational resources in popular reporting, news, informal discussions, and even academic work that intends to indicate an expanded availability of a particular valued resource. Such usage of *accessibility* permeates contemporary culture with little, if any, connection to disability. The very discursive flexibility of *access* has too often allowed it to pass unexamined, conferring cultural value even as it may constrain civic, cultural, and technological possibilities.

One unifying feature of all of the uses of *access* is that they convey a positive outcome—*access* is routinely understood as an individual benefit or a public good. A second commonality lies in the tendency to talk about access or accessibility as something that can be possessed or "had." These assumptions must be challenged in order to build a robust theorization of access, as they threaten to constrain analyses through their positivist slants. Thinking critically about access requires consideration of it as a relational, unstable phenomenon that both grants benefits and interpellates individuals into larger social systems that may be empowering, exploitative, or both.

The benefits of access to computer and other forms of digital media have routinely been tied to social equality, political participation, and economic gain. Nico Carpentier posits that access is a necessary precursor to participation in media and, from there, in democratic civic structures.[16] Access to participation in mediated culture can support the public values of equality, democracy, or cultural competency.[17] Regarding disability in particular, access is a kind of public good, tied to the formation of a "newly imagined and newly configured public sphere where full participation is not contingent on an able body."[18] *Access* can thus serve as a means by which to discuss and promote democratic civic engagement and cultural inclusion, an ideological use that recurs in many debates surrounding media policies, disability rights movements and associated policies, and media and disability studies themselves.

The political potential of participatory culture demonstrates both the appeal and the dangers of this theoretical framework. It offers an attractive vision of a near future, or even present, in which increased access to cultural production, political participation, and social collaboration produces more just, egalitarian forms of culture as well as new forms of political engagement. This is a world in which, theoretically, anyone can potentially be heard, transform the status quo, and build upon the work of others outside of longstanding social and political hierarchies. In short, participatory culture can be tied to the development of progressive civic cultures and forms of engagement, in which case it demands theoretical expansion beyond the limited figure of the "user."

However, this understanding of participation requires deeper consideration. As Carpentier argues, we cannot assume that increased participation is always beneficial, as this assumption ignores the ways in which media participation is linked to democracy. This de-articulation is at the core of critiques of participatory culture theory, which often indict its acceptance or encouragement of global capitalism, its conflation of different participatory spaces and practices, and its limited global and demographic applicability in the context of glaring digital divides between and within national contexts.

Participation can also prioritize neoliberalism, markets, individualism, and consumerism over the kinds of public values or civic dispositions discussed above, in which case it demands grounded study of the specific contexts, technologies, and uses in question to prevent overgeneralization. Rather than refer to equality, it can be invoked in media policy contexts in order to justify expanding consumer frameworks and serving the interests of commercial media conglomerates. There is a tendency for access to reinforce individualism and consumerism within a marketplace of optional services, counteracting competing values of "equality, democracy and citizenship."[19] In their place, people are called upon to act as "consumer-citizens"[20] and "expected to think of themselves as consumers of 'products'" and to interact within a marketplace of such products and services.[21]

Given the dual connotations of *access* described above, the study of mediated culture must attend to what is being accessed, and for what purposes, prompting ongoing critique of the political dimensions of access and its instantiation via cultural discourses. To preserve the value of *access* for progressive political purposes, it is not enough to conceive of it in terms of availability, affordability, and choice. These concepts, though they can support public values and civic cultures, slide too easily into their neoliberal counterparts—passivity, marketplaces, and consumerism. In the combination of these discursive elements, the discourse of "media access" appears as a synecdoche for the functions and ideologies of media in a capitalist democracy; it is closely tied to both public values of equality and participation, as well as to neoliberal and consumer-driven forms of identity and business. To move beyond the deceptive positivism of access requires attention to uses, and the conception of access as a phenomenon-in-progress rather than as an end state.

Thinking through Use

The ability to participate culturally and civically depends not only on the availability, affordability, or choices provided but also on the fundamental ability to meaningfully *use* a given medium or technology. As communication and information scholar Leah Lievrouw has argued, "[A]ccess depends on people's individual capacities to convert availability" into something usable.[22] Without the capacity to make a telephone call, surf via a web browser, or remote-control a television, there is little opportunity to glean meaning from content, to interpret and engage with that content, or to respond to it or produce new content. Yet, access as use has been routinely overlooked in discussions of media access and telecommunications policy, despite its necessity to the furtherance of public values in this arena. The study of disability, conversely, forces consideration of access at the level of use; though radio, for instance, offered information to "shut-ins," those who could not see or manipulate the dials continued to lack meaningful access to the full range of content and the full experience of the medium because they were materially excluded from some of its uses.[23]

Access must encompass use, and it must also be conceived of not as an object or state of being but as what disability scholar Jay Dolmage refers to as a "way to move" in the world.[24] It is not an end goal but is a process of fits and starts, accommodations and innovations, learned skills and puzzling interfaces. As Margaret Price indicates in *Mad at School*, an exploration of mental disability and academia, access as a way to move does not require a set of specific practices or a linear progression but entails the creation of multiple paths along which people may move toward access.[25] Access, here, becomes a resource that is drawn upon not only by people with disabilities but by all participants; the conditions of access allow for certain possibilities, and these scholars call for expanding the range of possibilities. Canadian gender and disability scholar Tanya Titchkosky expresses this eloquently in her book *The Question of Access*. She writes that "anything said about access can be read for how it reflects a host of questions: Who has access? Access to where? Access to what? When? Every single instance of life can be regarded as tied to access—that is, to do anything is to have some form of access."[26] Similarly, Titchkosky observes that only people with disabilities are regularly discussed in regard to access needs; people presumed not to be disabled are presumed not to have needs regarding access. By figuring access as a relational analytic, potentially relevant to all people, Titchkosky opens the door to more nuanced study of access and its value, as well as to the use of dis/ability not only as a topic of study but as a lens through which to study a variety of cultural artifacts and practices. This perspective is echoed in what disability scholar Alison Kafer conceives of as a "political/relational model of disability" in which disability is produced through the relationships of bodies, minds, and social and physical environments;[27] access is produced and made meaningful through similar interactions.

These arrangements are inherently unstable, and the naturalization and universalizing of access as commonly done in studies of media, digital culture, and software interfaces renders ability invisible and pathologizes disability as an individual failing that requires accommodation to rectify. Throughout this book, I argue that access is not a matter of disability but is a means through which ability and disability are made meaningful and influence opportunities for broader participation in culture and civic structures.

Access is not a single thing; it is produced in the intersections, and articulations, of diverse realms of study. Industries and manufacturers, identity groups and content producers, individuals and public institutions may all be involved in the production of access at a particular time, place, and social location. Access is irreducible, but it may be studied at a macro level through the search for articulations between the meanings, processes, and practices that characterize access to a given goal or experience. As explicated by British cultural studies luminary Stuart Hall, an articulation is "the form of the connection that can make a unity of different elements, under certain conditions. It is the linkage which is not necessary, determined or absolute and essential for all time."[28] Thus, the study of access benefits from a cultural studies perspective in which connections are crucial, but mutable, and political consequences are felt as a result of a range of social practices regardless of their alleged intention.

In the articulations that constitute access (or the lack thereof), we can see possibilities for and limitations on potential participation in cultural and civic communities. Exclusions from participation ought to be understood as politically problematic, exercises of power in which the arrangement of culture, bodies, and technologies closes doors rather than opens them. If, as I argued earlier in this Introduction, the progressive value of access lies in its connections to participation, democracy, and equality, then deeper understandings of how access may work and how it may be fostered are crucial to the ongoing study of media.

Digital Media Accessibility: A Cultural and Disability Studies Approach

The adoption of a relational, use-based understanding of access enables the study of previously opaque areas of mediated culture. Accessibility is not a typical area of investigation for scholars of film, television, digital media, or even media industry or policy. It is, quite literally, a mediation between means of access and interacting with media forms and content. As such, this book is particularly indebted to the theoretical and methodological ecumenicalism of cultural studies, which has enabled me to identify a particular juncture at which issues of disability, identity, access, cultural and political participation, and neoliberal modes of being coalesce in digital media texts, artifacts, and practices.

Construction of this area of inquiry is based upon two ideas: disability and accessibility. For the purposes of this book, *disability* is understood to be any physical or mental condition that makes it difficult, if not impossible, to utilize default social, institutional, or physical structures without some form of accommodation. This definition makes it possible to discuss disability as an analytic category; when discussing disability as identity, I rely upon individuals' self-identifications, as the claiming of disability identity is a personal and political decision. Throughout, I primarily employ "people first" language, generally preferred in the United States, referring to "people with disabilities" and other permutations of phrasing that prioritize personhood before ability status.[29] I have also consciously adopted a pan-disability perspective because of its prominence in disability studies and its utility in liberal identity politics, and because it tends to be how accessibility policies are written.[30] *Accessibility* in this text refers to the ability of a person with one or more disabilities to make meaningful use of a media technology, whether through assistive technologies or through modification of mainstream technologies. The accessibility of a given digital media platform or text relies upon its code, and in turn upon professional and amateur developers, the offerings of popular hardware, websites and software packages, and the policies that govern digital media accessibility. Thus, it is impossible to locate accessibility in the context of a single industry. Similarly, *accessibility* cannot be simply defined for all users; different impairments, different technological contexts, and even different times of day may result in users'—or even a single user's—having very different experiences of accessibility. As I was told many times in conducting this research, one cannot declare that a technology "is accessible." Instead, one might say that a technology "is accessible" to some degree, for some people, in particular circumstances. The irreducibility of accessibility at both the sites of production and reception, industry and audience makes for some tricky linguistic turns throughout this text. However, this is also precisely the site of the theoretical richness of accessibility, in that this concept refuses to be flattened, unified, or separated from the intensity of human variation that gives it purpose.

Disability and accessibility come together in this project through experiences of digital media accessibility, and particularly through the origins, development, and influence of web content accessibility.[31] Web content accessibility entails the provision of accessible online content, originally through use of HTML and CSS,[32] though now this concept extends to scripting languages and dynamic web content. The Web Content Accessibility Guidelines 1.0 (WCAG 1.0) were released by the World Wide Web Consortium (W3C) in 1999. The W3C is a nonprofit organization dedicated to the creation and promotion of web standards; it acts as a kind of governing body or locus of best practice for web-based technologies. As such, it does not release "policies" or "standards" but "guidelines" that are entirely voluntary. The second major governor of web accessibility in the United States is Section 508 of the Rehabilitation Act of 1973 (as amended in 1998), and its attendant documentation. Often called simply "508," this law requires that federal government agencies and their contractors, as well as organizations that receive federal funding (including, for example, universities) make their web content and other information technology accessible to employees and members of the public with disabilities. The binding standards for 508 compliance were released in 2001 and are largely based on those of WCAG 1.0. Finally, I look to WCAG 2.0, an updated set of guidelines released by the W3C in 2008, with a new focus on technological interoperability beyond HTML, which has led it to be adopted in many contexts that move beyond the World Wide Web. As of 2015, the Section 508 standards are undergoing a substantial "refresh" by the United States Access Board, which will bring them into alignment with WCAG 2.0 and other relevant international accessibility rules.

Though technological details and affordances are important to this work and are referenced throughout, this is not a story of technological artifacts. Rather, I focus on the ways in which digital media accessibility for people with disabilities has been constructed, often in opposition to mainstream digital media technologies and practices, and has been a site of negotiation, innovation, and resistance over the past twenty years. Although many people with disabilities use mainstream technologies, and many people use accessible features without thinking of them as such, the divergences in the meanings of disability, participation, and media reflect and establish differences in value, access, and opportunity. Following French poststructuralist Michel Foucault's description of discourse as "a practice we impose upon" things and events,[33] the discursive evolution of accessibility reveals the ways in which bodies, media, technologies, and identities have been positioned in relation to one another and naturalized according to particular hierarchies. In exploring the meanings attached to *disability* and *digital media accessibility*, I attend to points of disjuncture, disagreement, and negotiation in the construction of digital media accessibility.

In order to trace these discursive threads, multiple forms of evidence were required, drawn from archival, popular, interview, and ethnographic research. The archival work done for this project involved the study of U.S. legal documents, archived documentation of academic and nonprofit institutions, and trade publications from within the digital media industries. The archives of the W3C are publicly available online, as are a host of government documents tracing the progression of Section 508 standards. These sources are particularly salient because old websites, with their accessible or inaccessible code, can only rarely be found. I instead located traces of web accessibility, including advertisements, policy documents, popular press coverage, and meeting minutes.[34] Beyond providing information about the technological development of digital media accessibility, these sources also enabled consideration of policy, and policymaking, as a technology of power that established discourse and shaped institutions, artifacts, and behavior.[35] Additionally, in keeping with critical cultural studies of media industries, I have consulted trade publications, textbooks, blogs, and other materials aimed at a professional audience of web developers in order to understand the ways in which accessibility was discussed among those tasked with producing it.[36]

Second, I found and analyzed popular texts in order to better situate this work in its shifting historical contexts, as well as to gain a sense of the discourses of disability and access that circulated outside of the field of digital media accessibility. These included news and entertainment publications, television commercials, a niche market of disability publications, and historical and contemporary websites and digital media themselves. Analyzed not individually but as part of a discursive formation, these sources speak to the ways in which digital media technology has been articulated to both normate and disabled forms of embodiment.[37]

I conducted nearly fifty interviews in researching this book. These oral history–style open-ended interviews helped to fill in gaps in available materials, give context to specific phenomena, and provide first-person accounts of digital media accessibility by people with disabilities. I benefited enormously from conversations with individuals pursuing digital media accessibility from within academia, government, nonprofit, and web development professions. These included representatives of the W3C, the U.S. government, research scholars, nonprofit employees, computer industry personnel, and accessibility consultants, among others. Additionally, I conducted open-ended interviews with selected participants from my ethnographic work in the disability blogosphere, described below.

Observing and engaging with the online activities of a disability blogosphere over nine months, between 2011 and 2012, allowed access to the writings, interactions, artistic creations, and complaints of users with disabilities. From a disability studies perspective, this work was essential to including the voices of people with disabilities, experts on their own lives. Furthermore, this kind of online ethnographic research pushes "against peculiarly narrow presumptions about the universality of digital experience."[38] With the goal of challenging universalism in digital media cultures, direct research with users with disabilities was essential to interpreting the possibilities of alternative experiences.

My ethnographic research site was a dynamically constructed "disability blogosphere." It was established using a modified form of web sphere analysis,[39] beginning with three seed sites (*Feminists with Disabilities*, *Disability Studies–Temple University*, and *Blind Photographers*) and snowballing to other linked sites, including Twitter and Flickr accounts and Tumblr blogs. At the conclusion of my fieldwork, this disability blogosphere included fifty-two blogs, thirty Twitter accounts, twenty-six Flickr accounts, and eleven Tumblrs. My research took the form of participant observation, including entry into the disability blogosphere, where I maintained a personal blog for a period of time, linking to and exchanging comments with other bloggers and my ongoing participation in Twitter and Tumblr conversations with research participants. This participation was counterbalanced by ongoing detailed observation and the regular recording of fieldnotes. All participants were contacted and offered the opportunity to opt out of this research prior to its start or at any time during the research.

Ethical accountability in this work intervenes in three forms. First, in keeping with the politics of disability studies and the methods of feminist ethnography, I incorporate the voices and words of people with disabilities whenever possible; drawn from blogs, Twitter accounts, ethnographic work, and formal interviews, these perspectives are presented on their own terms. Though I may analyze or extrapolate from these statements, I try to avoid speaking for those whom this work aims to empower. Second, all use of ethnographic and interview data has been shared with participants ahead of publication, allowing them to confirm that their perspectives and meanings were preserved and to ask for alterations or omissions where these goals were not met. Finally, I hope that the language, style, and presentation of this text enable multiple entry points, from the academic to the activist, amateur, or technologist. I wish to make this book itself as accessible as possible to people with disabilities, those who work in digital media, and others who may find it useful by incorporating multiple perspectives and copious examples. This "access strategy"[40] extends to encouraging readers to make use of online extensions of this text, in which media texts and examples are linked or displayed along with condensed explanations, additional information about ethnographic and interview research is provided, and links to accessibility resources are offered.[41] These resources are intended to facilitate the use of this book in teaching, learning, and implementing accessibility as a practical skill and a progressive political strategy.

Digital media accessibility in the United States serves as a case through which to investigate the ways in which discourses and material realities of disability, digital media, and access intersect to produce opportunities and exclusions, expand and contract cultural and civic participation, and challenge entrenched ways of thinking about mediated culture. The history of accessibility in the United States weaves through this text, highlighting the concerns, policies, technical innovations, and experiences that shadowed a more conventional history of the web. This is supplemented by the rich experiential knowledge of bloggers with disabilities, accessibility professionals, and other stakeholders for whom digital media access is not a thought experiment but a way of life. Digital media accessibility, access, and disability are all concepts in flux. In their movements, we can learn quite a bit about moments of media circulation and forms of embodied difference that are not often the focus of media and cultural studies.

Interrogating Access: The Whole Kit and Caboodle

The investigation of digital media accessibility through theories of cultural and disability studies reveals that access itself may be treated as an analytic framework through which to make sense of the infinitely varied articulations of media, culture, bodies, and technologies, with respect to difference, power, and democratic values. Access, as a relational and inherently unstable phenomenon, emerges in the articulations of intersectional identities, media technologies, and cultural discourses. As a result, the study of access can enable the unearthing of dynamics too often glossed over in existing methods for the study of media or disability. The study of media too often elides the moment of access; the proposed analytic framework provides a means by which to make sense of a range of cultural artifacts, practices, and interactions with respect to access. Through richer analyses of media with respect to access, media studies may gain more nuanced perspectives on the role of media in civic and cultural participation. Through studies of media access, similarly, disability studies may find more productive ways of engaging with the technological and cultural mediations of disability experiences.

As explicated earlier in this Introduction, a robust theorization of access must draw on availability, affordability, choice, and use while integrating the relational, variable perspectives of disability rights movements and disability studies. Yet, even once that theorization is in place, employing it for the study of disability and media poses a challenge because of the branching and overlapping elements that may be relevant to a study of access. This book advances theorizations of access by building upon such theories and using research on digital media to offer a framework for conducting such study. It is a kind of "access kit," a modular grouping of different perspectives, methods, and interrogatories that may be picked up and deployed individually or in concert.

The "access kit" is organized as shown in figure I.1. There are five categories—regulation, use, form, content, and experience—each of which contains three guiding questions. This organization emerges from the theoretical cross-pollination of circuit models for the study of media culture, from theorizations of access to information and communication technologies (ICTs), and from theories of disability and new media. Circuit models of the study of media culture were particularly influential in developing this kit, as they propose approaches to analysis of media circulation and delimit specific conjunctural spheres (production, regulation, social context, text, audience, industry, etc.) in which discursive practices converge and use those spheres as guides to this analytic method.[42] Additionally, models of access to information and communication technologies were useful in their attention to the uses of digital media and the range of factors involved in individual adoption of technologies.[43] Neither body of literature, however, offered both the specificity and flexibility needed to understand digital media accessibility; theories of new media—particularly those emphasizing modularity, recombination, and dynamic integration of different elements through remediation, or remixing—provided the necessary bridge in formulating this "access kit."[44] As software studies scholar Lev Manovich asserts, one characteristic that distinguishes new media from its predecessors is "variation," by which "*a number of different interfaces can be created from the same data*" (emphasis original).[45] The very complexity and flexibility of digital, or "new," media thus complements and reinforces the variability of relational understandings of access and disability. New media and disability studies both speak to the variability of embodied and technological cultures, reaffirming the need for a framework of study that could address varied contexts with specificity. This, then, forms the theoretical core of the kit, with elements of circuit and ICT models incorporated to varying degrees throughout, either to enhance flexibility or to draw attention to specific elements.

The proposed "access kit" offers five categories of questions to direct researchers' attention to particular dynamics and articulations that may arise in a given case. These are portable sets of questions, grouped within broad areas of inquiry; they are not prescriptive but suggestive of the means of study and the kinds of articulations most relevant to using access as a means of deepening scholarship related to media, disability, and possibly other phenomena and embodied forms of difference. The interrogatory kit may be understood as a set of analytic lenses, related but distinct, brought together for their utility in uncovering articulations and circulations of power within the case of digital media access for people with disabilities. The categories are conjectural, pried apart for analytic purposes, but are ultimately constructed by the researcher and always deeply connected to one another. Like taffy, the question of access is of a piece; it may be pulled in many directions, twisted, folded, and otherwise reshaped, but its holistic essence remains unchanged.

Now, a note on language. I refer to this framework as an "access kit" precisely because it is intended to increase our ability to study access and because it provides avenues by which to access particular cultural dynamics in our research. More important, however, in calling it a "kit" I am deliberately eschewing the language of models, methods, or tools. The deeply connected research perspectives discussed throughout this book do not provide abstracted representations of real-world dynamics as might a model. They do not offer straightforward, unitary theoretical perspectives or didactic instructions, as might a purely methodological text. And finally, they are not objects to be wielded pragmatically in the (de)construction of an artifact or an argument. My interest is in identifying potential avenues to enable the serious study of media access; if this union of cultural, media, and disability studies is to produce worthwhile new scholarship, it will do so through the formulation of new questions and new perspectives on old ones. Thus, in naming this framework an

An Interrogatory Kit for the Study of Access

Regulation

How is a medium, and access to it, defined, and by whom, in this case?

What are the structures that limit or expand access in this case?

What official and unofficial sources of power exert discursive authority?

Use

What is a given medium "for"? How is it meant to be accessed and used, and by whom?

What are the assumptions or defaults of the user position in this case, in terms of bodies, cultures, and technologies?

What alternate uses and user positions are there, and how are they found, negotiated, or discouraged?

Form

By what means does one access a medium in this case?

What material, technological, cultural, or social structures shape this medium's material, technological, or designed components?

How do these means of access, or structures, interact (or interface) with the bodies of those who use them?

Content

What is the information, meaning, or experience being pursued and why?

What are the cultural values surrounding that content?

How does this content, as a set of motivations and meanings, relate to the form in which it is delivered or received?

Experience

How is a medium experienced and defined by various groups or individuals, in relation to particular embodied identities, material forms, or social contexts?

What are (some of) the variations in access — to content, via technological form, in regulatory definition, or in terms of use — revealed by experience?

By what processes, and in what contexts, can access be taken advantage of or extended?

Five categories, with three questions each, that can guide the study of access in a cultural and disability studies framework.

interrogatory kit for the study of access, I intend to indicate that it is an assemblage of items (or, in this case, ideas) that are brought together for a purpose, but that may be utilized flexibly as needed or desired.

Further discussion, perhaps, is useful here. Many groups of objects are referred to as kits: travel kits, first-aid kits, model airplane kits, kits for specific craft projects (everything you need to build a ship in a bottle!), survival kits, and so on.[46] In all cases, the word seems to retain reference to a grouping of supplies, related but distinct, brought together to serve a *common purpose*. The small sewing kit seen in figure I.2 is a useful visualization. Its contents are diverse—scissors, safety pins, needles, straight

A photograph of a sewing kit, with scissors, thread, and measuring tape. Like many kits, this is a collection of disparate objects united by a stated purpose but available for repurposing.

pins, thimbles, a tape measure, thread, and fabric—and these contents can be variously combined and utilized. Though they share a larger purpose—the joining of materials or creation of new articles—the contents of a sewing kit are not always equally useful and may be recombined in numerous ways as called for by the situation. The use of this sewing kit for affixing a button to a sleeve is quite different from how it might be employed to sew a new garment, and both uses are different still from how the contents of the kit could be reappropriated and used for unforeseen purposes, such as medical stitches, punk rock appropriations of safety pins, or the restorative surgery that can rejuvenate a bedraggled, much-loved stuffed toy. Kits, then, are brought together to serve a purpose *but are not limited by that purpose*; their contents retain individual characteristics and are open to a range of possible use. This scholarly kit, by extension, is constructed in service of a given purpose (the study of media access) but is not reducible to that purpose and is open to recombination and modification as needed. This flexibility and theoretical openness is particularly appropriate to the project of cultural studies, in which theory and context are "mutually constituted, mutually determining" and questions inevitably lead to the strategic use of theory and method.[47]

Over the course of the following chapters, I deploy the "access kit" to analyze digital media accessibility in relation to ideologies of ability, neoliberal contexts, and cultural and civic participation. The specific underpinnings of each category, and its questions, are explored in greater depth within those chapters. For now, simply remember that these categories are intended not to reveal the "truth" of any kind of media access but to reveal tensions, power dynamics, and articulations that might otherwise be invisible. Each has been selected for its ability to raise distinct (though always interrelated) lines of questioning. In this spirit, each category is set in motion through an interrogatory, a set of questions that can guide research. Methods, theories, and possible sources of evidence are also discussed in relation to each category in subsequent chapters, though these are obviously not exhaustive possibilities.

Regulation

Chapter 1 begins with the questions grouped under "Regulation," exploring the discursive and policy developments of digital media accessibility. The questions guiding this chapter are as follows:

How is a medium, and access to it, defined, and by whom, in this case?
What are the structures that limit or expand access in this case?
What official and unofficial sources of power exert discursive authority?

These questions interrogate the ways in which a particular medium is regulated and how it, in turn, exerts discursive authority to regulate particular cultural dynamics. This of course includes legal strictures, international agreements, and other forms of official policy and regulation. However, the site of regulation may also be understood to include informal, private, and community-based forms of regulation. These could include professional norms, internal corporate standards, or grassroots activism. In the case of digital media accessibility, multiple sources of authority develop different notions of accessibility, reflecting different structures of power and experience. The history of web content accessibility demonstrates how legal and extralegal forms of authority constructed accessibility as a technical phenomenon aimed at aiding people with disabilities. Examples from industrial and grassroots contexts show how accessibility may be tied to other meanings. Industrially, it is both a source of risk to be minimized and a potential ethical good among web developers. For activists and people with disabilities, it is often figured not as a technological or legal phenomenon but as a question of fairness or citizenship. By and large, regulatory forces have defined accessibility as a technological phenomenon that "fixes" individual deficits. Even as industry personnel and people with disabilities attempt to redefine access in relation to more progressive politics of disability as variation, or social construction, they lack the authority to fully transform dominant meanings.

Use

"Use" unites the questions posed in chapter 2, in which the ideal uses and users of technology are analyzed in respect to the non-normative and creative uses and user positions developed by people with disabilities. The interrogation of use proceeds through three central questions:

What is a given medium "for"? How is it meant to be accessed and used, and by whom?

What are the assumptions or defaults of the user position in this case, in terms of bodies, cultures, and technologies?

What alternate uses and user positions are there, and how are they found, negotiated, or discouraged?

Popular media, user-generated online media, and first-person accounts of user experiences provide the majority of sources in chapter 2, as I explore how popular discourses aid media technologies in establishing what I refer to as preferred uses and user positions; systems are set up for particular audiences and tasks, often in such a way as to privilege normative articulations of bodies, technologies, and culture. Such positions, however, like a preferred reading position, are not determinate; there are possibilities for negotiation and oppositional uses and user positions.

Form

Chapters 3 and 4 work in concert to both utilize and problematize the separation of "form" and "content." The ability to separate form and content is central to the kinds of variation and recombination that many theorists of new media celebrate, and it is foundational to the very possibilities of digital media accessibility. However, posing questions about these elements reveals the difficulty—and necessity—of distinguishing them from one another.

Interrogating "form" begins with the material dimensions of media technology, the structures of code, and the presentation of the interface. It is based on the following questions:

By what means does one access a medium in this case?
What material, technological, cultural, or social structures shape this medium's material, technological, or designed components?
How do these means of access, or structures, interact (or interface) with the bodies of those who use them?

Chapter 3 asks how material and encoded structures restrict access for people with disabilities and how they might be constructed differently. Brief cases are used to illustrate various understandings of form and access. First, the graphical user interface (GUI) is studied in reference to the assistive computing technologies of the late 1980s and early 1990s; here, the design of a formal structure made it unusable by visually impaired users, requiring extensive work to retrofit the software. Second, I turn to the ways in which HTML and Flash were understood oppositionally in early web accessibility work, drawing attention to the site of form as both a question of function and a question of style. Third, I look to mobile media, an area of innovation that drew explicitly upon accessible web technologies and has resulted in increased convergence between people with disabilities and mainstream audiences in their use of technology. Finally, I describe some current accessibility initiatives that are explicitly aimed at promoting the convergence of digital media forms and the integration of disability with a range of common concerns, including personalization, privacy, and cloud computing.

Content

The site of "content" is the focus of chapter 4. Digital media accessibility and accessibility initiatives in other media have often stressed that they do not intend to change the content, or cultural meanings, of media. Rather, they intend to change its presentation into a mutable form that allows for access by diverse populations. Questions regarding content are:

What is the information, meaning, or experience being pursued and why?
What are the cultural values surrounding that content?
How does this content, as a set of motivations and meanings, relate to the
    form in which it is delivered or received?

In answering, however, I am forced to ask in what ways form *must* change content and whether it is possible to consider variations of content as essentially equivalent. Issues of copyright, freedom of speech, and hierarchies of taste cultures intervene in the accessibility of content. Additionally, in studying the site of content I begin to consider the wide range of material that people with disabilities may want to access; how are these cultural motivations accounted for (or discounted) by larger technological and cultural institutions? Closed captioning of online material and the accessibility of video games are the dominant case studies throughout this chapter. Ultimately, I argue that content is a crucial motivator in demands for access, and that access to mutable content offers valuable, but not necessarily identical, experiences.

Experience

"Experience," a deliberately amorphous term, is the focus of chapter 5. The site of "experience" is intended to incorporate phenomenological and identity-based elements of people's encounters with media. It seeks the differences in experience, the unexpected outcomes, and the collaborative potential in media access. Theoretically, this chapter relies upon feminist theories of intersectionality as they have been adopted within critical disability studies. The questions guiding interrogation of experience are:

How is a medium experienced and defined by various groups or individuals, in relation to particular embodied identities, material forms, or social contexts?

What are (some of) the variations in access—to content, via technological form, in regulatory definition, or in terms of use—revealed by experience?

By what processes, and in what contexts, can access be taken advantage of or extended?

This chapter begins with investigation of the access strategies deployed by people with disabilities. Then, I discuss the notion of "cultural accessibility." This and similar phrases were used by many bloggers with disabilities to describe their own definitions of digital media accessibility. Though these incorporated technical elements—as did activist forms of regulation, in chapter 1—they were equally attuned to the emotional, cultural, and political dimensions of access to digital media. Extending "cultural accessibility" would require that accessibility initiatives attempt to integrate into their structure elements of participatory culture, a range of identity positions, and a range of technological expertise. I argue that identity and access are closely related features of encounters with media. When one or both of these elements are taken for granted, it is too easy to generalize about the nature of media and its users or audiences.

Collaborative Futures

The Conclusion will return to three central themes of this work: Access is a variable and relational phenomenon that structures media experiences; most media are designed, regulated, and discursively constructed around a normative user position that marginalizes communities such as people with disabilities; and intersectional study and attention to variability are crucial to realizing the progressive potential of media participation, as they prevent the easy assimilation of diverse experiences into a single privileged "user." Building upon "cultural accessibility," I analyze three contemporary initiatives that facilitate collaborative forms of accessibility and thus enable coalitional politics based on shared interests and needs. Coalitional modes of being and participating are particularly necessary counterweights to the neoliberal modes of individualism and division that characterize much of contemporary culture.

In concluding this Introduction, which has established the kit that will guide the book, I cannot resist a note on the oddly persistent phrase "kit and caboodle." Though one would be hard-pressed to find any other uses of the word *caboodle*, or to define it outside of this phrase, it offers a pleasant finishing touch to the construction of this "access kit." The (whole) kit and caboodle is understood most simply as referring to "everything," or "all of the things." Historically, however, *caboodle* referred most often to a group *of people*.[48] Used with *kit*, it suggests a coming together of things and individuals into a collectivity for a given purpose or activity. Thus, I bring it up in this context because a kit comprising ideas ought always to be accompanied by the caboodle of individuals, identities, and attendant forms of agency that are implied by those ideas. Considering this connection encourages the grounding of cultural research in the material and embodied and connects my "access kit" to the lived experiences of the diverse individuals who participated in my ethnographic and interview research, populated the texts I studied, wrote or enforced or benefited from legal structures, and developed or used digital media technologies, as well as those who stand to benefit from a deeper understanding of the variable intersections of bodies, media technologies, and culture.

One member of this caboodle, of course, is the researcher, who makes decisions regarding the means of study, sources of information, and ultimate arguments drawn from this analysis. A degree of self-awareness is particularly important in the study of access, which depends upon one's own embodied relations with media and technology and which may be influenced by these factors. I come to this project with a professional background in web development and an academic grounding in cultural studies. I write from within academia, with access to copious resources and reference materials, and with the advantages that such a position may confer on others' willingness to participate in this project. Furthermore, my "relationship to disability" is as a scholar and ally; my minor physical ailments are not disabling conditions in my life.[49] A similar phenomenon is discussed in race and disability scholar Sami Schalk's work on "identifying with" disability studies as a nondisabled scholar, which she uses "to mean having acknowledged and prioritized political and personal connections to a group with which one does not identify as a member."[50] As, coincidentally, I wrote much of this book while increasingly pregnant and later with an infant at my side, I also experienced an increasing identification with disability. Experiences such as the stare, the medicalization of bodily functions, the embodied physical discomfort, and the experience of the body as social property became far more relevant to me as I begin to experience them from outside of a normate subject position. Pregnancy, like fatness, can be connected to disability on the basis of medicalization, social and moral condemnation, and political claims of identity. As feminist scholar April Herndon explains, "[M]any women have times in their lives when they gain weight and/or become disabled."[51] She argues that such possibilities force consideration of how bodies exist in flux, destabilizing our lives and identities. Pregnancy offered a window into both fatness and disability, increasing my ability to "identify with" the political project of disability studies and culture not only as a scholar but also as an embodied woman experiencing a shifting social location. This is not to say that those without such a window, who may not (yet) identify with disability, cannot enter into this text; my aim is to produce an intersectional analysis in which individuals may locate their own positions and draw from my research in ways that are meaningful to those contexts.

In bringing together the questions and forms of research joined in this text, I argue that disability—as identity, embodiment, and legal structure—forces consideration of both the flexibility of digital media and its normalization. It demonstrates both the limits and the potentials of participatory cultures and the technological frameworks upon which they rely. The study of digital media accessibility is important in its own right, as absent or flawed accessibility features work against the inclusion of bodily variation in new media spaces. After all, as seen in the "CAPTION FAIL" videos, mangled content and inappropriate media forms do no favors to anyone. Interpreting "A 100% organic free range black bean vegan burrito" as "Oracle organic free range but being in retail" is at best confusing and at worst a stymied lunch order. Digital media accessibility is thus both an example and a teacher, enabling the development of a framework for the study of other moments of media access and thus enabling greater accessibility technologically, academically, and politically. From the study of digital media accessibility, we may come to learn nuance, value variation, and apply these lessons to discussion of access in all of its critical contexts.

1

Regulating Digital Media Accessibility

#CaptionTHIS

In June 2012, d/Deaf and hard-of-hearing Twitter users called upon media producers to "#CaptionTHIS." Using social media as a venue for protest, they demanded increased captioning of streaming video in a range of online contexts. The protest launched on June 6, 2012, with a video explaining arguments for online captioning (including legal regulations). Between the 6th and the 10th, there were more than 10,000 posts on Twitter employing the #CaptionTHIS hashtag.[1]

These activists did not rely upon any official definitions of accessibility but invoked their status as consumers of information and entertainment, employed the language of fairness and equal rights, and talked about their feelings in the face of inaccessible media. Adam Jarashow, who was one of the leaders of this event, recalled, "It dawned on me one day; people shouldn't suffer like this, being denied their basic right to access. If this makes me feel like a second-class U.S. citizen, in no way anyone else should [*sic*] experience this barrier."[2] In this statement, Jarashow positions himself as both consumer and citizen, invoking the public value of equality and also drawing from the knowledge gained through his own experiences of frustration. Accessibility in this statement, and in the protest at large, is conceived of as a "right" that is not explicitly tied to laws but is invoked through a commonsense idea of fairness, of being treated "like everyone else."

#CaptionTHIS tweets directly addressed media entities, including television networks and channels such as ABC News, CNN, Fox News, and Nickelodeon, as well as news organizations such as the *Huffington Post*, the *New York Times*, and the *Washington Post*; online video providers such as Amazon, Netflix, and Yahoo!; and conglomerates such as Vivendi and TimeWarner. In this way, the campaign relied upon individuals' status as consumers, even as users asserted that they were outraged at "unfairness," "inequality," and the denial of their rights as citizens. Only a small portion of tweets attempted to target government officials, with most aimed directly at President Barack Obama. This blended activism of citizen-consumers has a long history in media activism[3] and reflects the duality of access as simultaneously politically progressive and inflected with neoliberal values.

Most of the protest messages came from individuals and organizations fairly closely connected to d/Deaf culture and accessibility needs. Deaf activist organizations participated, including the National Association for the Deaf, and a number of accessibility organizations participated, including VITAC (a closed captioning provider), and Knowbility (an accessibility consulting group). Jarashow recalls that "we never had any doubt about how our message would be received by the deaf community. Of course our friends, allies, and anyone with hearing issues would appreciate better access."[4] However, he and his co-organizers were disappointed at the lack of response and media attention to the protest, as there was no sense that their needs and experiences were speaking back to the regulatory and institutional bodies that oversee digital media access.

The #CaptionTHIS protest demonstrates that closed captioning, despite its prevalence in the U.S. mediascape, is once again a site of regulatory uncertainty and activist concern. Though captioned television content was pioneered in the 1970s and gradually expanded through the 1980s and 1990s, the rise of digital media formats has thrown existing systems into disarray. First, the transition from televisual exhibition to online streaming meant that laws about closed captioning did not apply. The Telecommunications Act of 1996 required all new programs aired by "television video programming providers" to be captioned by 2006, and thereafter uncertainty arose around the legal status of streaming content and service providers. Second, the civil rights protections of the Americans with Disabilities Act had only recently been established as applicable to online media, with enforcement still pending. The legacies of activists, users, and innovators in closed captioning for broadcast media were all but forgotten as the digital context complicates and recreates existing definitions and practices within governments and industries and among users themselves.

Disability similarly complicates existing conceptual and regulatory frameworks, particularly when it is understood not as a category of individual deficiency but as a social category that is inherently flexible and political in its meanings. Media regulations presume a relationship between industries, technologies, and a default abled user; when access is considered in relation to disability, numerous concerns that were otherwise invisible are often opened up. Although online streaming media enabled more on-demand access for many users,[5] as shown in the case of #CaptionTHIS, it curtailed the access that d/Deaf and hard-of-hearing users had enjoyed to preceding media forms.

This chapter interrogates a range of regulatory contexts in which digital media accessibility has been defined, limited, extended, and authorized by both official and unofficial authorities. Forms of regulation explored include legal documents and processes, extralegal collaborative processes, industry standards and practices, social and community norms, and grassroots and activist perspectives. The captioning of online media emerges as a particularly useful case study for the ways in which digital media accessibility is subject to myriad regulatory forces and engaged in ongoing negotiations surrounding the rights of people with disabilities, the interests of regulatory bodies, and the neoliberal contexts in which media industries and audiences come into contact. What emerges is a persistent double bind. While the government has the advantage of enforcement, its regulatory requirements prevent the kinds of flexible, progressive understandings of disability that may create innovative accessibility solutions. Simultaneously, the flexible and nuanced approaches that industries and accessibility professionals can adopt do not carry the weight of enforcement. In the face of this stalemate, several different processes of self-regulation are coming to define accessibility for government personnel, industries, activists, and accessibility professionals alike.

Interrogating Regulation

In the "access kit" discussed in the Introduction to this book, regulation is the first of five categories through which one might study the vicissitudes of access to media. It is a conjectural space, useful for setting aside particular concerns in order to look at the ways in which access is produced via a range of policies, forms of enforcement, and cultural norms. Like each of the other categories in this kit, *regulation* is defined not by inflexible official structures or specific methods of study but by the following three questions and the contexts and methods needed to answer them:

How is a medium, and access to it, defined, and by whom, in this case?
What are the structures that limit or expand access in this case?
What official and unofficial sources of power exert discursive authority?

These questions attempt to unearth the sources of power that produce and enforce ways of understanding and accessing a medium. These are often familiar sources of regulation, such as national laws, industry standards, international agreements, and various policies. But access to media is regulated by a wide variety of institutional and cultural forces, often through mechanisms that are informal, invisible, and individual.

Many sources of regulation operate through governmentality by which the functions of government in the management of populations are offloaded onto other institutions and, ultimately, onto individuals themselves. As theorized by French poststructuralist Michel Foucault, governmentality produces powerful results by encouraging self-regulation of one's behavior and of one's biopolitical life. Governmentality and biopower are provocative tools for analyzing the forms of power that surround disability, which is always a matter of bodily classification, self-management, and institutional governance of bodily norms and behaviors. Such forms of self-regulation support the project of neoliberalism,[6] making it particularly productive in the study of industrial and professional practices. Feminist cultural theorist Rosalind Gill demonstrates that self-regulation is endemic to new media labor, in particular, as it lacks traditional institutional structures for the establishment and enforcement of professional norms. Instead, individual workers must manage their work and identities while producing their own conformance.[7] Though self-regulation may be associated with the decline of the state, the rise of neoliberalism, and the expansion of consumerist and celebrity cultures, it may also constitute a progressive space of political negotiation and ethical behavior. Finally, self-regulation need not be individual but may be a collaborative practice, shared by a community.[8]

Even corporate contexts can be interpreted as local communities engaged in self-regulation, particularly when studied from the perspective of employees rather than executives. Internal industrial policies, or best practices, constitute a form of collective self-governance, augmented by corresponding social and cultural norms. Additionally, research may draw out "vernacular policy."[9] Unlike formal policies, vernacular policies are rules and norms of being enacted at the level of the individual, the family, the community, or the activist movement. Such practices and norms may exist in harmony with more official regulations or may emerge as counterdiscourses that challenge the regulatory actions of the powerful. The site of regulation is, simultaneously, a site of negotiation at which meanings, practices, and authority are involved in ongoing contestation. Media policy scholar Bill Kirkpatrick discusses this process in terms of policy translation, "involving metaphors of outcomes, constructions of community identity and power, and tensions between utopian and dystopian discourses."[10] Translation and negotiation offer alternatives to an overly simplistic notion of policy as deterministic; though policies may exist, in a variety of contexts, their effects are not always predictable. Through exploration of sources of policy, policy documents, and subsequent debate and practice, a fuller picture of regulation emerges in which the production and maintenance of particular norms may be understood as necessary to the operations of regulatory power.

Though governmentality signals a shift from the rule of law to the rule of the norm, this does not render the law irrelevant; instead, the law itself operates increasingly as a norm, alongside and in combination with other normative structures.[11] Thus, the study of law and policy remains central to the site of regulation, as these documents, their development, and their implementation exert productive force upon the material and technological forms of media, as well as upon their industrial practices and possible uses. Just as technological artifacts have politics, or "arrangements of power and authority in human associations,"[12] so too the processes of policy development that shape technologies' meanings and uses are political engagements with various concepts, ideologies, and forms of governance. Laws, the process of their formation, the standards by which those laws are enforced, and court cases that interpret those laws collectively form a legal discourse around a medium and structure access in particular ways.

This chapter integrates theories of regulation, governmentality, and critical cultural policy studies in order to understand the construction of digital media accessibility as a specific discourse and field of practice and in order to trace the negotiation of these meanings by interested parties. This is made possible through reliance upon archival sources, U.S. legal and government documents, policy documents produced by industry and nonprofit organizations, social media content, ethnographic and interview research in a disability blogosphere, and interviews with professionals involved in digital media accessibility in various capacities.[13]

Legal Policies and Discourses of Digital Media Accessibility

Within the United States, legal sources for the regulation of digital media accessibility are located within civil rights, employment, and telecommunications law. Study of the legal corpus indicates that as a source of discursive authority, these official policies attempt to define disability, and accessibility, narrowly for the purpose of enforcement. In doing so, they struggle with the variability of disability as an experience or social construct. Laws therefore may find more success in direct regulation of consumer industries than in use of a civil rights model.

The first federal law to regulate digital media accessibility was Section 508 of the Rehabilitation Act of 1973, first passed in 1986. The Rehabilitation Act of 1973 was an employment nondiscrimination law pertaining to federal contexts. It offered the first legal definition of disability based upon a social, rather than medical, model of disability. Section 508, as amended by the Workforce Investment Act of 1998, required that employees and members of the public with disabilities "have access to and use of information and data that is comparable to the access to and use of the information and data" by peers who do not have disabilities.[14] Congress established an enforcement plan by which the Federal Acquisition Regulations Council, the Office of Management and Budget, and the Architectural and Transportation Barriers Compliance Board (the Access Board), among other federal agencies, would write policies and directives that incorporated 508's mandates. The Section 508 standards were revised and then published in final form in the *Federal Register* on December 21, 2000, and enforcement of the standards began on June 21, 2001.[15]

Because of the constraints of law, particularly the need to have clear standards for interpretation and enforcement, the scope of 508 was limited to a focus on employment in the federal sector and public access to federal information. Although the standards drew most of their web provisions from the Web Content Accessibility Guidelines (WCAG) 1.0, they also dropped some and added other provisions.[16] Such changes were made because of the necessity of removing subjective judgments from legally enforceable standards; for instance, one WCAG 1.0 guideline stated that the color contrast of page elements must be "sufficient" to prevent difficulties, which was an impossible standard to enforce via legal structures. Beyond removing subjective elements, the 508 standards also confronted the impossibility of making technology equally accessible to all forms of disability simultaneously,[17] leading to less emphasis on universal design and similar philosophies and resulting in the prioritization of visual disabilities in the final document.

For many involved with Section 508, *accessible*, in practice, means "in accordance with accessibility standards." Though this seems circular, such a definition effectively reflects the necessity of definitional precision in legal regulations. Simultaneously, however, it glosses over the complexities brought on by the diversity of disabilities, needs, and practices that could be relevant to web accessibility, forcibly simplifying this domain in order to conform with the norms of legal language and enforcement. Yet, despite its emphasis on clarity for the purposes of enforcement, the web accessibility portion of Section 508 is enforced only through the option that employees and members of the public have to sue federal agencies for noncompliance. This puts the onus of enforcement on people with disabilities themselves and means that those agencies which have not been targeted by such suits may produce inaccessible content with few consequences. In this regard, it is similar to accessibility protections granted by the ADA: Legal regulation via antidiscrimination and civil rights measures requires definitional simplification but does not guarantee rapid compliance or meaningful social justice outcomes.

Perhaps as a result of the tensions between definitional simplicity and weak enforcement in Section 508, recent advances in legal regulation have focused on direct regulation of specific industries, rather than on digital media technologies and content more generally. The efficacy of such an approach is visible in the Telecommunications Act of 1996, which mandated closed captioning of television content and provision of TTY services for d/Deaf telephone users and ushered in a new era of compliance by regulating industries directly rather than by relying upon judicial enforcement.[18] In 2006, it was announced that the standards for compliance with Section 255 of the Telecom Act, which mandates accessible features in telecommunication and mass media devices and services, would undergo revision alongside the Section 508 standards. This decision was made, in part, because where these prior standards referenced product types such as web, software, and telecommunications, "many of these technologies have evolved and many of their various functions have converged and overlapped."[19] The Access Board convened The Electronic and Information Technology Access Committee (TEITAC), which recommended a new organization based not on product types but upon their uses. After the completion of the TEITAC report in 2008, the Access Board began work on turning those recommendations into new standards.

In February 2015, the Access Board released a Notice of Rulemaking, the penultimate step in producing new standards for the enforcement of both Section 508 of the Rehabilitation Act and Section 255 of the Telecommunications Act. The goals of this rulemaking, routinely referred to as a "refresh," include keeping abreast of changing technologies, addressing convergent and multi-purpose media and technologies, and harmonizing with WCAG 2.0 and many other voluntary and legal standards around the world (in recognition of the global reach of many computing technologies).[20] The Notice of Rulemaking—like the 2010 and 2011 Notices of Proposed Rulemaking on the 508 Refresh—offers members of the public a period in which to comment on the changes, after which the Access Board reviews comments, considers and makes changes, and moves forward with rulemaking. This process entails regulatory and cost assessments, voting by the Access Board on any revisions, and then approval by the U.S. Office of Management and Budget, after which the final rule is published in the *Federal Register*, with enforcement beginning six months later. The 2015 publication of the Notice of Rulemaking indicates that the 508 Refresh will likely be in effect sometime in 2016.

However, the work of the Access Board is only one area of ongoing standards-making for digital media accessibility within the federal government. On the twentieth anniversary of the ADA in 2010, President Barack Obama announced the intention of the Department of Justice to establish standards for digital media accessibility under Titles II and III of the ADA, which, respectively, require provision of effective communication for people with disabilities and provision of accessible places of public accommodation. Enforcement of accessibility via the ADA will require the establishment of concrete standards, which likely will be closely tied to the standards developed by the Access Board, and thus this process is also ongoing. Furthermore, Congress passed the 21st Century Communications and Video Accessibility Act (CVAA) in 2010, requiring additional closed captions for online television content, caption display options for mobile devices, and a range of accessibility features for Voice over IP services and other emerging media technologies. Thus, the Federal Communications Commission joined the Department of Justice and the Access Board in needing to develop new consistent, enforceable accessibility standards that will regulate meanings of disability, access, and digital media in the coming years. Such expansions of accessibility regulation indicate increased attention to the variety of services and contexts to which Americans with disabilities require access in order to fully participate in society; they reflect the convergence of media types, the overlap of public and private services, and the impossibility of predicting and containing uses of media technologies.

These emphases in legal regulation of accessibility have led to critique, as the narrowness required to make a law enforceable conflicts with the varied experiences of users, who have a breadth of accessibility needs, and the range of experiences of professionals, who may implement accessibility differently. As digital culture scholar Helen Kennedy observes, following her ethnographic work with web developers, it is possible that the "ethical origins of accessibility get lost when attempts are made to develop accessibility legislation."[21] The law can become a constraint, prohibiting innovation or experimentation with accessibility. When technological specifics are incorporated into law, as in the case of Section 508, requirements can become outdated and hamper true utility for people with disabilities. Additionally, narrow definitions tailored for enforcement may prohibit more comprehensive notions of access embraced by disability activists from being taken up on a large scale. Matt May, an accessibility expert and advocate currently serving as Adobe's "accessibility evangelist," describes laws and their standards as several "levels of abstraction" away from the ultimate goals of accessibility, aimed at preventing harm rather than increasing the social good.[22] Similarly, companies often hire accessibility consultants in order to avoid lawsuits by adhering to the minimum standards needed for compliance. This limits implementation of more expansive accessibility practices and reinforces an instrumental understanding of accessibility as a burdensome means of avoiding risk.[23] Laws, it seems, may not provide the necessary motivation for widespread implementation of accessibility, even as they can provide punishments for its absence. Such policies, and oversights, signal an opportunity for other forms of regulation to emerge from outside the government, without public oversight.

Extralegal Regulations

One of the most discursively powerful sites of web content accessibility regulation is the World Wide Web Consortium (W3C). As discussed in the Introduction to this book, the W3C is a nonprofit governing body for the World Wide Web; it oversees the establishment of best practices, the formation of new technologies and protocols, the updating of markup languages such as HTML, and the conduct of outreach.[24] The W3C is an active international organization that is looked to as a leader in web technologies; as such, it has a uniquely privileged regulatory position despite its lack of formal authority.

Section 508 and WCAG 1.0 and 2.0 are both accessibility "standards" in the sense described by Lawrence Busch, a sociologist of standards and society. Both "are means of partially ordering people and things so as to produce outcomes desired by someone. As such, they are part of the technical, political, social, economic, and ethical infrastructure that constitutes human societies."[25] Busch rejects the distinction between voluntary and government-produced standards, as both types serve to organize both physical and ideational social structures.[26] Both, essentially, function as regulatory measures by which accessibility is defined and according to which it may be produced and evaluated. Furthermore, these regulations exist in close conversation and are mutually influential in the construction of the meanings of accessibility.

The very origins of web content accessibility could be traced to the April 1997 chartering of the W3C's Web Accessibility Initiative (WAI) at the White House. WAI was established "to promote and achieve Web functionality for people with disabilities."[27] The practice of web content accessibility existed prior to the establishment of WAI, but it was not clearly defined or codified. For instance, in 1995, the Trace Center at the University of Wisconsin–Madison released its first web accessibility standards, titled "Design of HTML (Mosaic) Pages to Increase Their Accessibility to Users with Disabilities Strategies for Today and Tomorrow." At this point, web technologies were new enough to refer to in terms of a single browser, and recommendations for accessible code were quite simple. Quickly, though, these standards changed; Trace refined its best practices and soon began to collect web accessibility standards being developed and circulated in various academic, governmental, and professional contexts, leading to the development of an eighth version, released in October 1997, which was adopted as the starting point for the W3C's web content accessibility guidelines.[28]

The W3C's process began in earnest with the formation of the WAI/ IPO Markup Guidelines Working Group (GL) that would "produce the official WAI markup (HTML/CSS/XML) guidelines documents to be used by Web authors and tools providers alike, to make their sites and products more accessible using the W3C recommended markup formats."[29] The group had representatives of industry, accessibility organizations, and disability advocacy groups and included several experts who were also, themselves, people with disabilities. It used a system of regular conference calls and an email listserv for ongoing communication, in addition to holding several in-person meetings at World Wide Web Conferences; day-to-day work entailed the proposal, critique, and revision of possible guidelines. At various stages, drafts were released for public critique and were then revised. The final guidelines, WCAG 1.0, were released on May 5, 1999. The document, frozen on release, laid out the principles of increasing web content accessibility by means of attention to specific elements of HTML, CSS, and scripting languages.[30]

Following the release of WCAG 1.0 and the Section 508 standards, cracks in accessibility regulations were immediately evident. The speed of technological change in the early 2000s, including the rise of Web 2.0 and the rapid spread of video and multimedia content, meant that WCAG 1.0 "was almost out of date by the time it was published,"[31] in the words of one WAI participant. These guidelines had focused nearly exclusively on HTML and CSS, ignoring or even recommending against other formats on the web. In laying out specific pathways to web content accessibility, these regulations had in fact constrained innovation in accessible media design and stymied their own implementation by appearing out of touch with mainstream online technologies and cultural developments.

It took nearly eight years for WCAG 2.0 to be released as a W3C recommendation on December 11, 2008. This delay is attributable in part to the rechartering of the working group, which mandated consensus as their decision-making process.[32] Though it took time, this resulted in deep, long discussions of various points of contention in the guidelines, including detailed attention to public comments, and ultimately produced a full-consensus document. Additionally, the W3C process incorporated a new stage, called Candidate Recommendation, during which "an evaluation is taken of the feasibility of the proposals based upon predictions of the implementation experience."[33] Again, though it added time, this permitted more extensive testing of the guidelines and allowed for final decisions to be made on the basis of experience and user testing.

Furthermore, the delay was attributable to the rise in user-generated content, which blurred the lines between web producers and consumers; it was less possible than ever to assume a level of expertise in web creators, and it became necessary to address a range of audiences and technologies. Initially, the WAI working group, by this point renamed the WCAG Working Group, attempted to address these challenges by incorporating more detailed and "future-proof" technological writing that avoided specific mention of technologies or coding languages. However, early drafts were widely criticized for their opacity and inability to communicate important information to a diverse audience that included not only professional web developers but also a range of people creating web content in their work or personal lives.[34] Ultimately, the guidelines adopted a principle-based structure in order to meet the challenges of innovation and difference. This was initially proposed by Gregg Vanderheiden, a leading accessibility and assistive technology researcher, and web accessibility specialist Ben Caldwell because, as Vanderheiden explains, "Everybody needs to be able to see the content, everybody needs to be able to operate it, everybody needs to be able to understand it. This is not a disability thing."[35] However, people with disabilities do need to use assistive technology and/or to have flexible interfaces in order to do such things and thus needed content to be robust, or flexible, enough to be used with atypical hardware and software.

Taken together, this became a set of four principles—Perceivable, Operable, Understandable, and Robust (POUR)—that guided the final organization of WCAG 2.0. This separation of these principles from the specific ways in which they should be achieved resulted in a more flexible set of guidelines that could evolve with new technologies and changing capabilities and uses of the web. Thus, varied development processes, technological set-ups, and embodied uses were supported by WCAG 2.0, providing that they served these principles. Beneath the principles, WCAG 2.0 offered twelve guidelines, each explaining a specific goal in service of a principle, and for each guideline provided "success criteria" at three levels of conformance (A to AAA, with AAA being the highest). Then, for each guideline and success criterion, WCAG 2.0 provided "sufficient and advisory techniques," flexible documents explaining how to meet criteria in sufficient or recommended ways.[36] While the principles and guidelines are normative, fixed elements, the supplementary documents are regularly updated in accordance with new developments, such as HTML 5 or WAI-ARIA, neither of which was finalized at the release of WCAG 2.0.

WCAG 1.0 and 2.0 are prime examples of regulation that is not legally binding, a distinction made plain in their insistence on the terminology of "guidelines." These documents are referred to as "guidelines" in order to suggest best practices without implying enforcement. Although this has allowed for flexibility in the techniques documents over time and has enabled the maintenance of human judgment as central to accessibility decisions,[37] the W3C's lack of formal authority and enforcement mechanisms likely contributed to a general lack of implementation of WCAG 1.0 guidelines. Though the guidelines were normative statements, they were also often subjective and not subject to formal enforcement, allowing many to see them as optional, additional, or otherwise nonstandard components of web development.[38]

Perhaps the most striking difference in legal and extralegal forms of accessibility policy is the principle-based structure of WCAG 2.0, which eliminated any easy definition of accessibility as compliance with particular standards, technological formats, or professional practices. The subjective elements present in WCAG 1.0 were, instead, expanded; there is a need for expertise, judgment, and flexibility in using WCAG 2.0 to produce web content, or in using it to evaluate web content accessibility. The guidelines document itself begins by stating that "although these guidelines cover a wide range of issues, they are not able to address the needs of people with all types, degrees, and combinations of disability."[39] Accessibility, here, is understood as variable and impossible to "guarantee"; instead, the regulatory power of WCAG 2.0 comes in its provision of a framework within which to move toward particular accessibility goals that will improve accessibility for a range of people with disabilities. This more flexible approach to accessibility relied upon a definitional link to the social model of disability and the values of universal design and inclusion in the digital sphere. Though not directly enforceable, these standards are available as the basis for self-regulation of communities of accessibility professionals, as will be discussed further below.

Industries' Internal Regulatory Practices: Standardizing Closed Captioning and Formulating Business Cases

The legal and voluntary policies discussed above are highly influential public documents, with extensive influence in a range of computing and web-related fields. In contrast, innumerable forms of accessibility regulation stem from local contexts. These forms of regulation include policy documents developed by companies for their own use, which may be proprietary, as well as collaborative policy documents that govern a particular industry via voluntary recommendations. In order to demonstrate the ways in which these local contexts regulate accessibility, and how those regulations may or may not accord with dominant meanings of accessibility, I briefly discuss two examples of industry regulation—growing standardization in online closed captioning formats and procedures and the formation of "business cases" for accessibility at large, for-profit companies.

Closed Captioning

The first example of internal industry regulation comes from the expanding closed captioning industry, in which television content producers, distributors, internet service providers, online sites and services, and closed captioning providers must now collaborate to produce captions for online video content. Following CVAA, and in anticipation of ADA standards, this industry has been in need of both technical standardization and the development of work practices in order to comply with shifting federal regulations.

Rather than wait for governmental standards to be established, industry representatives have collaborated on regulatory documentation via the Digital EMA (Entertainment Merchants Association). Founded in 2008 "to build a community for collaboration among professionals supporting the distribution and retailing of digital audiovisual media," Digital EMA has already produced a standard for audiovisual metadata, published a glossary of industry terminology, and hosted a repository of research on its website.[40] In June 2013, the EMA Closed Captions Working Group released a draft document, "EMA's Best Practices for Closed Captioning of Internet Protocol–Delivered Video Programming." This working group was made up of industry professionals engaging in self-regulation, including representatives of Google, Netflix, Amazon, Microsoft, and Best Buy. The group's goals included developing best practices for both compliance with federal law and caption conversion. Thus, this initiative may also be understood as a response to and an attempt to negotiate with federal regulations, by demonstrating the ability of the industry to move toward compliance voluntarily.

Such actions were particularly necessary following the 2012 lawsuit *National Association of the Deaf, Western Massachusetts Association of the Deaf and Hearing Impaired, and Lee Nettles vs. Netflix, Inc.*, wherein the plaintiffs sued Netflix for discrimination on the basis of disability under Title III of the ADA, which requires places of public accommodation to be accessible. The company claimed that it complied with CVAA, which it argued superseded the ADA. The U.S. Department of Justice issued a Statement of Interest, asserting that Netflix fit the definition of a public accommodation and thus was required to provide accessible services, and noting that the CVAA does not preempt or conflict with the ADA.[41] The trial court agreed that the ADA applies to all of Netflix's streaming content.[42] Following this ruling, in October 2012 Netflix chose to settle and agreed to caption all of its content within two years. This decision looked to have far-reaching effects, as Netflix, as of first quarter 2013, was a leader in streaming media with more than 29 million subscribers in the United States.[43] Subsequent court cases, however, have not been definitive; in March 2015, the Ninth Circuit Court of the United States rejected an appeal in the case of *Donald Cullen vs. Netflix, Inc.* (2012) on the grounds that the ADA has been held to apply only to physical places of public accommodation.[44] Given these disparate outcomes, the ongoing (as of 2015) Department of Justice rulemaking concerning the applicability of the ADA to online contexts, and the mandates of the CVAA, the legal status of captioning for online video remains in a kind of purgatory.

Yet, despite this confusion, many in the captioning industry have realized that, in the words of longtime captioning professional Larry Goldberg, legal enforcement "is going to happen, . . . better get involved and cut the best deal possible."[45] The Digital EMA offered a way to do this, as the industry could produce its own standards as counterparts, or reference points, for eventual legal standards. In the "EMA's Best Practices," captioning policies and techniques were explained, justified, and summarized in simple checklists. For instance, the group suggested that the onus should be on content owners to indicate to distributors if a video file is exempt from captioning laws, using a checklist of legal exemptions.[46] This is part of a larger move toward placing the responsibility for captioning on content owners, rather than on distributors.[47] Such best practices regulate professional practice in the industry, clarifying and unifying expectations (and likely increasing the speed and predictability of interactions). Additionally, however, with much content migrating from television to multiple online distributors, there has been a need for technological standardization; in its absence, one captioning executive recalls being required to convert and provide more than twenty formats of captions so that a single client's content could be distributed on multiple streaming sites.[48] Therefore, the "EMA's Best Practices" also recommended preferred technical formats for online captions. Though several formats were deemed acceptable, the recommended technical process was conversion from the CEA-608 protocol used for televised captions to SCC (Scenarist Closed Caption, .scc) because of its growing ubiquity and open source nature.[49]

As with the other best practices set out in the EMA draft document, and as seen in the success of WCAG 2.0, the establishment of technical best practices through this collaborative, industry-driven process may increase their adoption. Furthermore, industry participation in this process, ahead of federal government regulations, may enable the industry to create *de facto* standards[50] that reflect its interests. In some ways, this is a takeup of responsibility in what legal and media studies scholar Siva Vaidhyanathan has called a moment of "public failure," in which the failings of the public sphere leave space for corporate interests to fill needs.[51] As governmental accessibility policies have failed to create widespread accessible web content, industrial collaborations may take up the slack and create self-enforced policies that come to define the regulation of captions and other accessibility features. This, however, is not an unqualified good; industries often act in the interest of risk reduction and profit maximization, which may at times conflict with the best interests of those who require accessible digital media. In the case of Google's autocaptions, for instance, there is a risk that quality will become de-prioritized in the absence of legal regulation, and the interests of digital media companies will be prioritized over those of people with disabilities.[52]

Business Cases

Another form of industrial self-regulation regarding accessibility occurs in the "business cases" developed for large corporations. A "business case," in this context, is a set of arguments, practices, and strategies used by accessibility advocates to encourage other stakeholders to prioritize access. These are industrial self-regulations that emerge from and reflect the local cultures, organizations, and workflows, even as they may reference or attempt to comply with W3C guidelines, Section 508, or other national standards. As digital culture and labor scholar Helen Kennedy notes, "[T]he clients, line managers or other decision-makers for whom [developers] are working may not share their commitment to accessibility."[53] As a result, advocates develop a "business case" in order to connect the benefits of accessibility and the values of the social model to the values and imperatives of their specific business context. Business cases often include arguments about cost, market share, and efficiency as well as address legal compliance, technical factors, and emphasis on the social good of accessibility.[54] Accessibility expert Karl Groves pins the formation of a "business case" to three questions: Will it make us money? Will it save us money? Will it reduce our risk?[55] However, as noted in the WAI's resource on building a business case, "a customized business case for a specific organization will have different content and style, and incorporate different aspects with different emphasis, focused on that particular organization."[56]

Accessibility professionals who have developed business cases and implemented large-scale accessibility initiatives at major corporations emphasize that their success stemmed directly from aligning accessibility with local corporate values. Elle Waters, an accessibility consultant at Simply Accessible who specializes in working with large corporate clients, explains that the key steps in formulating a business case are "identifying those key members who are decision makers . . . and figuring out what their measures of success are, and then aligning accessibly as the answer to those problem statements"[57] across multiple divisions of an organization. This strategy is seen in many successful accessibility initiatives. At one financial institution, for instance, upper management was extremely data-driven and motivated by competition; accessibility advocates thus presented the results of accessibility tests on their site as well as their competitors'. This demonstrated a quantifiable problem, as well as a possible area for competitive growth and resulted in significant buy-in from management in the form of training and resources. A major player in a different service industry, by contrast, was focused on preventing risks; as a result, accessibility advocates tailored their business case to a presentation of the risks and costs associated with non-compliance. In these and other cases, advocates recalled that business cases were often most persuasive when tied to "softer" values as well—corporate interest in "excellence," a user-centered focus, and the knowledge that this work would help people often contributed to increasing buy-in at all levels.

The business case does not end with convincing decision makers of the value of accessibility, however, but entails the formation of procedures, budgets, and even standards to support implementation. In some cases, accessibility functions as its own small division, with new web products and revisions routed through specific personnel in order to check compliance. In other cases, accessibility becomes part of a larger user-testing or even marketing department, with new procedures and checkmarks in place. Alternately, some institutions integrate accessibility checks in each stage of development, following extensive training of those involved. Regardless of the specific procedures, corporate contexts often develop their own standards or testing tools. One reason for this is that in response to frequent questions, experts within a company may create summary documents to aid implementation. A related impetus is the need for clear, developer-centric standards designed for easy implementation and reduced confusion among employees across divisions.[58] Beyond these pragmatic reasons, in-house standards development is often an attempt to reconcile the outdated 508 standards with current best practices in web development; by-the-numbers implementation of the 2001 Section 508 standards is no one's ideal, and in the absence of clear corporate standards, that could be the outcome of requesting accessible development without providing guidance. Accessibility law specialist Linda Dardarian has seen such outcomes from instances of "structured negotiation," in which people with disabilities work with companies to produce more accessible digital media experiences. She explains that "it often takes the regulatory process way, way, way too long to actually mandate what we have and what the companies we deal with through structured negotiations have agreed to years and years before. We can't be hamstrung by the regulatory process."[59]

The examples of industrial regulation discussed above demonstrate different means by which accessibility is defined and encouraged in industry. The Digital EMA captioning best practices are an ongoing attempt by major players in the industry to standardize procedures and technical formats in advance of upcoming federal regulations. It is both a collaborative form of industrial self-regulation and, presumably, an attempt to influence more discursively powerful regulatory documents, such as legal standards. In contrast, the formation of a "business case" and the implementation of internal standards at major corporations demonstrate the ways in which accessibility regulation may take place at a local level and the ways in which corporate policies may actually outpace more formal means of accessibility regulation. Closely tied to the goals and values of their contexts, such as risk reduction or profitability, business cases are a form of accessibility regulation that functions as a pragmatic means of improving attitudes and organizing workflows, not as a public, or collaborative, process of regulation. Both examples, however, indicate that industries may engage in multiple regulatory practices in addition to participating in the formation of and complying with dominant legal and W3C standards. These industrial practices are based upon avoiding legal risk, adopting specific technological practices, and potentially changing attitudes through exposure to the social model of disability. They are tied both to the neoliberal imperatives of the new media industries and to the progressivism of the social model; this tension is regularly moderated through an emphasis on technological solutions and recourse to bureaucracy. Flexibility, while possible, is not often desirable in contexts of industrial self-regulation.

Self-Regulation, Professionalization, and the #a11y Community

"Self-regulation," as discussed earlier, entails the management of an individual or an organization via intrinsic or communal motivations and criteria. At its most basic level, self-regulation is a practice undertaken by individuals—developers, users, policymakers—by which they manage their beliefs, knowledge, work, and professional status within specific groups or contexts.

Under this conception of self-regulation, WCAG 1.0 and 2.0 are policies that rely upon the self-regulation of accessibility professionals in order to take effect. As accessibility expert Molly Holzschlag states, "[I]mplementation trumps specification";[60] the effects of accessibility policy are realized through the interpretations and implementations of a diffuse professional community. In such an environment, Helen Kennedy argues, "standards-adherence can be considered as a form of self-regulation."[61] By following standards, developers control their own conduct, the results of their work, and their image or reputation. This is but one case of the self-regulatory practices that characterize new media workplaces, including the management of one's self and one's labor in accordance with neoliberal imperatives to be always available for work.[62]

Professionals, however, do not rely entirely upon implementation of standards in their regulation of accessibility; there is a community of accessibility professionals who self-regulate through collective interactions in various venues. This community exerts a powerful influence upon the meanings and practices of digital media accessibility that only partially overlaps with official regulations. Furthermore, new practitioners are encouraged into the community via the transmission of "industry lore"[63] and enculturation into the field. For instance, textbooks transmit legends of accessibility history, ethical and political instruction in disability rights, and the state of accessibility as a subfield of web development.[64] Though this community includes isolated developers worldwide, it also includes experts who participate in legal and W3C standards formation, corporate employees, consultants, and others who straddle boundaries between the forms of regulation discussed in this chapter. Thus, the community becomes a prime space in which to observe the negotiation of various forms of accessibility regulation, even as it is, itself, a channel of regulation. Through experiences in this community, individuals may take on identities related to accessibility and may adopt specific ideologies and practices regarding accessible web development.

This community is seen in the conferences, websites, and social media use of accessibility practitioners. Many have adopted the Twitter hashtag "#a11y" to indicate tweets related to web or digital media accessibility. This tag shortens *accessibility*—abbreviated into the numeronym *a11y*, where the number 11 stands in for the number of letters omitted—in a way that is both conducive to a 140-character medium while referencing the notion of being an "ally" to users with disabilities. It thus signifies at both practical and political levels, reinforcing the ethical dimension of accessibility as "the right thing to do."[65] Alternately, the community has been referred to as "the tribe,"[66] indicating its status as a close-knit group of people who are distinct from broader cultures of professional web development. The community, via the hashtag, regularly provides news, job announcements, and educational opportunities related to web and digital media accessibility. As a result, it fosters self-regulation by indicating the kinds of information and skills that are valued within the industry and by providing guidance to newcomers. Accessibility consultant Elle Waters recalls getting involved with accessible web content in 2008 and turning to social media to learn the basics and get her questions answered.[67] The use of hashtags links online professional resources into a single, communal self-regulatory practice. What does it mean to practice web accessibility? #a11y comes as close as any other form of regulation to answering this question at a pragmatic, quotidian level.

However, this kind of professional self-regulation can have the effect of shutting down participation and excluding people from the community. Accessibility consultant Karl Groves has criticized the notion of a "special club" of accessibility professionals who "would rather spend their time telling others how wrong they are."[68] The emergence of professional consensus can lead to inflexibility, and—by producing the community along specific lines—social regulation can also produce exclusions. This remains a challenge for the accessibility community, which remains largely white and dominantly male; women of color,[69] people with disabilities, newcomers to the field, and others may find the term *tribe* to be unfortunately apt in its suggestion of separatism and homogeneity.

One case in point is that of aspiring web designer Marissa Christina. Christina, who has a vestibular disorder that affects her balance, energy, and ability to handle some animated graphics, became interested in web design as a career several years ago. She read online materials and listened to podcasts, where professionals would "talk about getting together with groups, and you should get out there and get an internship, and you should, you know, go to these conferences, and get out there! And a lot of that stuff, in the back of my mind, I sort of dismiss because it's not *possible* and I constantly hear that. The way for you to get started in web design is to get out there and join a design agency—OK, so what happens if that's not possible, you know?"[70] Christina had been negotiating with the Department of Rehabilitation in her area, which had specific rules for the kinds of continuing education that it would financially support. She eventually emailed web usability "guru" Jeffrey Zeldman, who co-hosts the *Big Web Show* podcast, describing her situation and what she described as "the disconnect between the web accessibility movement and those that are actually disabled."[71] Zeldman invited her to be a guest on the podcast, where Christina began by asking, "Is a career in web design accessible?"[72] She described her efforts to learn web development skills, answered questions about her disability and web use, and got advice from the co-hosts and callers. Since her appearance, Christina has enrolled in online courses through Treehouse's reduced-cost student plan, and she remains optimistic about her prospects and the future of accessibility within these careers.

Though she and others with disabilities understand the importance of accessibility, practically and politically they may not be able to integrate easily with a professional community that is focused on technology and professionalization. Their experiences with inaccessibility and their love of web media would seem to make them excellent candidates for positions as testers and developers, but there are now more structured paths to success in web development, most of which involve a computer science degree and experience in a design agency, which are not always attainable for people with disabilities. Self-education may no longer be sufficient. Similarly, flexibility is often a concern; many people with disabilities interested in accessible web design would prefer to work from home and pursue credentials on their own time. For instance, Blake Watson is a blogger who has mobility impairments. Although he has a computer science degree and has had jobs in web development, at the time of our interview he was struggling to find a job that would allow him to work from home.[73] In the meantime, he kept up his skills through limited freelance work.

In response to both the regulatory power of an inclusive professional community and its countervailing tendency to exclude those not already experts, members of the industry are currently working to create a professional society and explicit credentialing structures for web accessibility. Such formalization of community regulation could address the inconsistencies and exclusions perpetuated by an informal, social form of community regulation. Discussion of professionalization has been ongoing and has exhibited "concern with control over knowledge, education and regulation."[74] Online credentialing programs, college courses, training modules, and other means of centralized education have been suggested as means of conveying how to "do" accessibility; presumably, these would be based on existing legal and voluntary standards.

Recognition for the field, and its authority, by other sectors of web and digital media development, as well as by corporate clients, appears to be a paramount goal; professionalization, many hope, will communicate the value of accessibility to those outside the community. It is thus unsurprising that these efforts recall the attempts to professionalize computing in the mid–twentieth century through the establishment of educational curricula, industry-based licensing programs, and codes of ethics.[75] Historian of computing Nathan Ensmenger argues that the appeal of professionalization in that case was an increase in social status, greater autonomy, increased chances for career advancement, and higher pay;[76] certainly, many of the same goals are relevant to accessibility professionalization.

This is especially true given that individuals often come to accessibility from other specializations, requiring what Adobe's Matt May calls a "volunteer spirit" within the field.[77] The growth of accessibility requirements and awareness means that such voluntarism is no longer sufficient, and there is a need to create and make visible highly qualified accessibility professionals. As May explains, "Without a professional society it's like we have . . . 'these are the accessibility gurus and these are the accessibility wizards and these are the accessibility medieval barbers.'"[78] Standardization is key to recognition for the community, and validation for its practices outside of its internal discussions. The goal, it would seem, is to produce accessibility professionals who "get it" at an ethical level and are competent to make the subjective determinations that are often required.[79] Centralized, collaborative professionalization would also eliminate the need for internal corporate accessibility trainings and would foster the development of consensus concerning what it means to "do" accessibility.

As of this writing, professionalization efforts have resulted in the formation of the International Association of Accessibility Professionals (IAAP). This organization describes itself as "a membership-based organization for individuals and organizations that are focused on accessibility or are in the process of building their accessibility skills and strategies. The objective of this association is to help accessibility professionals develop and advance their careers and to help organizations integrate accessibility into their products and infrastructure. The IAAP will provide a place for accessibility professionals around the world to gather, share experiences and enrich their knowledge of accessibility."[80] The IAAP has thirty-one founding members, including major technology firms, large banking corporations, advocacy groups, accessibility consulting firms, and assistive technology providers. These members, and their individual representatives, have contributed to the development of educational resources, put together events, and oversee the development of certification programs, the strategic plan, and more elements of IAAP that remain under development.

However, in the formation of the IAAP, members of the accessibility community seemed keenly aware of the political dimension of professionalization. Questions of which experts, and which industry leaders, would devise credentialing programs are fraught; professionalization is a move toward further standardization, in which "standards create winners and losers."[81] Inevitably, it seems, some forms of accessibility knowledge and practice will be privileged over others, which will be cast aside. In the largely self-educated field, this produces a tension, as it seems that the flexibility and expertise required by the current regulatory environments might be constrained by the very community that has heretofore supported self-education within the industry. The breadth of organizations involved in the IAAP, the variety of member levels (from inexpensive student memberships to nonprofit to corporate memberships) and the sentiments of professionals involved all suggest that there is an awareness that this professionalization could produce exclusions and an effort to retain the openness of the preexisting informal communities. Andrew Kirkpatrick, Group Product Manager of Accessibility at Adobe and participant in the development of the IAAP, stated, prior to the organization's debut, that it was "important for us to try and do it well and that means including people, listening to different ideas, and trying to achieve a consensus about the best approach."[82] As in more formal regulatory processes, an ethos of openness and collaboration was evident as accessibility professionals began to more concretely construct themselves as such.

The self-regulation of accessibility professionals via an informal community and increasingly formalized structures bears many similarities to the regulations instantiated through legal, extralegal, and industrial policies. The meaning of *accessibility* is once again tied to ideas of inclusion through technology, tying the social model of disability to detailed technological practices. However, unlike the sites of regulation previously discussed, self-regulation within the professional community involves a crucial element of identity work. In part, this has to do with the neoliberal management of the self and labor within web development and accessibility, in particular.[83] There is a strong strain of entrepreneurialism and individual initiative, seen not only in accessibility consultants but also in the crucial role played by internal advocates—or "evangelists"[84]—in making accessibility a priority in a variety of contexts. Alongside such self-regulation in the interest of career success, however, the self-regulation of the community produces an imagined community of professionals, bound by practices, ethical stances on disability and inclusion, and cultural touchstones. The power of this site of regulation is not in simply defining accessibility but in conveying what it means to be a person who "does" accessibility, who "gets it," and who is a "good" developer.

In the fostering of particular cultural and professional identities, a shared sense of the industry is formed, maintained, and challenged over time. This collective imagining, and the identity work that supports it, may also produce exclusions, indicating the importance of not merely celebrating self-regulation but interrogating its connections to categories of identity and hierarchies of power. Particularly in the case of accessibility, which rests on a social model of disability and an ethics (or politics) of inclusion and equality, it is crucial to consider what kinds of access are encouraged, for whom, and in what ways. Cases like that of aspiring web developer Christina suggest that the inclusive values of accessibility have not necessarily entailed the formation of an inclusive professional community. Instead, the self-regulatory professional practices and expectations may enable the continuance of a charity model of disability, in which it is something that "we" (able-bodied developers) produce for "them" (people with disabilities). As part of this problematic framing, it seems that accessibility is routinely understood as something that is "done," or produced by developers; users are placed on the other side of the equation, as recipients of accessibility, and users with disabilities may not be conceived of or welcomed as participants and producers of accessible digital media. Of course, such exclusions are not the goal of the community and work against its stated norms. This is only an indication of the ongoing importance of interrogating regulation for both its intended and unintended consequences and of recognizing the roles of identity and experience in shaping that regulation.

Regulation in Activist Contexts

The final site of regulation to explore in relation to digital media accessibility is found within activist contexts. Where the regulatory forms discussed earlier in this chapter exert fairly high levels of discursive influence through their ties to government, industry, and other sanctioned institutions—and tend to replicate the understanding of accessibility as a process of technological inclusion for people with disabilities (understood through the social model)—activist constructions of meaning exhibit quite different emphases. Grassroots and activist perspectives display a combination of disability politics and user-centrism that lead accessibility to be understood in terms that incorporate experiential and affective dimensions.

In fact, it is perhaps more apt to talk about these as counterdiscourses, policy translations, or negotiations; they recognize, but do not always partake in (and may explicitly contradict), dominant definitions of accessibility. Considering the discursive meanings of accessibility produced in activist contexts affords one an opportunity to see such translation in action and to consider how the nuances expressed in these contexts might speak back to dominant discourses.

Generally, people with disabilities and activists are much more likely to understand accessibility as closely tied to a user's experience, often with no mention of standards or technical specifications. Curtis Chong, a blind man and longtime board member of the National Federation of the Blind and co-chair of the 2008 TEITAC, delved into this difference: "[W]e can make all the technical specifications we want . . . [but] . . . what I'm focused on is—what is the net effect on the end user? What is the result of all of this work for the person who has to use the technology who has a disability? Is it working or isn't it working? And the stories I'm getting are telling me that it isn't working in a lot of cases, and this is frustrating to me."[85] Such prioritization of user experience is common in activist contexts, where accessibility is often discussed in terms of "the extent to which someone can access or use something"; or serving "as many people as possible." Many of these definitions do not explicitly mention disability but position accessibility as a means of meeting diverse needs, reflecting a coalitional disability politics. Like Chong, many users with disabilities are more concerned with results than with policies or professional practices and less concerned with how the technology works than with whether it works when and how a user needs or wants it to. These emphases were visible in the #CaptionTHIS protest, where feelings, experiences, notions of fairness, and both consumer and citizen identities were on display.

Other forms of activism concerning the closed captioning of streaming media have made similar interventions. The aforementioned lawsuit filed against Netflix demonstrated the utility of civil rights law in pursuing the accessibility of media and communication as consumer services. Following the settlement, National Association of the Deaf CEO Howard Rosenblum stated, "[T]his legal ruling is a major decision that ensures the ADA remains current with this technological age and makes it possible for deaf and hard of hearing people and people with disabilities to have full access to the same programs and services available to everyone else."[86] This statement is based in fairness, which allows it to unite progressive and neoliberal conceptions of access, treating access as a measure of citizen equality to be expressed through availability of consumer choices.

While the colloquial notions of accessibility and access rights that circulate in activist and grassroots contexts deftly blend experience, emotion, and consumer and citizen rights, they may not be instantly understood as regulatory forces. Yet, the more official and elite forms of regulation discussed above do not always filter down to the level of everyday discourse and lived experiences. Instead, informal ideas about accessibility that circulate through social media become important sources of information, knowledge, and politics for many people with disabilities. This is a continuation of the politically educative potential of online media for people with disabilities. Notably, online media offer venues for learning about the social model and other conceptions of disability through the lens of individual experience;[87] bloggers tend to produce nuanced self-representations of experience that do not neatly fit into theoretical boxes.[88] In the sharing of self-representations and the circulation of ideas enabled by a networked online media environment, discourses are produced and strengthened; just as readers may learn of the social model, they can learn about techniques for accessibility and about what *accessibility* "means" within this culture. Blogs, Twitter, and other social networking spaces thus function to regulate identity in much the same way as the professional contexts of accessibility, except that they construct what it means to be a person with a disability, to need access, and to advocate for change on these grounds.

Such discourses may, in turn, feed back to the development of more powerful regulatory forces. This negotiation can sometimes be glimpsed, as in the first comment received on the 2010 Advanced Notice of Proposed Rulemaking (ANPRM) regarding online accessibility under the ADA: "I wish to see Netflix and Hulu to be fully captioned."[89] This comment is quite similar to those seen in #CaptionTHIS tweets, valuing a particular online experience and making a combined appeal as both citizen and consumer. Presumably, it could influence the formation of standards going on at the Department of Justice and the Access Board, though its general nature and technical agnosticism work against its incorporation in legal accessibility policies. The involvement of activists in policy formation also functions as a channel for negotiation of grassroots and official regulations of accessibility, though these processes often reveal tensions and incompatibilities in the goals and mechanisms preferred by nonprofit, government, and industry forces. Ultimately, it is perhaps less useful to attempt to track lines of direct influence between colloquial regulations and other processes than to consider the coexistence of perspectives as an ongoing source of possible misunderstandings, differences in expectations, and alternative possibilities regarding the meanings and practices of accessibility.

Conclusion

Legal, extralegal, industrial, professional, and activist forms of regulation are but a few ways in which a medium, and its paths to access, may be defined, delimited, and otherwise made meaningful and coherent. Regulation may occur through formal channels of policy and enforcement, as well as through informal discourses and disciplinary management of the self as industry, individual, or community. In the case of web and digital media accessibility, regulation has revealed the coexistence of competing frameworks and differing understandings of what constitutes access.

Most notably, examination of the sites of regulation discussed in this chapter has indicated that access to the web and other digital media is often, but not always, understood as a matter of technological structures. The recommendations of policy documents, the instructions of training manuals, and the practices of web developers center on the particular technological decisions that render a web page or other medium accessible to people with disabilities. Though regulation in this form may seem esoteric, it exerts quite real and material power once it is instantiated in practice, hardware, and software. Accessibility standards such as those growing out of WCAG 2.0 are "filter standards," which differentiate those things that pass a certain benchmark from those that do not.[90] As such, they quickly become subject to enforcement through a variety of mechanisms, not least through their instantiation in particular forms of hardware, such as integrated screenreaders on iOS devices. Though control in this form offers little possibility for direct resistance, the diversity of sources of protocol, or regulation, is a fissure through which resistance to totalizing control may erupt.

Yet, technological standards are not the only site of accessibility regulation, and not the only framework within which to define accessibility. Looking to the self-regulation of professionals and the alternate discourses perpetuated in activist and grassroots circles shows that accessibility may alternately involve the formation of specific identities or attention to personal, affective experiences with digital media. In the case of the professional community, attempts to cultivate a shared identity and culture, and to define what it means to "do" accessibility, have resulted in the strengthening of accessibility as a field. However, in defining and producing that community, it is crucial to be aware of oversights and exclusions, particularly as professional self-regulation moves toward more formal structures of education and credentialing. The place of disability in this community is particularly fraught, as the community espouses a politics of disability based upon the social model and notions of equality, even as its practices reveal the potential for exclusion. Similarly, activist and grassroots communities regulate accessibility not through policy but through the production of vernacular understandings of accessibility and its connections to everyday uses of web and digital media. These communities emphasize individual experiences, and even affective dimensions of access, over the technological components. As instantiated through these channels, accessibility of web and digital media becomes a quite different phenomenon than is conveyed through official policy documents.

Last, examination of these sites of regulation reveals that access in the context of digital media retains its connections to both public and neoliberal values. Activist organizations routinely invoke the model of the citizen-consumer to make their arguments, basing those arguments on public values of equality and participation, even as they petition the media industries directly. Additionally, the emphasis on industrial collaboration in legal and W3C policy contexts indicates a blending of these frameworks, where neoliberal ideals of competition and innovation are invoked as a means to more politically progressive ends. Though the regulation of accessibility has certainly been the site of conflicts among stakeholders, who often have different political relationships to disability and different levels of technological expertise, there is a general sense that progressive goals and business imperatives are not, necessarily, at odds. Instead, within the community of experts and policymakers, there is a sense that everyone is, in the words of accessibility evangelist Matt May, "working in the common spirit"[91] toward a shared goal.

Ultimately, that goal seems to be one of technological participation, understood in cultural, economic, and political senses. Accessibility, throughout these sites of regulation, is defined as a means of making web and digital media more available to consumers, so that they may pursue goals of their choosing—and some of those goals may even further public values and expand the involvement of people with disabilities in society at large.

This chapter has attempted to make clear how regulation is not a single process but a web of meanings and practices within which particular meanings of technology and access are achieved and come to be powerful. Though there may be overlap, there are certainly ongoing negotiations, in which competing regulations are brought into contact and sometimes conflict. Similarly, the varied regulatory influences on accessibility exhibit different strengths and realms of influence, with activist understandings being both the least technological and the least privileged. Thus, while elements of official regulations may filter down to this level, there seem to be relatively few efficacious means of challenging these authorities' understandings of accessibility. This does not make counterdiscourses powerless but merely indicates that the process of negotiation and discursive change is an ongoing and unpredictable one.

By asking questions about access and regulation, one may identify discursive forces that come to define a medium and the paths by which it may be accessed. Through study of policy, definitional discourses, and informal regulation of communities and identities, it becomes possible to pry apart what a given medium "means" and what access to that medium is thought to entail. This process also enables analysis of the differing authority and modes of power exhibited by various regulatory forces. Although legal regulations such as those in Section 508 may have more enforcement, the authority granted to the W3C standards is visible through their circulation and harmonization in a variety of contexts. Even as regulation, however, defines a medium and structures access to it, it is not totalizing. Regulatory bodies and practices are but one site through which to gain an understanding of media access; the co-constructive activities of users, the technological forms in question, the content that is conveyed via that medium, and the experiences of users all speak to the ways in which a specific case of media access is made meaningful and can be understood. Even in the example of Netflix streaming, which began this chapter, regulation is at best half the story; #CaptionTHIS hints at the range of uses and users, technological forms, types of content, and overall experiences of access that characterize this growing site of cultural consumption and civic engagement. Thus, though it is often a first stage, regulation, it seems, does not get the last word in the creation of that which it attempts to define.

2

You Already Know How to Use It

Technology, Disability, and Participation

"What is iPad?" So begins a 2010 television commercial for Apple's tablet.[1] The commercial introduces the viewer to this new technology not through specifications but through a series of phrases and images that deftly tie iPad to aspirational values while employing signifiers of race, class, gender, and age to present particular kinds of uses, and types of users, as normative.

iPad is "thin," "beautiful," "goes anywhere," and "lasts all day." Such language could easily describe fashion or other accessories and contains a suggestion of sexuality, indicating desirability of this technology. Multiple shots of people holding and using iPad accompany the male voice as it explains iPad in these vague terms. In each shot, the head is conspicuously absent; instead, we see torsos, often with hands holding iPad, or a view of the knees on which iPad rests (with feet below). The ad features a number of different settings, from outdoor seating areas to offices, and even a moving scooter with two riders, one of whom carries an iPad. The varied backgrounds communicate quite a bit about intended uses and users: We see a man showing a graph to others, all wearing business suits; we see a professional woman using an iPad in what appears to be a design studio; and we see a number of casual male and female ensembles, indicating a youthful—but not rebellious—aesthetic and lifestyle. Professionalism, creativity, and leisure time are thus emphasized in these early images.

Throughout the commercial, race and class are employed in a way which suggests that the "proper" users of iPad are affluent, and that users may employ this technology for either work or pleasure. This is reinforced later on, as we see a black man in a gray business suit looking at images of a young girl, presumably a daughter, and flipping through books on an iPad. He does not fit the dominant racial imagery of the ad, which is white, but his class status appears to compensate, granting entry to use of this technology for both personal and professional purposes. Though he is the only person of color to be a major focus, there is greater diversity of skin tones and dress seen in the ad during a rapid cut sequence in the middle of the advertisement, in which the voiceover explains that there is "no right or wrong way" to use an iPad and that it is "crazy powerful" and "magical." The first phrase suggests a variety of uses and, in combination with the rapid editing, also suggests a diversity of users. The latter two phrases, however, emphasize that iPad is being positioned as a consumer technology, usable by non-experts, and as providing a pleasurable experience.

Along with signifiers of race and class, images of children and women also serve to emphasize the possible diversity of use and users of iPad while affirming its connections to an affluent, largely white audience. In addition to the photographs of the young girl mentioned previously, there are also images of children's books, and in one notable sequence, the torsos of a white woman and young girl, wearing pink and purple clothing, using iPad together. Parenthood may be functioning in some ways as a stand-in for class status and like the suggestions of sexuality earlier may act as an aspirational marker for the target audience of affluent young or middle-aged adults balancing career and family. Yet, the image of the young girl and (presumably) her mother also coincides with the only "instructions" in the advertisement; as they share iPad, the voiceover declares, "You already know how to use it." This suggests, again, that this is a consumer technology usable by "anyone." The fact that the accompanying image is entirely female, and multi-generational, reaffirms this message by recalling stereotypes about women's lack of skill with technology and using youth to indicate a lack of knowledge or experience.

Taken as a whole, this advertisement positions iPad technology as appropriate for particular uses and users. It is a consumer technology, for entertainment and workplace uses, not a tool for technological development or innovation. It is pleasurable, associated with phrases and images that convey an affluent, easy lifestyle with associations of sexuality and family. It is for "you," an imagined advertising audience of one and many, simultaneously. It is to be used in "your" hands, or on "your" lap, suggesting the way in which the technology is to be handled and used by "your" body. Notably, disability, per se, is absent from this commercial. The bodies seen exhibit many other forms of visible difference, but differences in ability and embodiment are not seen or otherwise referenced.

The analysis of this commercial begins to demonstrate the ways in which *intended uses* are communicated via discourse and come to structure expectations of a medium's use and users. In this chapter, I trace several examples of the cultural construction of intended uses and users in order to discuss *preferred user positions*, hegemonic arrangements of uses, users, and circumstances through which a medium and access to it are constructed and reinforced. The danger in a preferred user position is the way it comes to stand in for "the" use, "the" user, and the default experience of a medium. Returning to the iPad ad, "you" already knew how to use it only if you were using it in the default ways demonstrated in the ad and for the purposes that were foregrounded. Alternative arrangements of bodies, motivations, and cultural contexts are absent from this dominant discourse, and looking to a marginalized audience offers insight into *actual* uses and user positions that reveals these assumptions and undermines their dominance. Disability destabilizes the preferred user position and forces consideration of specific arrangements of bodies, technology, culture, and power.

Interrogating Use

The interrogatory kit established in the Introduction to this book establishes five perspectives from which one might study media access: regulation, use, form, content, and experience. Though these domains are primarily conceptual frameworks, constructed on the basis of context and in respect to methodologies and research questions, their separation and elaboration allows a deep, nuanced, and potentially conflicting image of media access to emerge. Following the previous chapter's focus on regulation—the processes by which a medium and access to it become variously defined and negotiated—this chapter asks questions related to "use." Here, it is imperative to consider what the standard, or intended, uses of a medium might be, how that medium might actually be used in other ways, and who is using and accessing it. Thus, the three questions that underlie this analytic domain (and this chapter) are as follows:

What is a given medium "for"? How is it meant to be accessed and used, and
   by whom?
What are the assumptions or defaults of the user position in this case, in terms
   of bodies, cultures, and technologies?
What alternate uses and user positions are there, and how are they found,
   negotiated, or discouraged?

The questions posed under the framework of "use" encompass *intended*
and *actual uses* and *users*. That is to say, this is a perspective from which
one may both investigate the ways in which a media technology is
intended to be used and accessed by a particular audience, and the ways
in which it may be taken up by quite different users for quite different
purposes. Australian media and disability scholars Katie Ellis and Mike
Kent offer a concise description of how the wide variety of user positions might be imagined:

> Each person ultimately accesses the internet on their own; each individ-
> ual computer screen is designed for a solitary user. . . . The hardware of
> the computer hosts the software of its operating system and other pro-
> grams. The fusion of these two elements enables the digital environment
> represented at the analog edge of the computer screen, this then inter-
> faces with wetware, or the person using the device and their knowledge
> and experience. . . . The fourth element—cultware—describes the digital
> and analog environment in which the user is embedded, and the value
> and characteristics of that environment.[2]

The moment of access is ultimately individual, but relational, existing
in connections between hardware, software, bodies, minds, and cultural
and material contexts. The prescriptive discourses of use may delimit
this moment, or users may take this opportunity to rearticulate these
elements and create new uses and new user positions. Thus, this chapter
looks to discourse, representation, and interview and ethnographic data
to consider media uses as co-constructed phenomena.

   Questions related to use ought to reveal the assumptions that underlie encounters with online and digital media; this should be a process
of denaturalization, in which variation and difference are uncovered
and restored to conceptions of the medium itself. Thus, this chapter

delves quite deeply into discourses and experiences of disability and technology, highlighting the ways in which default modes of engagement and access are not, in fact, universally accessible or desirable. A crucial component of this work lies in unpacking the metaphors of disability used in discourses of new media, revealing their ideological foundations and implications in these contexts. Disability can serve as a sign of collapse when employed metaphorically, emphasizing the normativity of the nondisabled body and mind.[3] Additionally, utopian discourses of the future often explicitly present disability as "eradicated" or overcome. In both cases, disability retains its stigma and serves as a dystopic counterpoint to the potential of the technologized future.

Given the creative and potentially political uses of participatory culture, it is particularly important that its uses and users not be taken for granted. As contemporary media scholars Henry Jenkins, Sam Ford, and Joshua Green conclude, "If we see participatory culture, though, as a vital step toward the realization of a century-long struggle for grassroots communities to gain greater control over the means of cultural production and circulation—if we see participation as the work of publics and not simply of markets and audiences—then opportunities to expand participation are struggles we must actively embrace through our work, whether through efforts to lower economic and technical obstacles or to expand access to media literacies."[4] British scholar Sonia Livingstone, who has long studied media access and youth audiences, similarly argues that in conducting audience research in an age of participation, "the conceptual shift is from an exclusive focus on the viewer to a focus on the interaction between text and reader or between inscribed and actual viewer/user."[5] It is not enough to consider the text, however, as a similar relationship is forged at the moment of access that precedes and structures subsequent relations. Intended use, actual use, and the contexts in which each take shape should be fundamental not only to understanding diverse media audiences but also to conceptualizing the nature of media access and the complexity of media and culture themselves. The study of disability at the site of use destabilizes easy generalizations about contemporary digital media technologies, forcing deeper engagement with what is possible, what is easy, and what is potentially transformative.

Diversity, Disability, and the Dot-Coms: Intended Uses and Users of the Early Web

The discursive construction of the web during its early years centered on introducing this new technology, and its possible uses, to audiences of possible consumers. As in the case of iPad, there was a persistent effort to paint this new media technology as pleasurable and usable by an untrained audience. Additionally, however, discourses surrounding the early web incorporated utopian discourses of the near future, often expressed via diversity and the overcoming of disability. Furthermore, while there are progressive political dimensions to these discourses, particularly concerning notions of equality, it must once again be emphasized that there are neoliberal elements present; advertising existed to sell these services to consumers, and both news and advertising routinely celebrated consumer agency and choice, as well as individual self-actualization via new media technologies.

The cultural climate of the early web has been described in terms of both utopianism and romanticism. Ted Friedman, a cultural studies scholar of new media, argues that "cyberculture" provided an opportunity for imagining different futures, though these images did not contradict multi-national capitalism.[6] Utopian discourses promised a better future through technology, and that better future was quite often articulated to greater diversity and meritocratic ways of being. In these discussions, technology is an agent of change, reflecting a technological determinism that saps agency from individuals' uses of technology and predicts uniform outcomes. Romanticism, in contrast, promised individual self-actualization via technology; "dreams of freedom, self-expression, and the dramatic overthrow of the powers that be"[7] powered much of the popular and economic enthusiasm about the World Wide Web.

Advertising for internet service providers and related services were one site in which disability was commonly tied to the possibilities of new technologies and forms of participation. These ads were aimed at a broad audience of possible consumers, with the understanding that early adopters were more likely to be affluent, white, male, and parents of young children.[8] The emphasis on children in the 1990s was no accident; educational possibilities were regularly highlighted as benefits of new media technologies. Additionally, as argued by feminist disability theorist Alison Kafer, children are often used as representations of the future; if disability is disavowed in futurist discourses, childhood is often both romanticized as innocent and associated with utopian possibilities. Kafer summarizes this phenomenon, describing futurist discourse as "the stories we tell ourselves as a culture—disability is a tragedy, children are our future."[9] Therefore, I look to how advertisements in the 1990s often incorporated images of both disability and children, along with gender and racial differences. Race and digital media theorist Lisa Nakamura examined images of race in advertising for early internet technologies, arguing that "the spectacles of race in these advertising images are designed to stabilize contemporary anxieties that networking technology and access to cyberspace may break down ethnic and racial differences."[10] As images of race counteracted claims of a race-less future, easing the minds of those who would prefer stable racial and ethnic relations, so images of disability confirmed the normalcy of an abled user position even in a radically inclusive technological future.

A series of 1993 advertisements for AT&T titled "You Will" presented visions of a networked future, including paying tolls without stopping a car, tucking a child into bed over a video call, navigating a car without asking for directions, or sending a fax from a tablet, among other things.[11] One in this series of advertisements offered a brief sequence that incorporated disability, childhood, race, and gender. It features an image of a black woman in a wheelchair being pushed by another person through a hospital hallway, and the camera pans to a white man being asked for "her card, please." The voiceover asks if you have ever "carried your medical history in your wallet" as a male doctor, looking at an ultrasound image of a fetus, informs the man that "[his] wife will be just fine."

This vignette packs multiple messages concerning disability, childhood, gender, race, and the utopian digital future. Associations with disability are made through the signification of the wheelchair, and the location within a hospital; although the ad clarifies that this is a woman going into delivery, these signs tie it to disability for a mass audience accustomed to this association through handicapped-parking emblems and similar representations. Furthermore, pregnancy and birth themselves may be understood in terms of disability as a political category, via experiences of medicalization. The black woman, pregnant and potentially situationally disabled, stands in for utopian ideas about diversity in the networked future. She embodies multiple forms of bodily difference and is partnered with a white man, which adds connotations of equity to the invocation of diversity. It is no coincidence that this is a scene of reproduction, in which the (presumably mixed-race) fetus signifies an optimistic future, transformed by networked digital technologies. Yet, neither the woman nor the baby is granted agency in this future. Her medical history card is not in *her* pocket but is handled by her partner in conversation with another man. This suggests that while images of disability, children, women, and people of color might be used in selling these technologies, these politically disempowered bodies are not represented as users in control of these tools. At best, they are passive beneficiaries of these advances. This representation locates agency and power within white and male bodies, constructing a normative user and relegating the invocations of disability, childhood, gender, and race to the status of window dressing.

Similar invocations of disability and childhood can be seen in contemporaneous advertisements. MCI's 1997 "Anthem" advertisement promised a future in which "People can communicate mind-to-mind. There is no race. There are no genders. There is no age."[12] With the next statement, "There are no infirmities," the ad shows a blond teenager communicating the message through American Sign Language, intercut with a computer screen displaying the words. The youth of the signer suggests an optimistic vision of the near future, while d/Deafness was invoked as one of many "spectacles of difference that the narrative simultaneously attempts to erase by claiming that MCI's product will reduce the different bodies we see to 'just minds.'"[13] This form of representation invokes difference through bodies without considering the means by which depicted groups might or might not have access to the technology being sold. Instead, national, racial, gender, and financial differences in access were elided for an uplifting image that supports the centrality of the already-empowered, financially advantaged, white, Western viewer.

The "Anthem" sequence suggests an overcoming of disability, a "fixing" via technology that extends old representations of overcoming disability through hard work, inspiring effort, or charitable intervention.

Overcoming narratives have been widely criticized because they retain messages about the deficiency of disability and may create unrealistic expectations of people with disabilities; failure to overcome disability may be thus understood as a personal failure, enabling greater cultural devaluation of individuals who do not exceed their life circumstances.[14] In the words of Kafer, when such narratives are extended into representations of otherwise utopian futures, "the value of a future that includes disabled people goes unrecognized, while the value of a disability-free future is seen as self-evident."[15] Such representations can, at their worst, be understood as eliminationist; in all cases, they promote assimilation with mainstream cultures and values and deny the worth of disability communities or cultures.

Both advertisements, however, erased the material realities of experiencing computer and internet technology as a person with a disability. Showing such differences would only weaken the universalist message, demonstrating alternatives to the normative ways of using this technology. In these advertisements, people associated with disability are "potential" users: We do not see the woman or child control her medical history; we do not see the Deaf teenager typing those words or otherwise using a computer. Invoking this diversity, while ignoring the methods and forms of use that would accompany it, is ultimately politically regressive. These images uphold the experiences of a nondisabled, adult, largely white, and affluent audience as an unquestioned default, even when that user position is impossible or inappropriate to the simultaneous representations of disability and difference. Representations such as these constructed and enforced a preferred user position, a set of normative relations between bodies and technologies, that ultimately reinforced ideologies of ability and perpetuated social hierarchies in which disability was devalued. The presentation of disability not only did not challenge the default uses and users of emerging technologies but further served to affirm those assumptions as natural and positive. Thus, the different technological needs and desires of people with disabilities were not incorporated, and, instead, representations emphasized the possibility of extending a normative user position to people with disabilities. The affluent, white, able user position remained central, allowing it to persist as a normative, assumed perspective on new media technologies' uses.

Web 2.0, the User, and "You"

Following the dot-com crash, popular discourses about the web and academic theorizing of digital media shifted away from the speculative and toward the figure of the user. Web development became increasingly concerned with usability and other forms of user-centered design.[16] The new centrality of the user reached its apex in the rise of Web 2.0 and the celebration of participatory culture. The user, often described as "you," was now an empowered figure, and the locus of the transformative potential of digital media. Still an individualist model, Web 2.0 and participatory culture exhibited an even greater emphasis on self-expression along with growing integration of the user into neoliberal business models, most often based upon advertising and consumer choice. Users, it seemed, were culturally and politically empowered citizens, even as they were exploited sources of revenue creation and targets for commercial advertising. Yet only some users were part of this discussion; the user of Web 2.0 and participatory culture is a curiously flat figure, and once again, considering where disability does and does not appear in these discourses reveals the normative components and political elisions of "the user."

Web 2.0 emerged in web-related industries as a way of talking about websites that provided scaffolding for users' content and activities, and as a business plan for reinventing the web. In his elaboration of "Web 2.0," technologist and publisher Tim O'Reilly declared that these services feature "an implicit 'architecture of participation,' a built-in ethic of cooperation, in which the service acts primarily as an intelligent broker, connecting the edges to each other and harnessing the power of the users themselves."[17] Value for a web company would be created through its ability to encourage users to share information or creative works and then to utilize this content and the connections between users to create added value and keep their users coming back. Web 2.0 implicitly differentiates websites and services in the early 2000s from their 1990s counterparts, establishing a new context in which users are central to the content production and monetization of online media.

In celebrations of Web 2.0, the empowered user is one who easily uses tools and services to create, circulate, or curate content. The differences among users go unremarked upon, in part because of the relentless focus on early adopters as ideal users. Early adopters, those with the technological and financial resources to pursue the latest innovations in online services and devices, represent a cutting-edge market and first audience for new sites and services but are ultimately a limited perspective on the possible users and uses of media technology. Though the "user" is ostensibly an unmarked category, its very inattention to difference within the category serves to uphold the same white, affluent, able, and Western perspective described previously. The users have power to produce online culture, and the means by which that power is granted, accessed, and employed remain largely invisible.

An incredibly powerful avenue by which the centrality of a privileged user position was maintained during the era of Web 2.0 was through the pervasive rhetoric of "you." The direct, second-person address of "you" rings of familiarity and hails masses of people in language that emphasizes individuality. Imaginatively, we can each be the subject of this address, which takes aim at individual identities and desires, suggesting an ability to fulfill unique needs and even to set "you" apart from the masses of others. The "you" hails readers and viewers as potential collaborators in the fast-changing online environment, allows us to flatter ourselves as creative producers, and flattens the vast differences in how we do and do not use online media. The invocation of "you" asserts an ideal, even utopian, conception of the user, ignoring questions of access, constraints, and desire that undoubtedly influenced the ability to use these services.

This idealized "you" was hailed by many Web 2.0 sites and services, themselves, drawing upon both the utopianism and salesmanship of this rhetoric. In logos, names, and taglines, repeated invocations of what "you" can do with social media—such as YouTube's "Broadcast Yourself" and Flickr greetings that exclaimed "Hej! Now you know how to say hello in Swedish!"—welcomed the user as an active, productive, empowered individual. These greetings' use of the second-person address suggested that Internet media were both immediate and fully under one's personal, unmediated control. The use of direct address encouraged a more personal engagement, a friendly relationship with media, and thus also conveyed a kind of liveness and immediacy that was augmented by the interactive potential of online media.

In corporate contexts, and as explicitly used in advertising for web-sites and services, the "you" peddled empowerment while bringing users into an economy in which not only their purchases but also their use data produced value. The "you" flattened differences of experience and embodiment, as is common in advertising discourses, where it promotes individual consumption rather than public achievements.[18] What "you" choose to consume, how "you" take up identities, and "your" relations to other people and institutions are prescribed (and proscribed) by adver-tising discourses that permeate neoliberal late capitalism and proliferate in digital media contexts. Beyond direct advertising, Web 2.0 and simi-lar twenty-first-century media monetized data and user preferences, uti-lizing labor that users may not even have known they were providing.[19]

Yahoo!'s 2009 advertisement "It's You" explicitly relied on the "you" to produce a vision of an active, personalized, and pleasurable online expe-rience.[20] It seemed less a sales pitch than a recruitment message, attempt-ing to draw users into Yahoo!'s free services so that they might become part of the user base upon which Yahoo!'s value to advertisers is founded. This advertisement—and other corporate uses of "you"—employed the utopian spirit of the early internet and discourses of Web 2.0 participa-tion alongside a celebration of consumerism.[21] It employed signs of di-versity, rapidly cutting between images of global landmarks, multi-racial and multi-ethnic individuals, and several images of children. In contrast to advertising that accompanied the early web, technology itself was not visible; there were no computers in this advertisement, no headphones, no suggestion of technological skill or development. What was being sold was not access to a utopia via technology but access to an individually centered smorgasbord of options for an active, consuming user.

The imagery in this commercial was centered on action—running, jumping, kicking a soccer ball, blowing kisses. These actions are plea-surable and unserious and suggested that the experience of web media should be the same. Such activity additionally suggested an ideal active (abled) user, an association only made stronger through the repeated emphasis on "you." The ad used the word seven times in its voiceover, and it was even spelled out by dancers in a club, as seen in a shot from above. The promise in this advertisement was not of collective advance-ment but of wholly individual fulfillment via chosen activities, com-pleted "In new ways. You ways."

In this context, the images of diversity and activity were presented not as indicative of what "you" actually do but as representative of the entertainment and consumptive uses "you" may command. For instance, the shots of Las Vegas–style showgirls that opened and closed the ad communicates a spectator position, offering both a dominant gaze and a passivity to "you." That this was an image of women was not incidental; this advertisement was less interested in what "you" do than in how you consume, with women's bodies offered for the consumption of a dominant, male-identified viewer. By implication, the viewers/users were placed in a position of control, their agency upheld through their ability to choose and consume from a wide range of options. Images of racial and ethnic diversity worked similarly, with South Asian scenes crafted not to entice South Asian users but to present a comforting image of the many choices available to a normative white Western user. Such invitations to "you" figured the user as powerful and downplayed the structuring role and profit motivations of the services in question. "You" may create, but for Yahoo!'s purposes, your consumption is far more central.

Digital media theorist Wendy Hui Kyong Chun engaged with the rhetorics of "you" in her 2011 book *Programmed Visions*. She wrote: "You. Everywhere you turn, it's all about you—and the future. You, the produser. Having turned off the boob tube, or at least added YouTube, you collaborate, you communicate, you link in, you download, and you interact . . . empowered. . . . But, who or what are you?"[22] These examples seem to indicate that "you" embody a default user position that was white, male, and wealthy. You were simultaneously an active agent, creating and participating, and a target market, shopping and creating value through user-generated content. You were assumed to be technologically empowered, with the necessary hardware, software, knowledge, time, and interest to jump into new online offerings, but you were not expected to have technical knowledge or specialized skills. Additionally, you were assumed to be capable of using default technological structures and interfaces, even as personalization at the level of content was encouraged.

This ideal user, discursively created and circulated via the "you" of Web 2.0, overstates the power of the user while underplaying differences in users and experiences. Media scholar Michele White argues that signs of agency and control, such as the pointer finger, are used by online media to construct an empowered user even as the use experience is quite specifically designed to be limited, even passive.[23] Invitations to action, the provision of choices, and the use of direct address ("you") imply opportunities for interaction and meaningful activity, even as sites and services offer only limited possibilities. Media theorist José van Dijck makes similar critiques in her study of social media, arguing that the figure of the user is often bolstered by false dichotomies between "active" new media and "passive" old media, without attention to the varied skills and contexts that characterize users and their uses of these technologies.[24] The ideal user, invoked uncritically, perpetuates the individualism and romanticism of digital media cultures as well as a neoliberal emphasis on the self as constructed through constrained consumer choices. Through its generalizations, it divorces online and offline activities, identities, and bodies from one another, cutting off investigation of the varied articulations that enable access.

From the standpoint of disability, the ideal user of Web 2.0 is another instance of an able-bodied norm's being taken as the standard for technological design, use, and meaning. The total absence of disability in the discourse of "you" is not a sign of a "better" future but an absence through which the centrality of ability is maintained. Web 2.0 sites and services depend upon users to contribute content and use features, producing salable data along the way. The inability to do so, due to inaccessible websites, incompatible assistive technologies intermediating the body and the web, or intrinsic experiences of physical, mental, or intellectual disability, positions users with disabilities outside of this discourse. Accessibility and the experiences of users with disabilities thus reveal the hollowness of "you" and the way in which only specific configurations of bodies, technologies, and culture were invited into Web 2.0. Such a narrow invitation is indicative of the hegemony (and durability) of a preferred user position in relation to online media.

The Preferred User Position

The preceding sections have focused on the construction of an ideal user via popular discourse; the in-control user is routinely contrasted with the "passive" spectator or viewer of film or television, and the user's interaction with technology and degree of control over the media encounter is privileged. However, assuming a universal "user" encourages what sociologist of media policy Thomas Streeter identifies as the perception that "'everyone' is on the internet, using email, using Facebook, and so on—in a way that systematically ignores cultural and economic barriers to access and differences in use."[25] It is again too easy to assume that users fit dominant physical and cultural norms and to perpetuate an able-bodied standard and the exclusion of people with disabilities from forms of cultural and civic participation.

Instead of reifying the figure of the user, it is necessary to consider how a user position is constructed, inhabited, and challenged through both discourse and particular uses of media technology by diverse users. The user position structures experiences of access, communicating what the experience of media access and subsequent use ought to be and equally indicating which uses, and user positions, are outside of that normative articulation. The user position is (like access itself) a relational construct, understood as the intersection of culture and technology, body and representation. Studies of "the interface," or "software," or "code" produce detailed analyses and critiques of the technological structures and uses that are set forth by a given site, service, or technology.[26] Yet they nearly always adopt a universalizing tone, looking to software as a "core" element that defines the incredibly varied uses of digital media. As argued by Wendy Chun, software does not offer such analytic transparency but is yet another variable in the study of new media.[27] Software studies, similarly, too often adopts and perpetuates a default relationship between users, bodies, cultures, content, technology, and media. By taking a relational approach to the study of use and users, software studies is disabled; it becomes impossible to study "the" interface without considering how that interface may be taken up and altered in various contexts, by various people. Instead, specific study is called for, enabling attention to the ways in which access and use are endlessly modular and reconfigurable in different circumstances.

This is not to say that some user positions aren't dominant. The assumed uses and users discussed in the previous cases are dominant, and they invoke articulations of bodies, culture, and technology that are easily taken up by some individuals and come to function as a norm against which all other uses and users are positioned. These may be considered examples of the construction of a *preferred user position*. A preferred use position allows us to think outside of determinist narratives and see the flexibility available in the articulations of culture, bodies, and technologies. It is analogous to the theorization of preferred reading positions of media texts offered by cultural studies theorist Stuart Hall. In respect to media and meaning, Hall positions encoding and decoding as relatively autonomous moments in the mediated communication process; messages are semiotically assembled and made sense of in relation to dominant and alternative frameworks.[28] Both stages draw upon and potentially reinforce naturalized codes of meaning and interpretation, allowing for the spread and strength of hegemonic meanings and structures of power. Hall identifies the dominant-hegemonic position as that which occurs when a viewer decodes a message in the same dominant terms with which it was constructed. This preferred reading position is one in which dominant meanings are reinforced, and this process can be so naturalized as to be invisible, granting those meanings the status of common sense inevitabilities. Hall additionally suggests that there are oppositional and negotiated reading positions, the first a deliberate attempt to read against the grain and the second arrived at through the interaction of cultural codes and individual circumstances.

A preferred user position operates similarly, but at the level of the physical as well as the interpretive. In using a particular medium or technology, such as the web, we must both interpretively accept the meanings of cursors, arrows, and other interface components, while also positioning our bodies to use default structures including keyboards, mice, and often vertical screens. Interfaces and hardware alike are, by and large, shaped around a set of assumptions about the bodies, capacities, and interpretive strategies of an end audience. From the analogy of the "desktop" to the operation of copy and paste commands, computer and internet use is largely based on metaphors that themselves draw upon particular Western cultural processes.[29] In making sense of these metaphors using dominant hegemonic frameworks, we are invited to take up positions as "users"—active, capable individuals. The design of interfaces, websites, and hardware encourages this set of meanings, as do representations and metaphors of technology as transparently aiding users in their goals. At the physical, embodied level of use, preferred user positions encourage sitting—at a desk, with a laptop, the user's body folded and seated—and gazing at a lit screen, using fine motor skills to type or control a mouse. Such disciplining of the body has ramifications, from the fatigue of long use to the fatness, carpal tunnel, and even disabling conditions discussed and boasted about by computer programmers.[30]

The preferred user position is a hegemonic structure, serving the interests of the powerful while creating normative standards against which others may be measured and measure themselves. Disability makes these material enforcements of hegemony obvious, as consideration of media accessibility can illustrate. A television set assumes an audience capable of receiving audiovisual material; captions are opt-in, and video description is only rarely available. Such technologies maintain the hegemony of the preferred user position through their materiality and their status as a default; in doing so, they uphold an able-bodied norm regarding media and society more broadly.

Preferred user positions reflect idealized access conditions, which are normalized as defaults around which policies and technologies are regularly formed. Therefore the study of use, and the study of preferred and other user positions, must move beyond the discursive and technological; in the words of David Morley, a cultural studies scholar focused on audience studies, "[W]e need to set ethnographic stories of domestic consumption in the wider context . . . and then see how people work with these technologies in and against these existing, powerful discourses which work to construct 'preferred readings' of their desirability and uses."[31] Discourses of industry, academia, and popular culture construct technology as desirable for particular users in particular ways. To denaturalize these discourses, it is imperative to not merely identify a preferred user position but also to explore alternative user positions and negotiations. Disability and the inability to use default interfaces or the need for alternative interfaces represents a fruitful area of inquiry into the atypical ways in which bodies become materially and symbolically articulated to technology. They reveal alternate user positions, and alternate uses, that exist alongside—and may challenge—the hegemony of the preferred arrangements. Hegemonic understandings of use and the user are strong, but they are flexible and open to potential challenges. Such challenges, however, are rarely easy. While users with disabilities (among others) certainly craft user positions that differ from the preferred user position and encompass different uses, it must be remembered that their doing so comes at some cost, whether measured in dollars, effort, or emotional labor.

It's Not You, It's Them

In the construction of a preferred user position, there are, inevitably, users who are excluded and must take up or construct alternate user positions. The "you" of Web 2.0 thus always implies the existence of "them": those who are not invited, those who are not associated with the pleasures and agency of these technologies, and those who cannot take up these user positions because of different articulations of bodies and technologies. One way in which people with disabilities have been consistently excluded from preferred user positions is through nonfictional media representations of technology as a means to "fix" individual disability through consumer choices.

During the 1990s, in keeping with the use of disability as a sign of a utopian future, news reporting emphasized the benefits of digital media for people with disabilities. The internet, and computers in general, was often discussed as a "lifeline" that could connect people with disabilities to the rest of the world.[32] Such a statement, of course, suggests that these connections did not already exist, referencing an assumed isolation of disability from broader public culture. Users with disabilities were presented as uniquely empowered online, as "things are getting better all the time,"[33] because the web could offer opportunities for employment for blind people,[34] or because it "has changed forever the lives of blind people."[35] A dot-com CEO stated, "[T]he Internet is a great equalizer for the handicapped and home bound."[36] These, and other news items, conveyed a certainty that consumer technology would remedy inequalities without requiring social activism or broader changes.

Furthermore, these claims, while *about* disability, were not made to an audience of people with disabilities. Instead, most of these stories were written as human-interest pieces, explaining web accessibility and the needs of people with disabilities to an audience that was assumed to be unfamiliar with these topics. As a result, these stories often began by explaining the difficulties of disability and technology: Computer technology was useful, but it was also "an endless source of frustration";[37] technology was accessible, but people with disabilities feared that it might become less so;[38] and advocates requested greater attention to accessibility features, as they were "being forced onto a side road."[39] These challenges, and disability as a substandard experience, served as the "before" stage, presaging the transformations that would "fix" (or eliminate) disability. Mainstream media stories presented access problems as likely to be solved quickly through voluntary industrial and consumer measures and not legal regulations. It was often argued that greater accessibility would lead to greater financial success, as "in the competitive rough and tumble of the .com world, widely accessible Web sites and service providers will have the edge."[40] Why would accessible sites have an edge? Because people with disabilities were regularly refigured as a "new" consumer group, compatible with the growing field of e-commerce. Articles promised that "cybershopping can open new opportunities"[41] for people with disabilities who were "eager to use the Internet and use [their] credit cards and spend [their] money on line"[42] and could "shop for products online and get as much information as they want."[43] Shopping via online media was presented as a means of elevating people with disabilities from their deficient positions, enabling them to take up a preferred user position.[44]

These statements, and reporting in this vein, illustrate what has been called a consumer model of disability, whereby people with disabilities are positioned as consumers who choose from a range of options and self-advocate for attention to their needs.[45] The consumer model of disability, like the charity model, often conflicts with rights-based or social models of disability, as the suggestion that governments actively protect the rights of people with disabilities by requiring their needs be met is incompatible with market- or charity-based perspectives in which the needs of people with disabilities are understood as optional.

Remarkably, even after the rise of Web 2.0 and discourses of participation from 2008 onward, these earlier trends remained firmly in place. News discourses continued to represent people with disabilities as associated primarily with serious uses of consumer technologies that offered to fix disability at an individual level. People with disabilities were not positioned as participants—"you" or "us"—but as passive beneficiaries of others' technological creations, as a special population—as "them." Popular coverage of issues related to disability and technology conveyed this address subtly by describing the experiences of people with disabilities for an uninformed nondisabled audience. Many bloggers and reporters thus created a situation in which they, and their audience, were aligned in a nondisabled perspective, looking out at disability. For instance, a *Computerworld* article titled "Blind users still struggle with 'maddening' computing obstacles" foregrounded the particular barriers, assistive technologies, and legal structures surrounding blind users' use of the internet.[46] Likely familiar to internet users who were blind or visually impaired, this information is presented as novel for a mainstream audience, positioning internet users with disabilities in opposition to the normative "you," the subject of the address.

Where the preferred user of discourses of participation and Web 2.0 was active, creative, and collaborative, popular press coverage of disabled people's use of the internet constructed a subject who was passive, consumptive, and collective. Many stories focused on hurdles for people with disabilities, then interviewed technological specialists or policy advocates about solutions to these problems, giving little voice to those users who had had these experiences and positioning them as recipients of various forms of aid.[47] Similarly, as when the technology website *Gizmodo* expressed concern that mobile applications might not be made accessible to blind users, people with disabilities were positioned as consumers and end users of hardware and software, not as potential producers of content and applications, thereby rhetorically cutting them off from potential uses otherwise tied to Web 2.0 and participation.[48]

Disability, it seems, was not easily incorporated into either utopian or participatory discourses of the Web. In both cases, it was represented as a special case, more serious and more consumer-driven than mainstream uses of technology. People with disabilities thus formed a "them," an Other against which the preferred user position could be compared. The specialized uses of technology by people with disabilities presented in these examples served to reinforce differences, regardless of possibly well-intentioned educational goals. Furthermore, these articles promised a future in which disability was made irrelevant and thus served to reinforce preferred user positions. Rather than consider how disability might challenge existing technological systems, cultural discourses, or default uses, these stories implicitly argued that Web technologies would enable people with disabilities to take up a preferred (abled) user position. Technology can be a double-edged sword in this regard, as it can serve to normalize people with disabilities by allowing them to take up normative subjectivities, but it does so only through reproduction of divisions between the normal and deviant.[49] In other words, news pieces about the utility of the internet for people with disabilities often depended upon affirming the value of a nondisabled subject position and offering technology as a means by which people with disabilities might, in some ways, take up that position and become normalized. Differences in opinion or experience were not made meaningful in these stories, and the stories certainly were not presented as a possible challenge to existing technological structures, political practices, or cultural assumptions about disability. Instead, both ideologies of ability and preferred user positions are upheld through the contrasting presentation of users with and without disabilities.

Disability Participation and Politicized Uses

Disability presents a challenge to preferred user positions, not least through the mere acknowledgment that people with disabilities may be users of mainstream digital media technologies. Too often, disability is conceived of as outside the normal range of civic and cultural experiences; asserting the presence of people with disabilities as users, using these tools in both normal and innovative ways, is itself a political action. The progressive potential of such interventions lies in their challenge to the preferred user position, their assertion of a disabled user position as inherently valuable to participation and democracy, and the furtherance of a cross-disability coalitional politics.

People with disabilities use many of the same Web 2.0 tools popular among others, and by adapting and using these media technologies they assert the existence of alternate user positions and kinds of use. The online network of Blind Photographers was a particularly direct affront to the dominance of a sighted user position. Photography, a visual medium, may seem incompatible with blindness or other visual impairment. However, users with a variety of visual impairments joined the Blind Photographers Flickr group, blog, photoblog, Twitter account, Tumblr, and informal Twitter network.[50] In all of these spaces, members shared their creative work as well as their creative and technical processes, ranging from artistic influences to specific camera adaptations and large-scale editing techniques. This behavior recalls the ideals of Web 2.0 or participatory culture, as the community encourages artistic self-expression, sharing, and mutual education. Disability at the site of use was strikingly similar to the uses pursued by nondisabled audiences, in these ways. The photographs themselves similarly resembled those that might be found in any photoset—landscapes, flora, urban scenes, portraits, travel photos, and so on. They produced what media and visual culture scholar Susan Murray describes as "a collaborative experience: a shared display of memory, taste, history, signifiers of identity, collection, daily life and judgement through which amateur and professional photographers collectively articulate a novel, digitized (and decentralized) aesthetics of the everyday."[51]

Yet, in the declaration of the group's disabled identity, the context of these photos is changed, and the use and users in question are marked as non-normative. Art historian Rosalind Krauss has argued that the artistic medium is no longer material but encompasses contexts such as the technologies of presentation and the discourses through which an art object is interpreted.[52] Blind Photographers dramatically altered the context of interpretation, forcing interrogation of Flickr, the photographic process, and dis/abled user positions. In sites beyond Flickr, participants' discussions of the multiple media and technologies used to take, edit, and share photographs indicated that the medium of "photography" is, in some cases, a hybrid of digital hardware, software, and assistive technology. For instance, many participants used large projection set-ups to view and edit their photographs before sharing them in standard size. This was an invisible part of the final work, as seen on Flickr, but constituted a part of the medium, the use, and the user experience of this photography.

The invocation of blindness additionally challenged mainstream expectations regarding users and uses of photography and the web and contributed to a collective social and potentially political identity. Though the group's name suggested a uniform identity and experience of blindness, it is in fact diverse, encompassing individuals with partial blindness, color-blindness, cataracts, and a number of other visual impairments. Yet, the shared identification with blindness suggested a perceived unity among group members. This indicates a social or political perspective on disability, rather than a strict medical or biopolitical categorization. For viewers of the Flickr pool, blindness was not a spectacle or medical diagnosis but provided one discursive limit through which meaning was produced and received. Knowing these images were produced by people

Well, this is beause his war injuries keep him from being able to use a keyboard.

A still from "McCain Can't Type," showing a white woman using a tongue-control system to interface with her keyboard. Below, there are captions of the spoken content—Rove explaining McCain's inability to use a keyboard.

who identify with "blindness" opened up reflections on blind identity, community, and the uses and users of participatory culture.

A more explicitly politicized use of participatory online media by people with disabilities was a 2008 web video called "McCain Can't Type."[53] This was one of many user-generated videos uploaded and circulated on YouTube during the lead-up to the 2008 U.S. presidential election. This election marked a tipping point in the importance of social media, online donations, and blog-based news sources in electoral politics.[54] The cycle saw several highly popular videos, created by people outside of the political structure, such as "I Got a Crush . . . on Obama," by "Obama Girl."[55] One popular video series, "Yes, We Can," featured celebrities using the eponymous Obama campaign slogan; the campaign denied involvement, and the video circulated on the basis of celebrity culture and shared cultural, rather than political, references.

Like these popular user-generated videos, "McCain Can't Type" was a response to a particular cultural moment. Republican presidential candidate Senator John McCain had admitted to being "computer illiterate" earlier in 2008. This led to increasing coverage of the senator's perceived unfamiliarity with email and other digital media technologies, a potentially damaging narrative given the rising profile of these technologies in the campaign and in the broader culture.[56] The news cycle culminated in a statement by campaign adviser Karl Rove on *Fox News Sunday* that McCain avoided using email and other internet applications because of injuries sustained while a prisoner of war in Vietnam that caused him pain when typing. This attempt to explain away McCain's relative technological illiteracy drew on and reinforced social narratives about the limits of disability. The potential effectiveness of this statement relied on audience belief in three premises: that disability is inherently limiting, that technology is unavailable for users with disabilities such as McCain's, and that he had no choice regarding this inability to use internet technology. "McCain Can't Type," posted to YouTube on October 11, 2008, with a fully captioned and described accessible version made available on October 17, forcefully rebuts these assumptions while making an argument for Obama as a candidate deserving the support of those interested in technological progress, disability policy, or both.

The video opens with a blue screen featuring white text that reads, "John McCain can't use a computer," and a female voice conveying the same information. The text gets larger, and a question mark is added, as her voice rises, incredulously repeating the phrase as a question. A cut takes us to Rove's appearance on *Fox News Sunday*. As Rove's voice goes on, the image cuts to a woman using a tongue-controlled device to type (see figure 2.1). Rove continues, saying that "[McCain's] war injuries keep him from being able to use a keyboard, he doesn't have the nimbleness, he can't type," as the visual cuts to other users with disabilities accessing computers and keyboards in various ways. The sound then syncs up with the last user seen, a middle-aged white man who is using voice recognition technology to write a letter to a soldier about to be deployed. A cut, and then the blank screen fills with tiled images of diverse users with disabilities, those previously featured as well as others. As these images appear, Obama's voice is heard saying, "Yes, we can," the ubiquitous slogan of his campaign. Music, clapping, and other voices join in as the chant gets louder. The last image to appear in the tiling, filling the right two-thirds of the screen, is of President Franklin D. Roosevelt in his wheelchair, as the chanting continues. The closing strains of "America the Beautiful" fade in as the chant ends, and a full-screen headshot of Obama fades in as the tiled images fade out, followed by simple text reading "Obama '08." After a fade to black, the credits appear, with the original YouTube poster, Marc Krizack, credited as having conceived the video.

The images and juxtapositions used in this brief video discredit the assumptions that undergird the claims made by McCain and Rove and emphasize the ways in which people with disabilities *are users* of computer and internet technology, even if they use it differently, establishing an alternate user position. Here, disability is not represented as a limitation, as suggested by Rove, but as a feature of life that does not define those whom it affects. "McCain Can't Type" foregrounds the agency of users with disabilities regarding digital media; while McCain may choose not take advantage of available options, many users with disabilities do value computer and internet technology enough to form alternative user positions and pursue various uses.

In this context, the chant takes on a duality of meaning. On one level, the repetition of "Yes, we can" references and affirms the messages of the Obama candidacy, a political position confirmed by the concluding endorsement. It recalls the "Yes, We Can" videos featuring celebrities that were released by the campaign, lending it a cultural relevance and prompting reflection through the replacement of celebrities with people with disabilities. On a second level, the words of the chant answered the question posed at the start of the video: John McCain can't use a computer? By extension, and through the rhetoric of Rove's comments, the implication is that users with disabilities cannot use computers. Through images and the chant, the creators of this video respond, "Yes, we can."

No longer "them," or even "you," this video makes its clams on behalf of the "we." This may signal the collective authorship of the video, via the images of many different users with many different disabilities engaging in different uses of technology. It may also be understood to address an audience primarily comprising people with disabilities, extending the offer of identification to these viewers. In this way, the preferred user position is not made central—alternative arrangements of bodies and technologies are privileged, and the "we" creates an uneasy position for able-bodied viewers. Unlike the welcome of "you," this "we" implies that the mainstream user may be outside of this community and may not be welcomed into the collective first-person address. This constitutes a challenge to the hegemony of the preferred use position, as it exposes the existence of alternative positions. In doing so, this video challenges assumptions about disability, technology, and agency that provided the cultural context for Rove's statements, intervening in dominant ideologies of disability.

Finally, the "we" connects to the cross-disability, coalitional politics that have characterized disability rights activism. Many different impairments and assistive technologies are incorporated into the video, and its production in an accessible, captioned, and video-described format demonstrates attention to an audience of people with disabilities whose impairments are related to audiovisual content. A shared disability identity allows for the formation of a strong identity politics through which to advocate for change. However, a shared identity can also overshadow the range of experiences and needs that require accommodation under the rubric of disability. Coalitional politics, with its emphasis on building shared identities and calls to action while acknowledging difference, is thus foundational to disability politics. In theory, this coalition could include nondisabled allies, as well. In the case of "McCain Can't Type," while a nondisabled viewer could watch the video and identify with this "we," it might be an uneasy identification across bodily and likely cultural difference. The political chant smoothes this transition, allowing the nondisabled viewer to identify primarily as an Obama supporter and secondarily with the disability issues at hand, making the video itself a powerful tool for the furtherance of disability politics and awareness.

Conclusion

If "you already know how to use" an iPad, it is likely that you are at least partially aligned with a preferred user position and may be anticipating default uses. Yet, there are many other uses for iPad, some of which allow it to serve as an assistive technology, enabling access to media, technology, and the functions of daily life.[57] These uses, and their users, are rarely incorporated into discussions of digital media; in their absence, preferred user positions become taken for granted and further institutionalized in social and technological structures. Representations are a key venue for the cultivation of the intended uses, and users, of media technology. Through what is, and is not, included in these images, expectations are set, and alternatives are gradually erased from public consciousness. Ultimately, representational venues such as those discussed in this chapter create dominant images, supporting preferred user positions to the exclusion of other articulations of culture, bodies, and technologies.

The dominance and resultant unremarkable nature of these representations make it all the more crucial to look for their exclusions and to locate user positions that do not align with expectations. When we do not interrogate the uses and users of a particular media technology, it is all too easy for both lived cultures and interpretive theories to be unfortunately limited, and limiting. In theorizing participation, politics, access, or disability, it is crucial that scholarship not take for granted a central use or user position. When what works for "most" is made central to culture or theory, it is too easy to ignore the extremes and over-generalize or mischaracterize that which we try to explain. Furthermore, particularly in the case of digital media technology and the context of the internet, the most interesting, transgressive, and cutting-edge uses and user positions may come from those extremes, where those unable or unwilling to take up a preferred user position innovate in their own interests. The examination of uses of the web accessibility and users with disabilities in this chapter thus speaks back to contemporary debates about digital media and access, participation, and democracy. When we begin from a standpoint that is not part of the preferred user position, it is possible to see the oversights and new directions that characterize these theoretical debates. Intended use, actual use, and the contexts in which each take shape should be fundamental not only to understanding diverse media audiences but also to learning the lessons of marginalized populations and using them to more fully understand the nature of media access, participation, and the complexity of media and culture themselves in a context of neoliberalism and political democracy.

3

Transformers

Accessibility, Style, and Adaptation

Adobe accessibility advocate Matt May began a 2013 presentation on design for mobile devices with a parodic job advertisement: "Wanted: Mobile Dev with 40 Years Experience. Proven expert at human factors, interactive design, and technologies that don't yet exist."[1] Yet, his text was not entirely facetious; the slide was soon followed by a picture of Gregg Vanderheiden, an engineer who has, in fact, been working in the field of assistive technology since the 1970s. In 1971, Vanderheiden was introduced to assistive technology through an electrical engineering project aimed at helping a twelve-year-old boy with severe athetoid cerebral palsy participate in class. He "quickly became fascinated," and he and other students formed the Cerebral Palsy Communication Instrumentation Group—renamed the Trace Center in 1973—which Vanderheiden continued to lead through his doctoral studies and up to the present day.[2] The group took on new clients and developed patented auto-monitoring techniques for communication boards, which were further developed under grants from the National Science Foundation and the federal Department of Education throughout the 1980s.

Work at the Trace Center initially focused on "augmentative communication" but quickly expanded to encompass a range of technologies and needs of people with disabilities. The Trace Center focused "on making off the shelf technologies and systems like computers, the Internet, and information kiosks more accessible for everyone through the process known as universal, or accessible[,] design."[3] This entailed developing means by which people with disabilities could use computers and standard software. Many inventive technologies emerged from this research and its applications; May's presentation explained how innovations pioneered at Trace and throughout the assistive technology industry—including pinch-to-zoom, onscreen keyboards, and voice recognition software—later crossed over to mainstream applications. Vanderheiden himself has remarked that many accessibility features built in to contemporary Windows and Macintosh operating systems, such as "sticky keys, mouse keys, all of those came from the Trace Center here."[4]

Vanderheiden is just one of many professionals engaged in transforming the hardware, software, and interfaces of communications and media technologies in order to enable access by people with disabilities. This work is often done out of rehabilitation, special education, engineering, and other applied fields, and referred to under the umbrella of "assistive technologies." Nearly uniformly, these research and design projects attempt to alter the material and encoded forms of technology in order to make it possible for people with disabilities to use them. These projects are not concerned with content, or the specific uses to which technologies may be put; their goal is facilitating the possibility of access by increasing technological flexibility and addressing the needs of non-normative users at the level of form.

Form, or the specific technological and material structures that govern access, is the focus of this chapter. The form of digital media includes a range of designed artifacts—hardware, software, and code—that structure the presentation of content (discussed in the next chapter) and the intended uses and users (discussed in the previous chapter). Hardware is often the most obvious form of exclusionary technology, as the design of material artifacts disciplines and constrains bodies in ways that may limit use. For instance, in 2014, sociologist of technology Zeynep Tufekci reflected that because of the size of her hands, "on the latest versions of the kinds of phones I want to use, I cannot type one-handed. I cannot take a picture one-handed. I can barely scroll one-handed—not very well, though. I can't unlock my phone one-handed. I can't even turn on my phone one-handed as my fingers cannot securely wrap around the phone while I push a button with a finger."[5] Extending these relations between specific bodies and technological artifacts to instances of disability, as in the communications devices developed at Trace, it is obvious that the designed forms of material artifacts may impede access.

Software, code, and markup languages may also act as technological forms that either expand or constrict access. The history of web content accessibility is based on creating code that can mediate between mainstream and assistive technologies, enabling machine interpretation of a range of expressive content. Screenreaders, alternative input devices, specialized displays, and other forms of assistive technologies rely upon these intangible elements to function properly.

Though taken up by the World Wide Web Consortium (W3C) and U.S. government, web content accessibility standards got their start at the Trace Center. On January 31, 1995, Trace released its first set of web accessibility standards, titled "Design of HTML (Mosaic) Pages to Increase Their Accessibility to Users with Disabilities Strategies for Today and Tomorrow." In the introduction, it explained the perceived need for such standards: "There are some features of the World Wide Web (WWW) which are not currently accessible to people with some disabilities using today's browsers (such as Mosaic). In addition, many of the data formats currently do not support accessibility annotations (captions, vocal and text annotations, etc.)."[6] The Center began collecting accessibility standards from around the country, merging them into what it named the "Unified Guidelines." The "Unified Guidelines" explicitly focused on "the source material," or the code and form of HTML pages themselves, rather than on accessibility issues involved with the server, the viewing computer, or "the pipeline" (web browser).[7] They were updated and refined over several years, and version 8.0, released in October 1997, was adopted as the starting point for the W3C's web content accessibility guidelines, which themselves attempted to regulate accessibility through the transformation of code and presentation.

Form, as used throughout this chapter, encompasses material, technological, and linguistic or encoded components of digital media. In three case studies, coding specifications, trade press, and interviews with accessibility professionals are used in order to analyze several forms of digital media in relation to accessibility for people with disabilities, while examples from ethnographic research on disability blogging are incorporated in order to communicate how form is relevant to users' experiences. First, I consider graphical browsers and related graphical user interfaces (GUIs) used in desktop computing—as well as the accessible methods used to circumvent them—as a matter of design, bridging culture and technology. Then, I look to the evolving relationship between HTML and Flash in the development of accessibility standards, and the ways in which *form* implies both function and style. Finally, I turn to mobile media, where web accessibility guidelines provided a starting point for the development of best practices for mobile software.

Interrogating Form

The five-part interrogatory "access kit" developed in the Introduction to this book grouped research questions into categories of regulation, use, form, content, and experience. Each category and attendant set of questions offer a particular insight into the dynamics of media access as a relational phenomenon, arising from combinations of bodies, technologies, cultures, and practices. Like disability, access here is understood not as something that is inherent, unitary, or fixed but as a contextual and shifting phenomenon requiring nuanced analysis.

In proposing questions related to the categories of form and content, I bring a major component of new media studies to the study of media access. Digital media, in which all material is encoded in interoperable binary code, have resulted in unprecedented flexibility. A newspaper, for instance, offers content bound up in a material form; there is no way to separate the words or visual design from the paper on which they are printed. A newspaper's website or tablet display, by contrast, allows for the production of content in a range of formats: optimized for a browser, simplified for a mobile interface, stripped of images for slow connections, heavy on images for a tablet computer application, and reformatted for easy printing. In this example, the content is the words, images, and other elements that convey meaning. The form is the means of presentation via specific material or digital structures. Form is thus closely connected both to hardware and software and, in the case of the web, to HTML and related markup and coding languages.

New media theory has expressed great interest in the idea of form and its possible transformations. Software studies theorist Lev Manovich emphasizes the separation of content and form as foundational to the variability that characterizes new media. As in the newspaper example, the modes of presentation and access differ and create differing experiences. Manovich further seems to equate the form of new media with a cultural and computer interface, functioning "as a code that carries cultural messages in a variety of media."[8] Thus, Manovich understands form to be bound up in cultural contexts and to influence meaning. By contrast, media theorist Alexander Galloway's theorization of new media form draws attention to the hardware and software that convey content without changing its "semantic units of value."[9] He describes these technical pathways as "protocols" that "encapsulate information inside various wrappers, while remaining relatively indifferent to the content of information contained within."[10] This allows Galloway to theorize protocols as a formal apparatus with social effects and political meanings by breaking down the elements of protocol into their constitutive practices and ideologies. The form of the web, he argues, is centered on an experience of continuity (similar to that seen in classic Hollywood cinema), in which the goal is to use the technology and formal apparatus to conceal the mediation and construction of content and meanings. I endeavor to reconnect Galloway's formal apparatus with the interface of bodies, culture, and technology described by Manovich. The site of form acts as a lens through which to understand the material and ideological relations enacted through specific technological arrangements.

The study of form, however, need not be limited to digital contexts. It is possible to consider how television, for instance, comprises many possible formal configurations: delivered via broadcast, cable, or streaming delivery to a television, computer monitor, tablet, or mobile device and controlled by dials, remote controls, touchscreens, or mice. Examination of the form of a media encounter is necessary to discussions of access precisely because in each of these circumstances the paths to access will differ, as will any prerequisites. Thus, the site of form can be studied through the following guiding questions:

By what means does one access a medium in this case?
What material, technological, cultural, or social structures shape this medium's material, technological, or designed components?
How do these means of access, or structures, interact (or interface) with the bodies of those who use them?

Form is quite closely connected to the research spheres of both use and content, but it is distinct from each. Form may be differentiated from use through its emphasis on the material and technical elements that constitute the intersection of an individual body and a particular media technology. Where the site of use emphasized intended and actual uses and users of a given media technology, the site of form is agnostic regarding individuals and their goals. In the second case, as will be further discussed in the next chapter, form may be differentiated from content through its emphasis on structures, rather than on meanings. Study of a media technology with respect to form may proceed in some cases with no mention of the content, or meanings, that is communicated. In other words, use primarily answers the question "Access by whom for what purpose?", form addresses the question "Access by what means?", and content provides an answer to the question "Access to what meanings?"

In the study of media access, analysis of the site of form is similarly concerned with those elements that structure a media experience, as in Galloway's analysis of protocol's formal apparatus. This may include elements of style, but it also includes code, software, hardware, and other structures that shape the means of interfacing with a given medium. Analysis of a film's form from this perspective might thus entail discussion of the technology through which it is viewed and the ways in which that technology structures the viewing experience. Watching a film projected from a reel in a theater is thus understood as a different experience from that of watching the same content on television, through a streaming internet service, or on a mobile device. Form, in this instance, is a variable articulation of media content, technology, and individuals, with control of form shifting between these locations.

Analysis of formal elements of media, guided by these questions, may encompass the construction of a given technology, the production of an interface using a particular cultural metaphor, or the establishment of a structure through which content is presented. Form is particularly essential to the study of media access, because it is here that we may consider the design and instantiation of the material, cultural, and technological paths by which technology is encountered and accessed. The moment of encounter, between an embodied individual and a given medium, is partially constructed through the designed forms of that medium and the resulting paths to access.

Designing around the Graphical User Interface

Form is closely connected to disciplines of design, including software engineering, architecture, and graphic design. In each of these fields, artifacts are understood to be constructed in particular contexts. Analysis of the design behind an artifact can reveal quite a bit about its formal structures. Design is often discussed in terms of affordances and constraints that direct but do not determine access and use of a given technology by an individual. Cognitive scientist and usability engineer Donald Norman, in *The Design of Everyday Things*, defines affordances in terms of the possibilities for an object's use and constraints in terms of how those possibilities are limited. Literature on the social construction of technology has invoked disability as an example of the failures of design, as when science and technology studies scholar Langdon Winner used the inaccessibility of the built environment as an example of how benign neglect can have the political consequence of excluding people with disabilities from public life.[11] Norman similarly challenges the assumption of an "average" person and provides examples of people who may face challenges when built environments are constructed with a so-called average person in mind: "Wheelchairs, for example, cannot easily manipulate curbs, stairs, or narrow aisles."[12] Thus, the arrangements of affordances and constraints in a given technological artifact convey politics, or "arrangements of power and authority in human associations."[13] These political arrangements mirror other areas of society, as in the case of digital technologies that have often reproduced and created disability through the creation of exclusionary structures.

The rise of GUIs on operating systems and on the World Wide Web itself is ripe for such analysis of disability, design, and form. Just as digital media accessibility does not end with web content accessibility, neither is that its origin. Prior to the launch of the World Wide Web, there was significant work on adaptive technologies for computer users with disabilities, including augmentive communication devices, sticky keys, and other innovations. With the introduction of the GUI, academics and professionals in computer or rehabilitation fields turned their attention to the accessibility of software. Software, or code, underlies the functioning of a range of programs. Software thus acts as a structure, a form, through which content is passed and interpreted; and accessibility innovations at the level of software—beginning with adapting the GUIs of operating systems—marked an important first stage in digital media accessibility.

On personal computers, DOS (Disk Operating System) interfaces were replaced by GUIs during the 1980s. Innovative operating systems on the Apple Macintosh introduced folders, trashcans, pointing-finger cursors, and similar graphic icons, relying on the metaphor of the desktop to make computing intuitive to non-experts. Soon after, Microsoft released Windows, bringing GUI features to the PC. In the formal transition from textual to graphical interfaces for operating systems, the paths to access were altered. GUIs reduced the need for specialized knowledge of computing commands and extended access to a large number of people, expanding the use of personal computers into a range of industrial and educational contexts. For many audiences, these affordances made computers more usable, as they required less specialized knowledge and provided a more feature-rich, enticing environment.

However, the GUI as a form of designed software acted not as an affordance but as a constraint for blind and visually impaired users, who could not reliably interact with a visual system in the absence of compatible assistive technologies. Many feared that if the GUI became standard, blind users would be confined to specialized forms of hardware and software, thereby becoming isolated from the mainstream.[14] National Federation of the Blind board member Curtis Chong recalled that in the 1990s, "I was beginning to realize that technological changes were happening in the mainstream world which were beginning to hurt us as blind people, in particular."[15] Though there were many assistive (also called "adaptive") technologies during the late 1980s and early 1990s, including speech synthesizers, screenreaders, and software to convert audible alerts to visual alerts, the new graphical interfaces were not initially compatible with these tools.[16] Specifically, there was no way to convert graphical information to text that could be interpreted by a screenreader or read by a voice synthesizer. In a 1991 issue of *BYTE*, technology writer and consultant Joe Lazzaro wrote that GUIs were introducing "windows of vulnerability" because although "over the past five years, the disabled have enjoyed a new electronic independence in the form of the personal computer. . . . As a person who is legally blind, I believe that some of this newly obtained and hard-won freedom is in danger of being revoked in the name of the graphical user interface (GUI)."[17] It seemed that not malice but neglect of blind and visually impaired users could lead to their expulsion from the future of computing and its benefits. In this way, a technological problem can become a political problem, as oversights become exclusions.

These concerns were shared by many in research and development sectors, and researchers and software engineers were already working to make GUIs more accessible by creating software that could connect these new interfaces with adaptive technologies. Organizations already embedded in the assistive technology field, such as the Trace Center for Research and Development at the University of Wisconsin–Madison, jumped on "The Graphical User Interface Crisis," explaining that "The graphical user interface (GUI) is both a powerful new interface for mainstream computer users and a source of serious concern for those who cannot see. Fortunately, graphic user interfaces can eventually be made as accessible to blind people as any of their current character-based forerunners."[18] They believed this could be done by translating the meaning of icons to textual form, as "it is not necessary for a blind person to perceive the shape of the icons to use them," but for the name of the application pointed at to be conveyed.[19] By 1991, IBM had begun work on technology that would do just that. By intercepting requests for graphics in the graphics engine and producing a readable model of the desktop from those calls, the GUI could be made usable by blind users with screenreaders. Just six months later, Richard Schwerdtfeger, a software engineer—and later CTO of Accessibility—at IBM, published a feature article in *BYTE* explaining innovations in this area. He wrote that these advances "forecast a new era of independence for the visually impaired community. For the first time, blind and visually impaired people will be able to perform tasks such as formatting a disk and running a spreadsheet calculation while they are logged onto a mainframe and listening to the daily announcements in a window."[20] Soon, accessible practices were spreading to many hardware and software development companies, in part because of the work of the Trace Center and the Industry–Government Initiative, which developed the computer accessibility guidelines used by the General Services Administration for federal information technologies.[21]

These adaptations of the GUI involved conversions at the level of form, whether through the implementation of accessibility features in out-of-the-box software, or through the interaction of software and specialized assistive technologies (often including additional hardware and software interfaces, such as screenreaders). Furthermore, in the fears and innovations surrounding the GUI, we can see how the form of software may rely upon and extend existing cultural biases. The desktop metaphor, for instance, used icons familiar from an office setting to convey what could be done with the machine. In this way, the Macintosh GUI was "a work of culture as much as technology."[22] This indicates the persistent connection of what Lev Manovich has described as the cultural and computer layers, which together constitute an interface through which digital media are understood. The formation of such a "techno-culture" creates formal structures that limit the imaginative scope and practical possibilities of a given media or technology.[23] Thus, design practices exert discursive force through the instantiation of particular metaphors. The desktop metaphor displays its biases in the valorization of specific forms of white-collar labor; those who lacked familiarity with office environments may have found the referents opaque and struggled to apply them to the computing context. Similarly, the inattention to the struggles of blind and visually impaired users with regard to the GUI reflected the larger cultural tendency to exclude disability from conceptions of a political or commercial public. Though the creation of digital disability may not have been intentional, the creation of this specific form of human–computer interaction perpetuated social and material relations of inequality. Designed artifacts, whether hardware or software, convey culturally based assumptions and culturally dominant perspectives, including discriminatory attitudes and practices.

While the accessibility efforts chronicled earlier in this chapter attempted to redress these oversights and inequalities, they were reactive attempts to design around a discriminatory form. Such forms of specialized access, reliant upon additional hardware or software, or upon the retrofitting of existing technologies, bring their own challenges. Certainly, this process of innovation has been unfortunately common; a new form of technology is developed, *then* assistive technology experts work to make it accessible by designing around or adapting inaccessible features, and finally people with disabilities gain a degree of access. As this retrofitting continues, people with disabilities are isolated from the temporality of new designed forms and are regularly reliant on slightly older technology because of the expense of upgrading to the latest in assistive technology.[24] The forms of media and technology direct access along specific channels—such as the point-and-click paradigm of a GUI—and in doing so can exclude particular bodies and forms of interaction. Though this may be addressed through the formation of alternate formal structures, these divergent paths do not always result in equality of experience or access.

HTML versus Flash, Function versus Style

In turning from the GUI to the forms of the World Wide Web, we find that many concerns remain the same. Both are software, or groups of software, through which users' possibilities for action are conveyed. As argued by software theorist Wendy Chun, computers' architecture and instrumentality create and maintain particular logics of not only using technology but also making sense of lived experiences.[25] They thus function as a form of productive power, with software acting as protocols via which normative structures of use and interpretation are conveyed and taken up. However, not all software is created equal; software suites can convey quite different forms of power and interpretation, and their meanings are subject to negotiation.

Here, I contrast the development of accessible HTML and accessible forms of Adobe Flash (previously developed and owned by Macromedia) in order to highlight the conflicts between form as protocol and form as style that characterized the early days of the Web and accessibility policy. In this history, these divergent perspectives at first seemed to re-create divisions between functional products for people with disabilities and aesthetically pleasing products for mainstream audiences. Accessibility policies attempted to separate form as style from understandings of form as function. Through the evolution of HTML and Flash, however, this division is repeatedly denied, blurred, and ultimately eradicated in pursuit of accessible forms of web content. Currently, the form of the web is one in which both function and style may be made more or less accessible to a range of audiences—not by designing "around" disability but by designing "through" it. In other words, the integration of accessibility features has made it possible to use software to serve different audiences simultaneously without necessitating entirely different forms.

In beginning this discussion, it is appropriate to make a few distinctions. First, HTML is a markup language (indeed, the initials stand for HyperText Markup Language); it is not code, which tells a computer to run a process, but a language used to tell web browsers how to interpret, format, and display a web page. HTML was used to build the earliest web pages and is still foundational to the functioning of web content. It is not dynamic, meaning that HTML is not used to create and display personalized content, to call information from a database, or to run a submission form. These actions require integrating coding languages that can control processes, such as PHP, ASP, and JavaScript, with HTML. Furthermore, while HTML was initially (and in some cases still is) used to control all elements of the display, including colors, fonts, and other stylistic elements, the W3C has long recommended that stylistic instructions be written in CSS (Cascading Style Sheets). CSS is a complementary language that enables control of the visual elements of a web page at a number of different levels, from sitewide control and control over individual pages, to custom stylesheets employed by the user of a web browser. The distinction between HTML and CSS has often been made in terms of the separation of *content* and *style*; a website called the CSS Zen Garden illustrates this by showing myriad ways in which an HTML file may be radically altered in its display using CSS, with the same page content rendered in a bright "mid-century modern" style, in blacks and grays with accents that resemble steel girding, in soothing green botanicals, and in more than 200 other visual styles.[26] Here, and on many other websites, stylesheets control the visual display, while HTML is used only to structure the page—its textual content, its calls for multimedia objects, and its calls to other coding processes. All of these coding and markup languages are formal elements that, together, constitute the structure and formatting of a web page. They do not constitute content but are protocols through which content moves.

Flash, unlike HTML, was not developed as an open standard for web content production. It began as a small animation-focused tool, it was purchased by Macromedia in 1996, and Macromedia was purchased by Adobe in 2005. In all of its iterations, Flash was a proprietary software package. It enabled users to develop a range of graphic artifacts, from animations to full web pages, and then to optimize those for use on the web. Through the use of a specialized coding language, ActionScript, Flash creations could include interactive components, such as buttons, links, and other features. ActionScript could be written by hand, or built into the artifact through automatic tools in the Flash software. Additionally, "plug-ins" were required for one to view Flash content. These extensions to web browsers added the capability to interpret Flash and ActionScript, which were often not included in off-the-shelf browsers.

From the perspective of a user in the mid- to late 1990s, the technical differences between HTML and Flash would have been largely invisible. Viewed through a browser, a front end that hides the apparatus, web pages displayed a seamlessness between HTML and other components.[27] Stylistically, however, the differences were stark; Flash-based graphics and websites exhibited more motion and more innovative visual design, incorporated audio, and were increasingly used by major corporate brands. Flash was central to the ongoing graphic and multimedia development of the web. As a result, there was a perception of Flash as being the style-driven, innovative side of web development, with HTML a stodgy standby with limited capabilities. This conflict between design and function would haunt attempts to increase the accessibility of web content.

The accessibility of web content was initially addressed through specific instructions for the proper use of HTML and other W3C technologies. In short, these guidelines were aimed at altering the form of software. This focus on the form of software persisted during the W3C formation of web content accessibility policies. In both the Web Content Accessibility Guidelines (WCAG) 1.0 and the Section 508 standards, recommendations often amounted to instructions for proper use of HTML tags as annotations that could make content available in a slightly altered form that would be usable by screenreaders. For instance, Guideline 3 of WCAG 1.0 recommended that developers "use markup and style sheets and do so properly."[28] This constituted a recommendation at the level of form, suggesting practices for developers to present the same content while using accessible, W3C-endorsed code. Such formal recommendations separated form from content in order to make content transformable and thus potentially more accessible to people using nonstandard technologies or means of accessing online content. Where they struggled was in the question of how style or graphic design related to both form and content. Was graphic design an element of content presentation or a formal structure that could be easily adapted?

Accessibility recommendations were almost exclusively focused on the functionality of web pages and not on their aesthetics. At the turn of the twenty-first century, many web designers felt that "'standards,' 'accessibility,' and 'usability' interfered with the creative process."[29] Accessibility advocates denied these claims, often through reference to the "myth" that accessible sites could not be attractive.[30] Reiteration of these denials, however, may only have strengthened the perceived distance between functionality and style.

Flash, though more attuned to the possibilities of stylish web design, was a disaster in terms of accessibility and was not incorporated into early accessibility policies. Accessibility advocate and developer Jim Heid decried the inaccessibility of Flash-created content as a growing concern as more and more content was developed using the software.[31] These finished products expanded to include animations, splash pages, multimedia offerings such as games written in ActionScript, and dynamic applications. None of these offerings included options for captioning, alternative text, or screenreader interoperability.

Instead of regulating such inaccessible proprietary technologies, WCAG 1.0 recommended that web developers use "W3C technologies"—essentially, HTML—whenever possible. The guidelines were widely interpreted as calling for text-only or minimally designed pages. But, however onerous this directive appeared to developers, it was at least as damaging to industrial morale. Flash, Ajax, Microsoft Silverlight, ePub, and a variety of other web authoring technologies and formats were rapidly increasing in popularity through the late 1990s and early 2000s. Though they initially offered little in the way of accessibility options, recommendations against their use threatened companies' abilities to improve accessibility features and compete in the new marketplace. Developers seeking to comply with WCAG 1.0 and, more crucially, Section 508, seemed likely to avoid these technologies in order to achieve compliance.

As a result, Flash began a major overhaul in 2001. In 2002, Macromedia released Flash Player 6 (the software that allowed Flash content to play in web browsers) and Flash MX (the authoring software). The improvements in these releases focused on the accessibility of Flash content, an understandable choice given the claim that 98 percent of web users had Flash player installed and the need to make Flash a usable option for government offices under Section 508.[32] Flash MX offered an accessibility menu that could prompt content creators to add descriptions of video, or labels to interactive controls, in addition to testing for color contrast and other fairly simply determined accessibility features.

The most notable increase in accessibility came in screenreader compatibility. Certainly, there was no guarantee that Flash content was always accessible, but formally, accessible Flash content had become possible.

These changes were positively received by the larger web community, as seen in two articles published on the web development blog *A List Apart*. Andrew Kirkpatrick, Corporate Accessibility Engineering Lead for Adobe, wrote, "People concerned with accessibility issues will find shortcomings in Flash, as is also easy to do with HTML. Rather than [deride] Macromedia, we need to work with them to progress toward better solutions."[33] Accessibility consultant Joe Clark concurred, writing, "Accessibility experts are, moreover, generally hostile to good visual design. There's a considerable bias within web accessibility toward 'universal' HTML and away from 'proprietary' software like Flash and PDF. People are just gonna have to get over that."[34] Both articles saw these accessibility improvements as repudiations of the focus on HTML in WCAG 1.0 and Section 508. Flash's attempts to implement accessibility features indicated that W3C technologies were not the only options for accessible development and suggested that a wider range of content than that enabled by simple HTML pages could be made accessible to people with disabilities without losing the creativity, innovation, and "hipness" of web design and development. Stylistically, Flash retained some of its cachet throughout these changes while also pivoting to incorporate growing concerns with ideas of "usability" and accessibility. As the number of Flash-based animations and splash pages declined, Flash grew in popularity as a multimedia container for games and video, as seen in its use to play videos on YouTube, launched in 2006. The form of Flash, it seemed, could incorporate the accessibility of both style and function.

From roughly 2004 to the present, accessibility policies underwent significant revisions, many of which incorporate non-W3C technologies and stylistic innovations as accessible possibilities. Macromedia and Adobe representatives continued their participation in policymaking groups, along with representatives of many other web-related companies. Many of these corporate representatives were explicitly advocating for accessibility policies that were technology-independent. This meant that instead of explaining which technologies to use in what way, accessibility policies would explain what goals all technologies would need to achieve in order to create web content accessibility.[35] WCAG 2.0, with

its principle-driven structure, was released in 2008 and adopted this revised organization. By requiring that web content be perceivable, operable, usable, and robust, WCAG 2.0 could be applied to HTML, Flash,
or a range of other new web technologies. In fact, many participants in
the WCAG 2.0 process have expressed their hope that this structure will
allow WCAG 2.0 to remain relevant for many years.[36]

Some evidence of this mutability of accessibility policies can be seen
in two technologies that emerged following the release of WCAG 2.0.
Both WAI-ARIA (Web Accessibility Initiative–Accessible Rich Internet Applications) and HTML 5 can be used and be in compliance with
these guidelines. Additionally, in this flexibility, there also appears to be
greater incorporation of style as a meaningful component of form.

ARIA is a W3C specification that enables the extension of HTML
through the creation of semantic elements. Semantics are code elements that convey meaning, like "headers," which have long been part
of HTML and have various levels that control presentation (the H1 tag
indicates the most important heading, which is displayed as larger than
H2, etc.). HTML has historically had few semantic elements, though
their use has long been a goal.[37] ARIA allows developers to indicate
meaning for accessibility purposes through the creation of new semantic tags. For instance, a color menu, cobbled together from HTML, CSS,
and JavaScript, would be confusing for a screenreader; by adding attributes to HTML using ARIA to indicate that it is a color menu, the developer makes this element comprehensible to a screenreader and thus
usable by people with visual disabilities.[38] ARIA was known to be in
development during the WCAG 2.0 process, and in order to function,
it needed WCAG 1.0–era restrictions on the use of scripts and CSS removed. Like industries' requests for technology-independent standards,
these needs were accommodated. ARIA "is now part of HTML 5 and it
is used almost ubiquitously around the world" as an accessibility API
(application programming interface).[39]

As of this writing, HTML 5 is the latest update to the HTML standard. Like ARIA, it extends the semantic potential of web technologies,
introducing elements such as "footers" rather than requiring the footer
of a webpage to be conveyed through a "div" (page division) like any
other. The major innovations of HTML 5 include the ability to create
graphic and animated content directly and to embed multimedia easily

using the new semantic "video" element. The latter affordance allowed the rewrite of YouTube entirely in HTML 5, rather than in Flash; though this project is in beta at the time of writing, it shows the potential for a W3C technology to be not only functional but also stylistically interesting. In fact, as part of the "Open Web Platform," a W3C project to make rich web content available on a range of devices, HTML 5 may soon be directly competing with the applications currently made in specialized formats for iOS and Android products.

The form of web pages is widely variable, incorporating HTML, CSS, Flash, and countless other development and display technologies. In the evolution of HTML and Flash, however, we can see how the site of form has been an arena of struggle over functionality and aesthetics in relation to accessibility. The site of form is broad enough to incorporate both technological and structural elements, as well as stylistic elements; in part, this is because it can often be difficult to separate structure and presentation as fully as hoped by the division of HTML and CSS. This tension has a long history in relation to products for people with disabilities. Interaction designer Graham Pullin argues that much design for disability in the physical world has aimed for invisibility, while fashionable design has been concerned with the creation of a particular image.[40] Thus, hearing aids have most often been ugly and useful, while earrings are beautiful without serving a clear purpose.[41] Additionally, beauty and innovation may conflict with a solution-oriented approach to "fixing" the problems of disability, which has characterized assistive technology research and development. This approach leads to the dominance of functionality, making considerations of form and aesthetics appear shallow or unnecessary. Yet in order to destigmatize disability and find in it inspiration for future designs, Pullin argues that the two cultures need each other. The evolving relationship between HTML and Flash, in which each side took steps toward the goals of the other, demonstrates what this accessible union might look like. Rather than maintain a strict division between those interested in functional accessibility and those interested in design and innovation, the arrival of accessible Flash development tools, ARIA, and HTML 5 demonstrates how the forms of the web might not just coexist but may complement one another. Unlike in the case of the GUI, in which accessible paths were designed around inaccessible graphics, the evolution of these forms indicates the growing accessibility of mainstream forms. Far from creating separate paths, these innovations allow for the same content to be accessed in a range of forms, with the transformative elements hidden from users' experience.

Mobile and Cultural Adaptation

Mobile devices, and the web content and applications developed for them, built upon existing innovations and policies for accessibility. Here, accessible design led the way to mainstream innovations, resulting in benefits for diverse audiences. In this trajectory, disability is no longer an afterthought but is intimately connected to the development of emerging forms of media technology through a process of ongoing cultural and technological adaptation.

Cultural adaptations may drive new technological designs, as users' behavior suggests subsequent adjustments to the hardware and software forms themselves. Gerard Goggin, an Australian cultural studies scholar who focuses on issues of disability and media, argues that the iPhone, in particular, "draw[s] from the grammar of mobile phone design, and combine[s] and rework[s] a number of well-established affordances, elements and technologies. And it also borrows from the well-established, distinctive traits of Apple 'i' technologies."[42] In this way, the iPhone is an adaptation of mobile phone and internet cultures, blending the technical and stylistic forms of each into something new. Goggin goes on to describe the ways in which the iPhone became domesticated, or integrated into daily life. This process often entails the grafting of other cultural traditions and practices onto media or technologies by users; in the case of the iPhone, users created new forms of use, such as hacking, jailbreaking, and the subsequent distribution of applications not approved by Apple. A parallel process of adaptation involving mobile devices brought together the forms and affordances of digital accessibility with the cultural desirability of cultures of telephony, computing, and design.

The process of adaptation linking mobile technology and accessibility began at the level of formal recommendations for software. In 2008, the Mobile Web Best Practices (MWBP) were released as a W3C final recommendation. These guidelines not only mentioned but were in fact an adaptation of many guidelines from WCAG 1.0 and the developing WCAG 2.0, as the introduction explained that "[t]hese recommendations are in part derived from the Web Content Accessibility Guidelines."[43] Fifteen of the guidelines in MWBP list a specific WCAG guideline as a reference. For instance, the MWBP guideline for web navigation suggests using consistent navigation features, or implementing "drill-down" menus. It refers to WCAG 1.0 guideline 13, which recommends that developers "Use navigation mechanisms in a consistent manner."[44] The overlap in these recommendations demonstrates the ways in which clear navigation mechanisms may be useful to a wide range of audiences and particularly the similarities in barriers encountered by people using assistive technologies and people using mobile technologies, both of which may not present web content in the same form as a desktop browser. The Best Practices Working Group (part of the Mobile Web Initiative) even created a separate document explaining the relationships between MWBP and WCAG. In a 2007 draft, the authors wrote that "Many WCAG guidelines, checkpoints, and success criteria correspond directly to Mobile Web Best Practices 1.0 provisions, and complying with one automatically ensures compliance with the other, with no extra effort."[45] The document was intended to speak across any division between specialists in accessibility and those in mobile development, demonstrating where their interests aligned and how that alignment might be useful in creating better business cases.

Soon after the release of MWBP, the working group turned from web content displayed on new forms of hardware to consider the applications being developed for use on mobile platforms. The Mobile Web Application Best Practices, released by the W3C in 2010, "collects the most relevant engineering practices, promoting those that enable a better user experience and warning against those that are considered harmful."[46] In its recommendation for design for multiple interaction methods, this specification notes that "new interaction methods are likely to emerge in the future, particularly in the fields of voice and assistive technology."[47] This indicates that the design and development of mobile applications and hardware were indebted to the field of assistive technology, and thus to the tradition of accessible computer and internet development. However, this recommendation did not emphasize its emergence from WCAG, partially because WCAG 2.0 was nearing completion and partially to avoid confusion about what constituted compliance with each recommendation.[48]

Instead, the working group collaborated with the Education and Out-reach group of the Web Accessibility Initiative to produce a document laying out "Shared Web Experiences: Barriers Common to Mobile Device Users and People with Disabilities." The final version was approved and went live in October 2008. It used the principle-based structure of WCAG 2.0—content must be Perceivable, Operable, Usable, and Robust (POUR)—to give examples of problems faced by both people with disabilities (or people using assistive technologies) and mobile web users, and then linked to the recommendations for fixing these issues using WCAG 2.0 and MWBP. For example, the problem of multimedia content with no captions is relevant in a disabilities context to users who are deaf or hard of hearing; it is relevant in a mobile context for users who have turned off sound in public or cannot hear in noisy places.[49] Linking ideas of accessibility to mobile devices was believed to be a useful strategy in spreading accessibility implementation, as the emerging mobile market was of high concern to many in the web and hardware industries.[50] In addition to the note on relationships between standards, and the Shared Web Experiences document, the working group and WAI Education and Outreach group released a short document about "Making a Web site accessible for both people with disabilities and for mobile devices." This document explained that "Following these two guidelines makes your web content more accessible to everyone regardless of situation, environment, or device. Designing to the guidelines together, instead of separately, can make the process more efficient—especially when considered early in the project."[51]

This language is particularly interesting as it suggests that accessibility is connected to a full context, some of which is determined by the forms of hardware and software being used. The growth of this perspective within the W3C led much of web accessibility and mobile standardization to focus on making "the same information and services available to users irrespective of the device they are using."[52] Referred to as "One Web," this goal is behind both the device-independence of WCAG 2.0 and the policies developed for mobile devices, a growing category of alternative formal presentations of content. The diversity of forms used to access web content requires strategies for accommodating those different forms as "the restrictions imposed by the keyboard and the screen typically require a different approach to page design than for desktop devices."[53] Proponents of One Web acknowledge that this does not always mean that content presentation is unchanged; the form, in terms of style and function, may require alterations in order to create effective user experiences on a given device. This process is called Content Adaptation, in which the *form* of content is altered so that the meanings may be accessed.[54] This constructs formal adaptation as an ongoing process, driven by regulators, developers, third parties, and users.

The adaptations of accessible and mobile forms of access to web content have not only involved the carry-over of innovations in hardware and software accessibility to mobile policies and forms but also have enabled mobile devices to function as assistive devices. In fact, mobile devices such as phones and tablet computers have become relatively low-cost access solutions for people with a variety of disabilities. These have the additional advantage of cultural cachet. As an example, using an iPad allows people with communicative impairments to minimize their visible differences from mainstream technologies and cultural relevancies, building commonality with other iPad users at the level of form (though their uses may be different). The recognizable technological form may draw people in, enabling greater social inclusion and comfort for users of assistive technology, as when Glenda Watson Hyatt uses her iPad as a communication device in professional settings.[55]

Among disability bloggers, mobile devices were particularly useful in creating alternatives to traditional keyboards. Typing was a source of difficulty: traditional keyboards, and attendant desk configurations, were unpleasant if not impossible configurations of hardware and software. Despite the availability of assistive technologies for typing, it is common for users with typing difficulties to "try to avoid typing as much as possible," a rational choice that resulted in the constraining of access to various content and experiences. Assistive mobile technologies can help to address this lack of formal access.

The most popular devices for typing difficulties were not assistive technologies, per se, but mobile devices such as iPad 2 and iPhone 4S. Blogger and student Anna Hamilton stated that her iPad was "immensely useful from a disability standpoint—typing, for example, is easier for me to do on the iPad than on a standard laptop keyboard."[56] Similarly, for a visually impaired blogger with residual vision, using Twitter and blogging on an iPhone 4 (with built-in assistive technology) was just as easy as, if not easier than, using a computer.[57] Mainstream media have also begun to notice the ways in which mobile devices may be a form that facilitates access. Dyslexics may find that options for spacing and brightness on a mobile device improve reading abilities.[58] The use of tablet computers by people (particularly children) on the autism spectrum has garnered much attention, as has the use of tablets as communication devices for people with a range of speech-related impairments such as those resulting from cerebral palsy.[59]

Apple products feature prominently in much press coverage, and first-person accounting, of these assistive uses of mainstream mobile technology. This is largely due to the accessibility of iOS products "out of the box"; with simple adjustments to built-in settings, many people with disabilities can access this consumer technology. Built-in features include voice-output, magnification, and nonvisual means of using a touchscreen. As a result, Apple products are the most popular mobile devices used by Americans with disabilities, particularly among people who are blind or visually impaired. A recent survey on mobile accessibility found that most users had an iPhone 4S and that all Apple products together accounted for the devices used by 71 percent of those surveyed.[60] Additionally, the *financial* accessibility of these products has resulted in enormous use by and interest in many people with disabilities. The price of an iPhone (even at $200–$400) is significantly less than that of notetakers with Braille displays, which can cost nearly $6,000.[61] This lower pricetag comes with more availability, and more regular updates and innovations than are available for blind-specific assistive technologies. Even if insurers do not cover the costs of mainstream mobile devices (and might cover explicitly assistive technology), the tradeoffs are such that many users prefer the commercially available mainstream technology and its accessibility offerings.[62]

The benefits of Apple touchscreen products led many in the disability blogosphere to write about these devices.[63] Some expressed desire for an iPad, while others blogged about the eye-tracker studies, the development of iPads that could use breath input, and patents for the integration of iPad and assistive technology. Upon the death of Apple founder Steve Jobs in 2011, an outpouring of gratitude was seen across these websites, as his death provided an occasion on which to celebrate Apple's accessibility efforts. Many disability bloggers spoke about the importance of Apple technology in their own lives. Immediately following Jobs's death, many members of the blogosphere posted to the Twitter hashtag #thankyoustevejobs, tying their memories of Apple's accessibility innovations to mainstream public expressions of appreciation. Bloggers with disabilities shared their memories of Apple products, including how they enabled the use of necessary assistive devices at various points in their lives. In the weeks following his death, videos and news stories about him continued to circulate in the disability blogosphere, including pieces emphasizing the possibilities of Apple products for people with autism, limited speech ability, and other disabilities. The attention around Jobs's death, and the recurrence of Apple products in discussions of accessibility barriers and solutions, suggests that contemporary experiences of disability online are increasingly grounded in the same technologies used by mainstream users, though they may be used in different ways. In the case of difficulty in typing, for instance, the widespread use of mobile devices made for a consumer audience, and not specialized disability-centered assistive devices, is an important shift in extending affordable access and cultural relevance to people with disabilities.

The advantages offered by mobile devices such as iPad, which can double as assistive technology and increase access for many people, come at a price. Beyond the $500 or so spent on the technology itself, users are brought into a consumer environment in which they may be locked in to relationships with service providers and given access primarily to consumptive uses of technology. Jonathan Zittrain, professor of computer science and internet law, refers to iPods and similar devices as "tethered applicances," as they are always connected to their parent company and often fulfill functions for users without requiring any knowledge of how they operate.[64] Consumptive uses of technology may not facilitate the kinds of technological literacies that are necessary for careers in these media and may entrench notions of people with disabilities as passive recipients of aid. Furthermore, while access to an iPad carries a cultural cachet, integrating people with disabilities by enabling them to use a desired mainstream technology, it is unclear whether that consumer access can translate to civic values or access to public forms of participation and creation.

As disability scholar Rosemarie Garland-Thomson has observed, accessible mobile media, particularly Apple's personal assistant, Siri, "let me in, allowing me to meet professional demands and to be a fully participating citizen, just as it and many other technologies do for thousands of the disabled. What's even better is that tools like Siri function for both those who are disabled and those who are not."[65] Mobile devices have adapted elements of software accessibility and assistive technology in order to offer a simple, transformable experience of the web and online applications to users of mainstream cell phones. As debated in MWBP emails dating back to 2005, the emergence of mobile technology meant that "[a] content author should no longer continue to assume they [sic] understand the access point used by visitors"[66] Formal pathways were no longer set in stone but were multiplying, requiring new access paths to be created for all users; to do this, developers needed to consider a range of formats and use contexts from the beginning. As mobile users grew in importance, overlaps with accessibility provided an example of how development culture could shift to "encourage the design-in of mobile friendliness at the start,"[67] rather than retrofit technologies and create a second-class web for mobile (or disabled) users. This led to evolutions of the forms of hardware and software that were flexible enough for a range of users and contexts to access desired activities and content, undermining the singular paths instituted and reified in other forms of media technology. Mobile adaptation has allowed for the blending of audiences, activities, and access that was not previously available, with positive effects for the equality that is the goal of participatory democracy. However, in doing so, it has also drawn new audiences into consumer relationships with tethered devices and service providers. Devices such as Amazon's Kindle and Apple's iPhone exist within technological and regulatory frameworks that enable continued control of the technology by the company and allow for only limited forms of interaction and only approved uses by outside developers. These arrangements reify consumptive uses of technology for people with disabilities and entrench a division between users and producers.

Convergence and Universal Design

The quickly emerging ubiquity of computing in the 1980s led Gregg Vanderheiden, then working on assistive technologies for communication, to be "worried about the fact that [computers] were going to someday be ubiquitous, and people with disabilities need to [be able to not] do just special things on them, but regular things."[68] To allow people with disabilities to meet goals through the use of mainstream technological forms was in some ways more challenging than developing separate systems to meet particular needs, but Vanderheiden correctly speculated that this convergent approach would be the only way to move forward as technology and its uses became part of daily life in American culture. The convergence, in this case, was between the needs of people with disabilities and the technological culture of the mainstream. Unifying concerns with formal design, utility, and marketability with those of accessibility and functionality remains a challenge but increasingly characterizes the current climate of development. Though this convergent perspective stems from universal design, it is now also discussed under guise of personalization, usability, or "accessibility 2.0," and it is increasingly influential in accessibility initiatives.

Characterized by a move away from the normate body and an emphasis on flexibility, the theory of "universal design" (UD) was first expounded upon by architect Ron Mace during the 1960s. Mace and his colleagues proposed that "universal design means simply designing all products, buildings, and exterior spaces to be usable by all people to the greatest extent possible."[69] If designers were expected to serve a wide variety of bodies—often cast as potential markets, but equally possible to understand in terms of a robust citizenry—universal design offered a way to do so without sacrificing aesthetics or requiring costly retrofits. Universal design was particularly important and influential given its rise during the mid–twentieth century, as these decades also saw the passage of several laws aimed at increasing physical access for people with disabilities. In order to comply with the Architectural Barriers Act of 1968, the Rehabilitation Act of 1973, and the Fair Housing Amendments of 1988, new construction projects needed advice on accessible architectural design and turned to theories of universal design. Such needs were even more pronounced following the passage of the Americans with Disabilities Act (1990), which drastically altered practices of architectural design and construction.

UD was taken up within computer hardware and software design, where digital technologies were understood through spatial metaphors, as "built environments"—built from hardware and code, not bricks and architecture. UD for technology was understood as "the development of information systems flexible enough to accommodate the needs of the broadest range of users of computers and telecommunications equipment, regardless of age or disability."[70] UD motivated assistive technology computing fields, which in turn produced tools for people with disabilities who required nonstandard equipment, including screenreaders, tonguetypers, and other alternate forms of input and output devices.[71] The flexibility of designed artifacts and their potential use by broad sections of the population are core elements of universal-design philosophies in computing technology as in other contexts. UD, of course, is not perfect; there is no expectation that a single device could realistically accommodate the full range of human variation and needs. Instead, the driving question is "How do I get more people to be able to reach and understand this?"[72] Accessibility and web development experts Wendy Chisholm and Matt May write in *Universal Design for Web Applications* that this approach has "the ultimate goal of providing the greatest benefit to the greatest number of people possible."[73] To illustrate the pursuit of this goal, they focus on mobile and accessible web design, which provide examples of a wide range of circumstances (and forms) through which individuals access web content.

Within computer and internet technology, UD has been accompanied by theories of usability and universal usability (among others), all of which are user-centered design practices that aim to include a wide range of users through the construction of simple, transformable forms of hardware and software. Usability, which rose to prominence in the early 2000s, emphasized the importance of creating simple, clear, and easy-to-use interfaces for all audiences.[74] It was part of a backlash against Flash and other complex forms of online interaction, attempting "to sell readers on the 'practice of simplicity.'"[75] As defined at Usability.gov, a site run by the federal government to promote user-centered design, *usability* "refers to the quality of a user's experience when interacting with products or systems."[76] Usability is not equivalent to accessibility; a site that may be easily used by sighted users may still lack accessibility features.[77] However, a number of accessibility advocates see accessibility as a subset of usability, defining accessibility in terms of "usability for people with disabilities,"[78] "a dimension of usability," or "the ability of a product to provide comparable user experience to those with or without a disability."[79] The ability of people with disabilities to *use*, and not merely *access*, the forms of computer, internet, and mobile technologies is thus made central to this design process. "Universal usability" similarly attempts to bring together these design imperatives, by "thinking about advanced interfaces that benefit all information and computer systems users."[80] Universal usability is sometimes imagined as a spectrum ranging from those with no difficulty using a particular form, to those who are unable to use it under any conditions; this would include, at various points, accessibility challenges.[81] Some designers and advocates choose to use the phrase "inclusive design" to describe these practices, and the W3C recognizes "inclusive design, design for all, digital inclusion, universal usability, and similar efforts"[82] as related to, but distinct from, accessibility (which retains a primary focus on the challenges of specific impairments).

Theories of UD have been taken up within disability studies for their political potential to increase access and inclusion. By emphasizing design as a process that serves people who "are all nonstandard,"[83] UD denaturalizes distinctions and hierarchies based on ability. Feminist disability scholar Aimi Hamraie asserts that universal design can even act as an epistemology, based in the social model of disability, under which social structures may be analyzed and challenged in order to further the inclusivity of material, institutional, technological, and cultural artifacts.[84] Furthermore, universal design has offered disability studies a way to move past understandings of access as tied to particular disabled bodies. Instead, access is understood as an ongoing concern for all, and universal design encompasses the creation of discourses, structures, and institutions that allow for various "way[s] to move" for a wide variety of bodies and needs.[85]

Given the overlapping needs and blurred biopolitical distinctions suggested by these approaches to UD, the growing convergence between accessible and mainstream needs, products, and uses of technology is particularly important. Advocates of accessibility are now attempting to connect it to issues of privacy, security, personalization, and user-generated content and practices, as these articulations could make accessibility more obviously relevant outside of disability contexts and facilitate its incorporation into default forms of technological and cultural artifacts, increasing access for all.

One of the most ambitious convergent accessibility projects is the Global Public Inclusive Infrastructure (GPII), an ongoing, collaborative, open effort to create personalized profiles of needed accessibility features and preferences, stored online "in the cloud," that can be automatically implemented on any computerized device. The introductory video indicates the GPII's potential to upend relationships between the form of technologies and users' abilities. Rather than offer ways one can adapt to existing forms, or work around them, the video asks viewers to "imagine if you could pick up any device, anywhere, and it would automatically adapt to you."[86] This suggests the centrality of users' needs and the necessity of creating forms of technology that are flexible, adjustable, and usable by a wide audience. Thus, the GPII is an attempt to standardize accessible technology development, integrate it with mainstream technologies and practices, and reduce the cost and effort associated with developing and purchasing assistive technologies for those who need them.[87]

The GPII adopts a universal design approach as it aims to "ensure that everyone who faces accessibility barriers due to disability, literacy, digital literacy, or aging, regardless of economic resources, can access and use the Internet and all its information, communities, and services for education, employment, daily living, civic participation, health, and safety."[88] Expertise based in disability is being brought to bear on a wide range of situational contexts in order to increase access and usability for diverse audiences. In describing potential benefits of the GPII, user profiles are offered that demonstrate how this technology will change accessibility conditions. The benefit of "instant setup" of assistive technology is described through "Mary":

> Today—Mary has moderate low vision and all of the settings that she needs are already built into the computer. Someone once showed her how she can adjust the font size and the contrast and use zooming feature and some other settings and the computer was a lot easier to use. But when she was done they needed to undo it all for the next person. Now she can't remember how to make all the setting changes or where the magnifier utility is. And it is way too complicated to do all those things (and then undo them) each time she uses a different computer. And if she does it wrong she would mess up someone else's computer for them.

Gregg Vanderheiden, a bearded white man wearing glasses, explains the GPII during a session at the CSUN Annual International Technology and Persons with Disabilities Conference, 2013. Author's photograph.

In the future, with GPII—each time Mary sits down to a computer, it automatically sets up just for her, with all her font sizes, contrast, etc. And when she is done, everything automatically changes back. So she is not afraid of using any public computer or borrowing someone's computer when she needs to.[89]

Other benefits of this project could include the ability to take assistive technology with you (via a flash drive or other easily integrated form of identification for your profile); on-demand assistance and descriptions of possible accessibility features; anonymous profiles and set-ups; pre-made set-ups that do not require a profile; privacy for preference, permission, and payment information; and the reduction of barriers in a variety of contexts.[90] These benefits are widely desirable, for a range of user abilities and contexts, even as they are based in accessibility and assistive technology work for people with disabilities.

The GPII is organized by an international group called Raising the Floor, run by Vanderheiden and inclusive-design researcher Jutta Treviranus; the name refers to the need to increase the ability of basic assistive technology to work with modern online software, sites, and services. Currently, the group has more than seventy-five members from industry, academia, consumer groups, nongovernmental organizations, and other invested stakeholders.[91] The organization is open, akin to the W3C, and actively seeks new potential participants from a range of stakeholder positions.[92]

The legacies of universal design and related theories are apparent in the GPII, but it goes further by adapting cultural and technological ideas of convergence, personalization, and privacy to the context of access barriers. Bringing these concepts to bear undermines assumptions about assistive technology as slow, cumbersome, or outdated and situates disability not as a singular deficiency but as one among many features that may drive individual preferences for particular forms of technology and paths to access. These strategies have also been the focus of "accessibility 2.0."[93] Adapting the name and user focus of "Web 2.0," "accessibility 2.0" has called for greater attention to user experience, a range of stakeholders, flexibility, and collaborative development of accessible computing and internet.[94] Australian media and disability scholars Katie Ellis and Mike Kent take accessibility 2.0 further, defining it as the ability to access content in the desired form within an unstructured, Web 2.0 environment. They argue that it "prioritizes the accessibility choices of individual users."[95] The GPII may be looked at as an implementation of accessibility 2.0 in many ways, as the foundation of both is based upon the variations of users' needs, treating accessibility as a process, and integrating accessibility with related concerns about access and contemporary online media.

Convergent accessibility initiatives, and theorizations born out of universal design, treat the site of form as a space within which to offer flexibility. Both a range of users and a range of paths to access are made part of these design processes. In addition to facilitating increased access and thus "wider participation in education, employment, commerce, and our communities,"[96] the GPII and similar projects demonstrate a willingness to look beyond accessibility as a solution for people with disabilities. Instead, there is a recognition that access is of concern for all people, even as it has been made invisible through the reliance of computer and web design on normative intersections of bodies and technologies.

Conclusion

Yet there is no reason to expect perfect accessibility of digital media forms in the near future. The rise of mobile devices and attendant apps (applications) that are developed for specific hardware platforms and sold in proprietary systems (such as Apple's App Store) has created a universe of "tethered devices" in which users have limited control beyond the exercise of consumer choice.[97] The kinds of hacks, workarounds, and specialized technologies that have been central to making media technologies accessible to people with disabilities become more challenging to make or access, less likely to be made, and harder to find when devices exist within their own corporate constraints. Projects like the GPII require interoperability and openness, neither of which is currently prioritized across the brands and models of mobile devices. Without such openness, each platform is a universe unto itself, with its own technological specifications, policies, and development communities. Users with disabilities may find that, paradoxically, these walled gardens contain both incredibly useful accessibility apps and many apps that are inaccessibly designed, resulting in users' inability to access popular content, such as games.

In the former category, apps such as ProLoquo2Go offer powerful and comparatively inexpensive means of communication for people with speech and some cognitive impairments. Currently priced at under $300, ProLoquo2Go is less expensive and more easily available than specialized assistive technology and has been used as a communication board, for text-to-speech conversion, and for connecting cognitively with children with limited verbal abilities.[98] Apple has even integrated accessibility apps into its outreach techniques, offering a web page dedicated to apps for visual, hearing, motion, learning, and speech impairments. Featured apps include a Braille screen interface (BrailleTouch), an app designed to improve motor skills (Dexteria), and apps that teach American Sign Language (Sign4Me).[99] Titled "Where there's a need, there's an app," this page suggests that apps can extend accessibility in innovative ways.

While this is certainly true of apps that function as assistive technology, many apps that convey media or cultural content remain inaccessible. Fewer than 15 percent of users with disabilities expect to find accessible apps, relying instead on recommendations, research, and testing out apps themselves.[100] Both Apple (iOS) and Google (Android) provide guidance for app developers regarding accessibility.[101] However, neither of these systems requires apps to be accessible in order to enter the marketplace. This strategy of encouragement, rather than requirement, recalls web content accessibility; these are regulations aimed at form, which are effective only if taken up by those involved in the production of those forms of hardware and software. Furthermore, given the proprietary nature of these mobile systems, and the walled gardens that they create through their application distribution systems, there are few options for end users to control the forms in which mobile content is delivered via apps.

The site of form is a site of possibility. Here, cultural meanings intersect with and direct particular designs and paths to access, while potentially excluding others. Devices, as we know, are never neutral; they reflect their contexts, are shaped by their uses, and become part of chains of cultural and technological adaptations. Within this process, "design is a meeting place of ideas and practices to do with aesthetic considerations, functionality, economics, and signs, as well as engineering and marketing."[102] The contrast between the innovative assistive technologies built for mobile devices and the continued inaccessibility of cultural expressions such as games illustrates once again the struggles of defining and modulating the forms of digital media. Form is a site of possibility not only for quotidian practices but also for the contestation of dominant ideologies of ability and digital media. Although mobile devices offer the affordances to create an accessible media culture, function may once again be separated from style or culture, limiting the extent to which disability and mainstream mobile cultures may be integrated. Without requiring accessibility of third-party app developers, the innovations built into the hardware and software of these devices are utilitarian but may not facilitate access to the kinds of cultural content desired by users, as discussed in the next chapter.

Questions about form challenge the ways in which content is presented and the pathways to access that are created by those presentations and forms of interaction. In looking beyond the circularity of mainstream and assistive design processes, and escaping the technological specificity of early accessibility policies, we see an increasing emphasis on form as a site of transformation and flexibility. The forms of digital media offer affordances and constraints that become opportunities, barriers, or the foundation for further cultural adaptation. They contribute to the construction of the moment of access and may structure entire experiences of digital media through their characteristics. While formal elements can solidify paths to access, they can also offer multiple ways to move toward digital media access and use. Within hacker and developer cultures, the words *possibility* and *access* are often used synonymously.[103] This is logical, as what cannot be accessed cannot be transformed. The variability of form is precisely what may extend access and enabled transformation. This makes digital media a compelling case for the investigation of media access, technological possibility, and the cultural meanings of disability. The study of form is thus a study of variation and transformation of access, as there is always more to the conditions of media access than meets the eye.

4

Content Warnings

Struggles over Meaning, Rights, and Equality

The Boston Red Sox won the Major League Baseball (MLB) World Series in 2013, their third win in a decade. In 2004, the team broke the "Curse of the Bambino"—a stretch of eighty-six years without a World Series win that followed the trade of Babe Ruth in 1919—and emerged as a regular contender, rewarding old fans and energizing new ones. However, for some fans, the 2013 season was quite different from those of 2004 and 2007. The difference wasn't simply in the meteoric rise of the 2013 team from a dismal 2012 season, the resonance of the victory following the Boston Marathon bombing in April 2013, or the players' wooly beards. For many blind and visually impaired fans, the 2013 championship season was the first that they could follow and participate in on equal footing with sighted fans.

Baseball, with its slow pace and long history of radio broadcasting, has a significant blind audience. However, in the early twenty-first century, MLB launched a number of online and digital offerings that dramatically expanded opportunities to follow along with individual teams and the league at large. Online ticketing, online shopping in the team shops, and most notably the launch of cable channel MLB Network and the online subscription service MLB.tv made baseball more available to fans across the country than had ever been possible. These changes unfolded with little attention to accessibility for blind fans. In 2008, blind Red Sox fan Brian Charlson found that he could not buy tickets or look at player statistics online. Charlson approached Major League Baseball Advanced Media (MLBAM), which operates all internet and interactive media features for MLB, about increasing accessibility to these and other features.

Charlson, the American Council of the Blind, the Bay State Council of the Blind, and the California Council of the Blind reached an agreement with MLBAM in 2009. This agreement was reached not through the courts but through a process called "structured negotiation" that has been used successfully to increase accessibility in a range of industries. Rather than risk a case being thrown out, or the establishment of a precedent that decides against requiring accessibility, structured negotiations allow complainants to work with industries to find mutually agreeable solutions.[1] Often, the process entails bringing clients with disabilities into meetings to demonstrate barriers to industry personnel. After industries observe these barriers in action and meet individuals who struggle with access, structured negotiations often proceed as collaborations. Terms are agreed to, over a specified time period, and complainants in some cases even become ongoing consultants, increasing accessibility over time. For complainants, the process often results in speedier and better accessibility fixes; for industries, the process avoids any decree of legal wrongdoing and gives guidance in pursuing accessibility.

In the case of MLBAM, the original agreement included all league and team websites and services such as GameDay Audio, MLB.tv, and All-Star Voting interfaces. The agreement specified that complainants would be able to review services no later than May 1 of each year and could bring concerns to MLBAM if anything appeared to violate the agreement, at which point MLBAM could respond and the organizations could collaborate on solutions.[2] Following commencement of this collaboration, accessible content allowed blind fans to participate in online offerings; Charlson stated that while he did not agree with all of the All-Star team selections, he "felt like a part of it for the first time," viewing statistics and casting his votes.[3]

The original agreement spanned 2009–2011, then was extended through Feburary 1, 2015. The extension called for MLBAM to look into closed captioning, transcripts, and audio description, extending the accessibility of online videos for d/Deaf or hard-of-hearing fans as well as blind fans. The revised agreement also encompassed mobile content. As with the web content, a process of review and ultimately dispute resolution was set up to ensure ongoing progress toward accessibility. MLB.com At Bat, the league's mobile application for iPhone and iPad, had accessibility improvements in both 2011 and 2012, enabling fans to keep up via these channels. These improvements were well received, as in an evaluation by a site specializing in apps for visually impaired users which stated that "If you are a baseball fan, MLB.com At Bat 11 will be your favorite app. . . . Truly the ultimate baseball app, MLB is accessible and ready for the opening pitch!"[4]

Though regulation, use, and form are relevant to this example, it is most valuably understood through the lens of content. The *content* of Major League Baseball drove attempts to increase accessibility—not merely the information conveyed by scores and statistics but also baseball's cultural meanings were at stake. Culturally, baseball has a long history and an enduring reputation as an "all-American" game, associated with the nation and citizenship, while its geographically dispersed teams represent local and regional communities, its fan bases support countless industries, and its past is connected to larger historical concerns such as racial integration, monopoly practices, and performance-enhancing drugs. The pursuit of baseball content is the pursuit of a particular set of meanings, cultural allegiances, and shared experiences. For blind fans, inaccessibility was not lamentable because it represented political inequality, the impossibility of daily activities, or the absence of necessary information but because it cut them off from these meanings. To fully participate in a communal cultural space, access to content and its attendant ideologies and social meanings is essential.

This chapter uses several different case studies drawn from the World Wide Web, social media, television and online closed captioning, and video games to investigate how content is imagined, produced, and received in relation to disability and technology. First, the privileging of information over entertainment is informed by cultural understandings of disability as disadvantage or deficit and reproduces social inequalities by extending access only to "valuable" content. As a result, advocating access to pleasurable content that is socially devalued can be a political act that affirms the worth of those who have been excluded and challenges hierarchies of content and bodies or identities. Second, the means of accessing content may or may not be understood as changing that content; this raises questions about free speech, copyright, and similarity that are not easily resolved. Ultimately, analysis of the site of content makes the myriad and contentious relationships between access, equity, and culture available for dissection.

The Site of Content

Analyzing media access from the point of view of content is just one of the five perspectives established in the interrogatory "access kit" featured in the Introduction to this book. The kit offers five lenses through which to consider access, each with an associated group of questions. Individually, each perspective—regulation, use, form, content, and experience—draws focus to particular elements that enable or constrain access to a given medium at a given time for a given individual or group. Taken together, however, the questions asked within this kit aim to direct research in such a way as to retain the inherent complications and contradictions of media access as a variable and important phenomenon. No perspective is necessarily more truthful, useful, or rigorous; each perspective indicates particular concerns and dynamics that may be more or less relevant.

This chapter works within the domain of content, which I use to refer to the cultural signifiers and meanings conveyed by a media artifact. Accessibility advocates and new media theorists often trumpet the ability of digital media to separate form and content; the technical and material components, such as code and hardware, constitute the form, while the content is the meaningful component designed, written, or developed for the purpose of communication. Content thus includes simple textual information and audio, visual, video, and multimedia artifacts. It is the blog post, the YouTube video, the listings of a retail website. Content is the communicative and cultural component of digital media. Content is *what* we access; it is the most frequent *motivation* for access. The interrogatory that guides analysis of content in terms of access is as follows:

What is the information, meaning, or experience being pursued and why?
What are the cultural values surrounding that content?
How does this content, as a set of motivations and meanings, relate to the
   form in which it is delivered or received?

Studying access through the lens of content entails holding several definitions and implications of content in tension, particularly when considering alternative forms of access such as accessible web pages. What constitutes access to a motivation or meaning? How is it valued and by whom? When content must be presented in an alternate form, does it retain original meanings? These tensions reveal the conceptual difficulty of separating form and content, despite many scholarly attempts to do so.

Media content has often been understood as the messages that travel through a particular "channel," and it is often imagined as moving fairly seamlessly. Communication scholar Joseph Meyrowitz describes content as those elements that move between people via media channels or conduits; the channel is a means of distribution, while content comprises messages, values, information, narratives, genres, behavior, and so on.[5] Content literacy, therefore, involves the ability to access, interpret, and analyze such material. Such notions of content as a process, rather than an object, have become common within literature on media literacy and digital media access alike. For instance, journalism and communication scholars John Newhagen and Erik Bucy begin their edited volume *Media Access* by asking, "[A]ccess to what?" Their answer is meaning; they dispute the inherent value of computer and internet access, instead linking its value to its fulfillment of users' wants and needs.[6]

Such processes and linkages indicate the importance of the site of content for the analysis of access. Access to content requires specific material conditions, literacies, and motivations that support the pursuit of an individual's desires. Content links technological uses and cultural meanings and is a site for the negotiation of relationships of power. As content is so closely connected to the cultural, it is the prime location of battles regarding ideologies, values, and representations in media. Therefore, it is a particularly tumultuous site of analysis at which media, technology, culture, and embodied users come into close contact and produce varied forms of audiences, identities, and citizens.

The study of content complements and complicates the previous chapter's focus on the formal elements of digital media; though we may separate form and content for analytic purposes, they inform and refract upon each other. Software studies theorist Lev Manovich describes this in terms of the cultural and computer "layers," which meet and blend computer and human meanings, digital and traditional means of representation, form and content and ultimately produce a new cultural relationship between the individual and media.

In his description of a new computer culture based upon programmability, Manovich advocates "software studies" as a successor to media studies, recognizing the ways in which software rather than "medium" transmits culture.[7] Content and medium, culture and computer become interdependent in such framings. Yet, if "medium" is no longer a fixed element, and digitization contributes to this fragmentation, software may be an equally slippery object of study. Many in new media, digital, or internet studies have turned away from the study of specific content in order to study the "guts" of new media—software, code, programmability, hardware affordances, and so on.[8] Yet, even if "all new media objects allegedly rely on—or, more strongly, can be reduced to—software, a visibly invisible or invisibly visible essence,"[9] the study of such formal components in isolation from content offers only an illusory mastery of digital culture. At its worst, it is technologically reductionist. More charitably, Wendy Chun argues that a focus only on software or related formal elements risks the perpetuation of particular ideologies of computing, many of which rest upon neoliberal economies and subjectivities. Similarly, a focus only on the cultural artifacts delivered by digital forms can facilitate the transmission of ideologies of technology as transparent and free from meaning. Therefore, in advocating the study of content *in concert with* the study of these forms, I mean to emphasize the possibility of prying apart these ideologies by considering culture alongside computing and motivation alongside mediation.

The expansive notion of content described above is at odds not only with purist forms of software studies but also with common understandings of content within technology circles. For instance, many multimedia digital formats—such as AIFF, MP4, and PNG—are commonly referred to as "containers" or "wrappers." Such file formats use specific code to indicate how metadata and other elements are connected within the digital file. Under such a technological ontology, the "container" format is meaningless; it merely fosters computerized interpretation of that which is "inside" it. Meaning and value come from that which is inside a particular file, from the content inside the container. Explicating such arrangements, Jonathan Sterne describes the MP3 format as a container for recorded sound (itself a container for "live" performance or sound).[10] This example seems to suggest that the container is the "technological" element, while its contents are the mediated, meaningful, cultural artifacts. The proliferation of content management systems (CMS) for building websites forces a similar separation of form and content in which the former is made invisible and the latter technologically irrelevant. In a CMS, the code, structure, and functions of the page are predetermined; business or personal users are asked to upload their "content" within this structure, using a WYSIWYG ("what you see is what you get") interface that obscures the technological underpinnings of the site. Pictures, text, information, and specific forms of interaction are thus framed as "content," mutable and consumptive, while the formal structure is fixed and produced by professionals. Similarly, the emphasis on the separability of "form" and "content" in web development and accessibility tends to treat technological forms as meaningless and content as self-evident and static.

The Hierarchy of Content: Information, Communication, and Entertainment

An expansive notion of content as a process of meaning-making and cultural significance opens the door to considerations of value, taste, and differentiation. After all, different types of content are not treated equally by the government, marketplace, or society at large. Access to content is often dependent upon such differentiations, which display and reinforce particular arrangements of cultural power. In the relationship between disability and digital media content, these variances and their political import are laid bare. It seems that "information" is prioritized for people with disabilities, with "communication" a distant second, while "entertainment" is often framed as a luxury. This hierarchy of content, as explicated below, perpetuates a politics of disability as deficit and access as charity.

According to the W3C, content is "the information in a Web page or Web application," which includes texts, images, audio, and the code (or markup) that defines the structure and presentation of a page or application.[11] This definition indicates the attempted clarity of standardization, as well as the division of such content from the "techniques" used to meet accessibility goals (the latter would alter the form/code of a web page or application). Thus, there is little direct attention to the cultural relevancies of content within the accessibility world. This is most evident in its categorization as "information"—by extension, interaction, representation, narrative, and aesthetics may be something other than "content." Such a restrictive notion of content implies a hierarchy in which "information" is privileged over other forms of textual or multimedia content.

This prioritization of "information" is common in discussions of digital media and "disadvantaged" audiences, including the poor, disabled, or globally dispersed, and plays out in the continued unequal access to different forms of content. Recent reporting on the Global Internet initiative, backed by Facebook founder Mark Zuckerberg, has demonstrated this tendency to "treat the Internet as something deeply noble and serious in order to substantiate its importance in an impoverished nation."[12] This displays a pervasive paternalism in which those without advantages are expected to pursue civic-minded, developmental, or practical material rather than more popular or entertainment-oriented offerings. For instance, in his study of technology for social inclusion, education researcher Mark Warschauer argues that people need content related to economic development, health care, and education more than they need information related to "community affairs and culture." For people with disabilities, he is even more specific in calling for content related to "rehabilitation programs, assistive technology, special education, workplace adaptations, legislation, and training."[13]

Increasing the civic, economic, and social participation by people with disabilities or other disadvantaged groups has been and continues to be a priority for U.S. policies related to digital media access. Recall that Section 508 requires federal agencies and their contractors to produce accessible web content for employees and members of the public. Similar regulations have been taken up in many states regarding state government resources, and 508 is often used as the basis for public universities' accessibility policies. It is therefore not coincidental that government, educational, informational, and similar resources have been made accessible at much higher rates than commercial, retail, entertainment, or social services, though these sites are far from perfect.[14] As newer laws presage an expansion in the content required to be accessible, they build upon telecommunications and mass media regulatory frameworks that have historically supported such content hierarchies.

The distinction between "content" and "conduit" has been central to much of U.S. telecommunications and mass media policy. Content has usually been understood through a broadcast, one-to-many model, as seen in radio and television regulations mandating that stations operate in the public interest in their trusteeship of the airwaves. Conduits such as telephone calls, contrarily, have supported interactive forms of communication and been regulated as common carriers. Communication scholars Benjamin Compaine and Mitchell Weintraub describe this as a difference in definition: "In brief, communications is a process. Information is a substance."[15] Communications processes (conduits) have been valued more highly, via common carriage policies and the prioritization of individual access, than has content or "information." Instead, information is understood as optional and has historically been harder to come by, available only at libraries or similar institutions.[16] Information (or content), it seems, is a "thing" that can be acted upon via various technologies, institutions, or individuals.

"Information," "content," and "telecommunication" are further separated at the level of policy by Federal Communication Commission (FCC) definitions and attendant regulations. Following the Telecommunications Act of 1996, telecommunications is defined as "the transmission, between or among points specified by the user, of information of the user's choosing, without change in the form or content of the information as sent and received."[17] Telecommunications services are defined as offering such capacities to the public for a fee, and telecommunications carriers are understood to be common carriers engaged in providing such services. With the rise of computing and internet services, the FCC found itself in a quandary. The Telecommunications Act of 1996 authorized the FCC to act in the interest of expanding "advanced services" and new technologies. However, it did not classify those services as telecommunications but as "information services" that offer the capacity for "generating, acquiring, storing, transforming, processing, retrieving, utilizing, or making available information via telecommunications, and includes electronic publishing."[18] This has meant that digital networks are not treated as common carriers and has allowed the possibility of selling access to the internet as a content service (such as cable television). Content, again, is regulated as optional and unnecessary, as opposed to the value placed upon open communications conduits.

In contexts of communicative content, people with disabilities are often positioned as accessing material for noble purposes, or self-help. At Disability.Blog, a site run by the federal government, social media are touted as offering people with disabilities opportunities for "brand building," networking, employment, self-education, disability aware-ness, and "like-minded networking" with others who share disability experiences.[19] Readers are urged to "jump right in and find ways for social media to empower you, whether directly related to your disability or not."[20] The emphasis on social media for "empowerment" indicates the presumed disenfranchisement of people with disabilities and val-ues access to social media as a means for uplift. People with disabili-ties are expected to use digital media in practical ways, with an aim of self-improvement.

The prioritization of serious "information" and uplifting forms of in-teraction limit access to digital media content for people with disabili-ties. For instance, although YouTube is renowned for its user-generated content, when Google announced the initial launch of its autocaptioning technology, it partnered with universities, including Stanford, Yale, and MIT, and reputable information sources such as National Geographic and PBS.[21] The content provided by these services was thus prioritized. First, this had the effect of positioning those who would benefit from captions as audience members and not video producers. Second, that it was educational, informative, or culturally valued material reveals the persistence of notions of uplift as a guiding principle in media access for disadvantaged audiences, including people with disabilities. Though YouTube hosts a range of user-generated content, as well as profes-sional videos such as music videos or film trailers (which are among the most-viewed videos), these were not chosen for initial inclusion in the captioning project. And though many people with disabilities produce video blogs, diaries, web series, ASL performances of popular songs, and other content that is hosted on YouTube, they were not hailed as users who might be interested in creating accessible content. Entertain-ment, cultural production, and pleasurable experiences were depriori-tized through this targeted rollout, perpetuating a politics of disability in which certain "types" of content or information are "important" to those who are at some social deficit, while other types of content are pleasur-able luxuries reserved for the already-advantaged.

If straightforward informational content is deemed "necessary" for the disadvantaged, other forms of digitally delivered content are implic-itly understood as a "bonus," or luxury, that people with disabilities may not "need." Such thinking has the effect of entrenching the disadvantages of disability, as the media environment available to mainstream audiences remains unavailable to those who rely upon accessibility features. Such a hierarchy reflects and reinforces ideologies of disability as a disadvantage and neoliberal framings of pleasure as a luxury for the already-privileged. It also reflects an emphasis on "uplift" that has characterized discourses of public broadcasting in the United States, in which elites imposed their own tastes and values regarding content that was "good" for the masses. In practice, this meant prioritizing information and "high" culture over the populist tastes represented in the commercial media in the interest of educating or "improving" the mass audience (implicitly, a less elite audience encompassing women, racial minorities, and the poor and working class).[22] This resulted in public television "for the people, not by the people."[23] "Proper"—and elite— forms of content were imposed, while popular, crass, melodramatic, mundane, or minority content was pushed aside, out of mediated channels and thus, often, out of a shared political sphere. In the prioritizing of accessibility only for "necessary" or uplifting forms of content, a similar paternalism is evident.

These stances toward disability and content are deeply political. An ableist ideology of disability as deficit is maintained through the emphasis on "important" content and the conceptualization of people with disabilities as passive recipients of charity and content alike. Online practical information, health and disability information, employment and educational opportunities, and other informational, economic, or civic forms of content are positioned as resources that can improve the lives of people with disabilities. This assumes, of course, that these lives are in some way deficient, undesirable, and in need of improvement. As digital communication scholar David Gunkel notes in his critique of the "digital divide," those who lack access "comprise [sic] the negative counterpart and undesirable version" of the "haves,"[24] a formulation that reveals a disturbing endurance of hierarchies of global, economic, racial, and gender difference. As those who have lacked access to digital media have been those in the Global South, the poor, the nonwhite, the poorly educated, or the female, the binary of the digital divide reflects and entrenches hegemonic power structures. Gunkel's observation equally applies to disability and its cultural valences of deficiency and dependency.

Furthermore, if those in disadvantaged positions are held to a higher standard of moral and content "purity" regarding their use of digital media—given access only to "necessary," uplifting, or insular community content—then they are never fully incorporated into the broader mediated society. The option to have fun, to "mess around," and to engage in pleasurable, recreational (or even morally dubious) activities is necessary to ensuring full social participation and inclusion.[25]

Cultural capital and attendant relationships of power circulate through the varied articulations of digital media content, its forms, its meanings, and its embodied users. For those who struggle to access a particular kind of content, the issue is not one merely of technology but one of cultural access, equity, and the production and expression of identity. Cultural studies scholars have long advocated for the serious treatment of pleasurable media and cultural practices. In respect to television, cultural studies scholar John Hartley argues that the medium had instructed audiences in their identities as cultural citizens and opened possibilities for the construction of a "do-it-yourself" identity.[26] Choosing from the "semiotic material on offer," individuals could make and remake their identities as citizens, allowing for a new diversity of modes of political activity. However, DIY citizenship itself is quite close to a valorization of consumerism and neoliberal modes of celebritized identity.[27] The DIY citizen was presented as an individual, outside of traditional collectivities such as the nation, or racial or gender identities; the ability to choose, and alter, identities turns access to citizenship into a kind of consumer activity. Furthermore, the DIY citizen was a potentially exclusionary framework as, like the ideal public sphere, it took for granted an equality of access to semiotic resources and performances.[28] However, for those who cannot identify with the cultural citizenship promoted in media, and for whom there are not adequate representations or relevant content to support DIY citizenship, the ability to participate in media content and its attendant political meanings is restricted. Australian cultural studies and communication scholars Gerard Goggin and Christopher Newell argue that such bricolage has been inaccessible for people with disabilities, who have limited access to media content and representation.[29]

Content distinctions that privilege practical and informative material for the "deficient" audience of people with disabilities perpetuate ableist ideologies and reinforce material inequalities. The emphasis on useful forms of digital media content works as a paternalistic form of accommodation, allowing only certain forms of citizenship, identity, and participation to flourish for people with disabilities. It is thus politically limiting, sanctioning only prescribed information and behaviors. Therefore, criticism and alternative forms of content have the possibility to be not only pleasurable but also politically transformative.

If we accept that people with disabilities are an oppressed group in society,[30] then we must also consider that the bodies and pleasures of people with disabilities can be threats to social control, undermining the established political and ideological order.[31] In pleasurable media use by people with disabilities, popular content—to use cultural studies theorist John Fiske's understanding of the popular as an oppositional form of discourse that may be vulgar, scandalous, or otherwise unsanctioned—is articulated to bodies that challenge social norms, resulting in a critique of the body politic and its discursive and material exclusions.

Fun, thus, becomes potentially transgressive in its revelation of the material power dynamics that are mapped onto particular kinds of content. The Pew Internet and American Life Project has conducted surveys about online media use in which "fun" includes content such as music, movies, sports, and interactive chatting; these content types are not considered "major life activities" or ways to receive "information." Lisa Nakamura, a scholar of digital media and race, criticizes this division for its implication that the popular is not of value and suggests that definitions of "information" need revision in order for us to fully understand and account for minorities' use of the internet.[32] For people with disabilities—routinely held to limited definitions of "major life activities" under the ADA and other state and federal laws, which provide aid only when a disability or impairment interferes with activities such as feeding oneself, tending to personal hygiene, or communicating[33]—consuming, circulating, or producing fun content is an even more explicitly political activity. To go further and conceive of popular culture, entertainment, or pleasure as a major life activity is to challenge the entire neoliberal structure of public, private, and personal activities in mainstream American culture.[34] The next section considers video games in terms of accessibility and disability representation, illustrating the ways in which an often denigrated, "unimportant," and fun medium may offer valuable opportunities for inclusion.

Gaming the Systems

Advocating for the accessibility of games is an intervention in the systemic elements of games, game industries, and gaming cultures. While much accessibility activism aims to redress serious, material inequalities that could be ameliorated via technological access, games activism is predominantly cultural. Games are not presented as assistive technologies, or as venues for charity or uplift; instead, they are framed as sources of cultural capital and sites of pleasure and entertainment. This aligns with dominant discourses of gaming, in which games have been conceived of primarily as an entertainment medium, appropriate for leisure time and evaluated in terms of pleasure. Thus, in the prioritizing of the pleasures of game content for a diverse audience of users with disabilities, these forms of activism are deeply political, expressing a right to pleasure and frivolity for a group whose access is often constrained by paternalistic notions of appropriate or "necessary" content.

Games may be defined as nonwork interactive rules-based systems, in which players take actions that in turn produce variable outcomes. However, this only scratches the surface of what games can be, do, and become in the hands of diverse creators and players. Formally, games may be digital, analog, or physical and may incorporate a wide range of mechanics, from racing to puzzle-solving to use of a controller handset. Game content might be understood as the systems of narrative, imagery, social interaction, and user feedback that emerge from the experience of play. Together, the forms and contents of games constitute cultural artifacts that are part of larger systems of media circulation and representation. People with disabilities are often materially and culturally excluded from both systems through inaccessible interfaces, a lack of representation (or offensive representations) in games' content, or a lack of awareness within the games industries. Inaccessible interfaces include games that lack a color-blind mode; consoles that require specific, controlled movements; and visual game content that cannot be aurally conveyed. Representational exclusion can be seen in the often impossibility of constructing game avatars with disability, in the use of disability as a game mechanic (as when an avatar is injured and the rules of play change), and in stereotypical representations of disabled nonplayer characters, which often focus on narratives of overcoming or on villainous disabled characters.[35]

These priorities are visible in efforts to put pressure on video game industries to increase accessibility. One particularly notable organization involved in this cultural activism is the AbleGamers Foundation. Its work involves both advocacy within the mainstream games industry and the provision of accessible "arcades" at conferences that allow people to try out assistive technologies and accessible games. The group relies heavily on volunteer participation and also acts as a resource and hub for an online community for gamers with disabilities. AbleGamers appears to have a pragmatic attitude toward accessibility; its accessibility reviews indicate that no game may ever be perfect for all audiences and instead focus on the specific affordances and constraints of the games under consideration. For instance, 2009's Mainstream Accessibility Award winner, BioWare's *Dragon Age: Origins* for PC, was rewarded for specific accessibility features, including multiple options for subtitles and captioning, multiple mobility options for interaction with the game and computer, color-blind–friendliness, cognitive friendliness (in the ability to stop and start combat action), and numerous small accessibility options such as multiple levels of difficulty and clearly marked terrain. Such awards may reward those in the industry who make accessible games, but they also serve communities of gamers as badges that identify a game as accessible and thus perhaps particularly enjoyable, for an audience that may require such accessibility features.

Accessibility reviews and features such as the annual holiday gift guide put out by AbleGamers both convey a politics of pleasure that asserts the worthiness of people with disabilities as media audiences and participate in a neoliberal consumer culture, figuring people with disabilities as markets. For example, items in the 2014 holiday gift guide were described as "the most important items you can buy for the gamer with disabilities in your life" and included many of the most popular consoles and game titles of the year.[36] It evaluated popular titles such as *MLB: The Show 14* (recommended for its "one-button mode where you can enjoy the action of home runs with only one button or switch") and *Call of Duty Advanced Warfare* (listed as "a game to avoid"), as well as listed several useful assistive technologies for gaming.[37] By including a range of genres, impairments, and access needs, the gift guide takes seriously the notion of variable preferences and interests among gamers with disabilities, treating them like consumers entitled to a range of choices. This is not a pursuit of the universal game but an effort "to get every title to have the broadest audience possible and make sure that, for those left out of a particular title, there are other titles waiting for them to play."[38] Thus, accessibility is important at both the level of individual video game systems and at the level of the larger marketplace and cultural system.

In order to meet these goals, AbleGamers' 2012 "Includification" project attempted to put pressure on game developers by providing a resource for accessible game development. This website and accompanying documents laid out strategies for thinking about, designing for, and producing accessible videogames. AbleGamers editor-in-chief and director of Community Outreach Steve Spohn explained that the document was "a reference not only about how important accessibility is, but a road map for the easy-to-implement, cost-effective and market-boosting steps [game developers] can take to enable gamers with disabilities."[39] Produced with the cooperation of five unnamed leading game studios, the materials offer rationales for accessibility and first-person accounts from gamers with disabilities and game developers who have incorporated accessible practices. Much like WCAG 2.0, it "does not explain the technical ways to design a video game. Instead, it explains the most important accessibility options that can be included [in] a video game and what each one of them means to the end-user."[40] The document also offers several thought experiments and development exercises for those new to accessibility, aimed at increasing consideration of the relevant barriers and the perspectives of gamers with disabilities. In these sections, as well as through acknowledgment that total game accessibility may not be possible, and certainly may never be profitable, the Includification document demonstrates a pedagogical form of activism, conducting educational outreach in order to foster desired change.

AbleGamers argues that "there should be no barriers to fun."[41] Its activism, however, focuses primarily on technological barriers and does not address the ways in which representations within games may act as cultural barriers for people with disabilities. Too often, disability within video games is deployed as a metaphor, or a particularly challenging form of gameplay; in either case, it is nearly always a temporary state experienced without any kind of disability community. In these ways, *Katawa Shoujo* (*KS*) is a remarkably different kind of game. The idea came from an illustration posted to the online forum 4Chan. From there, it grew into an open source project completed collaboratively by an international group of writers, developers, and artists over a period of nearly five years. Set at a boarding school for students with disabilities, *KS* is a desktop game based on the genre of the Japanese dating simulation. These games typically involve the player's avatar's being put in a position to choose among several nonplayer characters with whom to pursue relationships. Translated, the game's title is "Disability Girls," and in accordance with the norms of the genre, *KS* incorporates romantic storylines and sexual encounters between characters with a range of disabilities. Fun, here, is tied not only to gameplay but also to sexuality, making this game a particularly interesting intervention in the politics of accessible content and pleasure.

The plot of *KS* begins with the player's character, a young man named Hanako, confessing his love to a female classmate and then awakening in a hospital to learn that he had an undiagnosed heart condition and experienced a heart attack. As part of his recovery, he is sent to a boarding school for teens with disabilities, where he soon meets others and learns about disability identities, how to interact across difference, and how to come to accept his own condition. Hanako's journey of self-discovery is populated by nuanced characters with disabilities. That nuance was an integral part of the development, because, in the words of one developer, "[W]e didn't want to make [disability] the character. . . . We said, 'Look, it's part of that character but it's not the only part, there are still other parts around it.'"[42] On the *KS* website, each romantic prospect is pictured with a short character description that illustrates this nuance: "Since Rin's arms are tiny stumps due to a severe birth defect and subsequent surgery, she uses her feet and occasionally her mouth to do everything, which includes painting. Because of her disability, using skirts is tough, so Rin is wearing a boy's uniform at school. Her creativity is matched by her philosophical streak: Rin is fond of occasionally getting lost in thought and giving voice to abstract ideas about man, the universe, and other things that thoroughly confuse people."[43] (See figure 4.1.)

At the hospital it was easy, but I still haven't sorted my feelings about having to live a "normal" life with this disability.

A screenshot from an early scene in *Katawa Shoujo* showing Rin in a hallway, with the text from the protagonist's voiceover: "At the hospital it was easy, but I still haven't sorted my feelings about having to live a 'normal' life with this disability."

These representations alone would be noteworthy, but it is the frank incorporation of romantic storylines and sexual encounters that poses a significant challenge to the meanings of disability and access usually conveyed through media content. Often, people with disabilities have been de-sexualized through institutionalization, oversight, infantalization, or assumptions about diminished physical capacities and desires. As a result, people with disabilities may be pathologized and denied access to their own bodies and interpersonal sexual experiences.[44] Furthermore, theoretical moves that value nonconventional sexualities have often done so by reaffirming the alterity of disabled bodies.[45] In such contexts, the eroticism of disability is rendered invisible or pathological. More positive understandings of disability and sexuality have come from the union of queer and disability studies, in which alternative forms of embodiment and desire come to be resources for challenging dominant structures of both compulsory heterosexuality and what disability scholar Robert McRuer refers to as "compulsory able-bodiedness."[46]

KS gives the player the option to turn off explicit content, but with all content enabled, its representations of sexual activity are humane, bawdy, and sometimes visually surprising. In an encounter with Emi, a young woman who uses prosthetic legs and uses blades for running on the track team, she leads the player into the equipment shed and propositions him, and (following acceptance) the scene that follows features obvious portrayals of her stumps without prosthetics. This bodily difference is not presented as making her in any way less desirable, nor is it obviously fetishized. The latter point is crucial, as representations of disabled sexuality can cater to an audience of "devotees," people who are sexually attracted to disability. Though devotees may be sincere in their desires, and some women have had positive experiences in such relationships, Alison Kafer's research has shown that "many women with disabilities have had frightening encounters with disability fetishists, including being followed and photographed without permission."[47] The erotic but not fetishistic gaze of *KS* is established through the necessity of interacting with the characters through conversation options throughout the game; their desirability is tied to personality as well as to embodiment, and the player must earn their affections through specific behavior.

The representations of sex and disability seen in *KS*, and experienced by the player, advance the concept of sexual citizenship and presents access to sexuality and pleasure as an important topic for scholars and activists interested in furthering access in other realms of life. Sociologist Kenneth Plummer argues that sexual or intimate citizenship requires people to have control over their bodies, feelings, and relationships; access to representations, relationships, and public spaces; and socially grounded choices about gender and sexual identities.[48] Such criteria are not easily met for many people with disabilities; as disability theorist Tobin Siebers notes, having "sex or a sex life implies a form of private ownership based on the assumption that sexual activity occupies a particular and limited part of life determined by the measure of ability, control, or assertiveness exercised by that individual. People with disabilities do not always have this kind of sex life."[49] Fostering sexual citizenship would thus require not only extending these capacities to people with disabilities but also rethinking the very criteria on which such citizenship is based. Individualism, particularly in its neoliberal forms, is not always achievable by or desirable for people with disabilities. As a result, sexual access may require assistance, interdependence, and unconventional arrangements that challenge normative understandings of gender and sexuality.[50]

Anthropologist of disability Russell Shuttleworth, who originated the concept of sexual access, indicates that "making sexuality an access issue, however, politicizes disabled people's sexual lives and, in doing so, demands a critique of the concept's prior restriction to rights-based discourse."[51] Access, framed in terms of rights and governed by laws such as the ADA, has struggled to be extended to "private" concerns such as sexuality. The ADA defines disability on the basis of interference with major life activities or bodily functions; following the amendments of 2008, major life activities "include, but are not limited to, caring for oneself, performing manual tasks, seeing, hearing, eating, sleeping, walking, standing, lifting, bending, speaking, breathing, learning, reading, concentrating, thinking, communicating, and working," while bodily functions include "immune system, normal cell growth, digestive, bowel, bladder, neurological, brain, respiratory, circulatory, endocrine, and reproductive functions."[52] Sexuality would seem to be potentially relevant to caring for oneself, bending, communicating, and reproductive functions, but it has not been explicitly incorporated into these frameworks. Thus, access to sexual expression is not protected in a rights-based framework in which such "private" activities are not available for public governance or assistance. Once again, pleasure is de-prioritized by the institutional contexts of access. Though *KS* is no challenge to these structures, its existence may foster a recognition of the sexual citizenship of people with disabilities among those who play it.

The two games-related examples above illustrate two ways in which the politics of disability and pleasure may be navigated through digital media content. AbleGamers and *KS* present models in which technological or representational access for people with disabilities is valued because of the pleasures of the content, not because of its utility or importance. Games are a particularly provocative site for this activism, as they are explicitly not governed by the mass media or telecommunications frameworks that create hierarchies of other media content. John Fiske identified early video game arcades as sites in which young people could take pleasure in resistance to the social control they otherwise experienced;[53] similarly, games' intersections with disability are a repudiation of what ideologies of ability would consider proper uses of technology and an affirmation of the full humanity of people with disabilities.

Free Speech, Copyright, and Content Transformation

The political import of questions related to content extends beyond the prioritization of content types and the progressivism of advocating access to pleasure. The lens of content also raises difficult questions regarding freedom of speech and the economics of media accessibility. Prescriptive regulations concerning content are almost unanimously ill-received in any media context, because of their perceived infraction of free speech rights and inhibition of creative expression. Thus, the U.S. government and the W3C alike have encountered the greatest resistance to accessibility when their recommendations (or enforced standards) touch upon not merely the form but also the content of online media.

Larry Goldberg, director of the National Center for Accessible Media (a research branch of Boston public broadcaster WGBH), succinctly sums up the first conflict: "[W]hen you talk about media and content and technology and seeking government control over that, right away people think about the First Amendment."[54] In the words of accessibility expert Joe Clark, requiring all web authors to make content accessible is "an outrageous infringement on Constitutional rights."[55] Thus, government efforts to address content and accessibility have largely progressed through what Goldberg describes as laws concerning "technology and the use of airways and public rights of way"[56] rather than through direct regulation of "content" or "information."[57] There is not an implied right to access content; civil rights and mass media regulations are incomplete at best when it concerns accessibility for people with disabilities. Instead, as discussed above, telecommunications laws regulate media accessibility and thus do so largely by attempting to regulate conduits and avoid questions of content.

This avoidance is particularly evident in the erasure of measures aimed at intellectual disability in the 2001 Section 508 standards. Where WCAG 1.0 had recommended that the "simplest language appropriate for a site's content" be used to convey content, the federal government rejected this guideline as too vague to be enforced.[58] These measures were perceived as subjective, open to various interpretations, and thus too close to infringing upon the textual and multimedia expressions of those individuals and institutions governed by the standards. Beyond official rationales, this move indicates how regulating content in the interest of making it accessible to people with intellectual disabilities was conflated with possibly infringing upon expression, speech, and public communication. As a result, federal web pages need not take substantive measures to make content comprehensible for people with intellectual disabilities ranging from dyslexia to Down syndrome or dementia. This is particularly troublesome given the increasing use of the web for tasks such as applying for Medicare, a case in which content barriers may have serious consequences. Though any site that is necessary to obtain or learn about government services must be written and presented in a "clear, concise, well-organized" fashion, this is regulated by the Plain Writing Act of 2010.[59] This law has no reference to disability, and it does not go far enough or encompass sufficient accommodations to address the content accessibility needs of many with intellectual disabilities.

The influence of the First Amendment was such that the federal government avoided regulating content accessibility in the early twenty-first century and in doing so avoided the backlash experienced by the W3C when developers and content producers encountered guidelines that dealt with content. Much of the resistance to accessibility came from a protectiveness toward online content, a resentment of the idea that websites' content would be forced to change for "normal" people in order to accommodate people with disabilities. One accessibility professional and WCAG participant recalls that when confronted with guidelines involving content "writers think we're telling them how you can or cannot write, so there's pushback."[60] As an industry accessibility expert explains, governing content comes down to "how information is authored [. . .] not just how the code is written, but how the words are used. And people definitely have a little bit more difficulty with that because it's encroaching on the author's way of delivering their own content."[61] Taken together with other perceptions about the dogmatism and lack of creativity allowed by accessibility standards, attempts at content regulation seem to reinforce an ideology of disability as deficit, and accessibility as imposition.[62]

Though the government has avoided such conflicts, the absence of a clear federal legal relationship between free speech and accessibility leaves open a range of oppressive legal interpretations at the state level. For instance, in 2013, the Greater Los Angeles Agency on Deafness (GLAAD) filed suit against CNN for the lack of captions on clips shown on CNN.com. The case was then filed in California State Court alleging violations of the California antidiscrimination law.[63] In response, CNN filed a motion arguing that the lawsuit violated California's Anti-SLAPP statute (Anti-Strategic Lawsuit Against Public Policy), meaning that the suit had the purpose of limiting its free speech rights and, as such, should be thrown out. The case moved to federal court, where the Anti-SLAPP motion was denied; the court determined that "captioning comes in after they've already exercised their free speech rights. Captioning is just about the mechanism by which they deliver their speech to the deaf community."[64] This decision reflects a clear separation of content and form, such that access measures are understood instrumentally and not as potentially relevant to the meanings of media. Though a productive way to enforce legal accessibility measures, this distinction is often difficult to maintain. Though equivalent access is desirable in the name of equity, it is sometimes difficult to ignore the ways in which rendering content accessible may, in fact, alter that content.

One way in which this tension between sameness and difference in rendering media content accessible has played out is via copyright battles. Amazon's Kindle 2, released in 2009, trumpeted a new text-to-speech feature, allowing users to listen to their e-books and potentially increasing access for blind and visually impaired readers who otherwise relied upon Braille or specialized audio formats. Readers with print disabilities were enticed by the prospect of access that did not require additional documentation or expense, as generally "print-disabled persons must either submit to a burdensome special registration system and prove their disabilities or pay extra for the text-to-speech version."[65] However, Roy Blount, president of the Authors Guild, wrote an outraged op-ed piece in the *New York Times* stating that "Kindle 2 can read books aloud. And Kindle 2 is not paying anyone [i.e., authors or publishers] for audio rights."[66]

The Kindle 2 placed copyright and accessibility practices in direct conflict by technologically converging what had been quite separate markets and versions of cultural products. The publishing industry had, historically, separated rights for print and rights for the creation of audiobooks; their content was copyrighted, and that copyright was strictly enforced through licensing agreements. Publishers (and copyright law) had long made books available in accessible formats, including audio.

However, these were understood to be for a limited, unprofitable audience and not intended for mass usage. However, the Kindle 2 used audio as an accessible format and as an optional feature, blurring the line between access for a market understood as without value (people with disabilities) and the desirable format and audience of the audiobook. As Blount expounded, Kindle 2 offered "an e-book and an audio book rolled into one. And whereas e-books have yet to win mainstream enthusiasm, audio books are a billion-dollar market, and growing. Audio rights. . . . are more valuable than e-book rights."[67] As a result, the Authors Guild, afraid that it could no longer charge the same license fees for audiobook creation, nor the same prices for audiobooks for consumers, encouraged the creation of contracts that would prohibit use of text-to-speech technology on specific Kindle titles. Furthermore, the Guild argued that having a book read aloud by a machine, in absence of audio rights, was a copyright violation. This argument surprised many blind readers, who "routinely use readers, either human or machine, to access books that are not available in alternative formats like Braille or audio. Up until now, no one has argued that this is illegal, but now the Authors Guild says that it is."[68]

By 2012, with the release of the Kindle Paperwhite, Amazon had disabled text-to-speech and even removed the audio jack, perhaps indicating that it was no longer interested in the debates about rights and accessibility.[69] As a result, what could have been a powerful mainstreaming of accessibility features became an even more exclusionary device, tethered to not only Amazon but also the interests of the publishing industries. Kindle apps for iOS and Android may be configured to work with VoiceOver or other screenreading software, enabling a degree of text-to-speech access, but the upgraded devices are less accessible than their 2009 counterparts.

That accessibility for people with disabilities regularly raises questions related to free speech and copyright suggests that content transformation cannot be as straightforward and value-neutral as hoped by those who would understand content as "information" housed within a particular form. Instead, it seems that one must understand content and form in relation to each other if one is to think through what it might mean to foster experiences of content access. In the case of the Kindle 2, author Neil Gaiman argued that text-to-speech could not "get the voices right" and therefore could not compete with audiobooks or reading aloud by a person, both of which augment the textual elements with affective interpretation.[70] This suggests that there is an element of transformation in moving from text to speech, a kind of cultural translation of content that goes beyond mere replication in a new form. Content accessibility, it seems, both is and is not a simple question of access and equality. It is not, legally, a transformative use of copyrighted material. Culturally, however, access measures affect content and are closely tied to the shaping of reading positions and interpretations.

Separate but Equivalent?

Though form and content may be productively separated as elements of our "access kit," enabling different lines of investigation, the study of content accessibility reveals a major conflict between what is the same and what is equivalent. If the form is radically altered—as when a web page is rendered aurally by a screenreader—can the content be said to be the same in terms of its meanings and potential interpretations? Conceived of as pure "information," content is stripped down to its denotative meanings, its utility, and its authorial intentions. Such a reductive understanding of content is at odds with the richer understandings of textuality and audience agency that have characterized cultural studies and broader humanistic studies of literature, media, and discourse. Despite its political desirability, we must ask if "mainstream" and "accessible" content can ever be equivalent. Or, is accessible content a case in which separate-but-equal may be the best possible outcome?

First, let's consider whether content is "the same." On the basis of poststructuralist understandings of the "text" and the "author," as well as subsequent work such as cultural studies theorist Stuart Hall's notion of encoding-decoding (see chapter 2) or literary theorist Stanley Fish's formation of "interpretive communities," there is ample argument against the uniformity of cultural meanings associated with a media text or communication.[71] Instead, it seems that cultural artifacts are "read" or made sense of within specific personal and community contexts and along differing ideological lines, defying any attempt to restrict meaning through inherent polysemy and the potential for what John Fiske calls excorporation.[72] These theories, notably, concern merely the variations among presumably able-bodied subjects; how much more unpredictable must be the meanings created among those who fundamentally access and interact with media content differently?

Though identical content access may be ideal, it is not clear that it is attainable because of the interactions of content, form, and use. Auditory screenreaders, for instance, create qualitatively different experiences of digital media, calling upon a different sensory system and alternate means of user-interface interaction.[73] Using an auditory screenreader differs from visual usage in several key ways: Content is heard instead of seen (or read, as might be said to be the case with Braille screenreaders); rather than a mouse, this software often relies on keyboard commands or the use of other input devices. On loading a page, one does not get a gestalt impression of the page content and site organization that is conveyed visually through images, layout, and navigation menus. Instead, the loading process initiates a synthesized voice, which reads through the page content by following the order of the HTML. In order to comprehend an entire page, one must listen closely, perhaps memorize some of what is heard, and construct a mental model after hearing a linear recitation of the content.[74] Especially for novices, this process can be "time consuming and fatiguing."[75] Though tab indices, well-placed keyboard navigation options, and other factors may make a page more accessible and cut down on some of this linear progression by offering options to skip through content, screenreaders offer a presentation of content that is significantly distinct from its visual form. Phenomenologically, semiotically, and technologically, accessible media provide content in a qualitatively different form, producing a distinctly different experience. Though this process will be discussed in greater depth in the next chapter, for now, "sameness" must be abandoned as a criterion for determining equitable access to media content (or meanings).

Instead, many accessibility advocates have argued for "equivalence" in access to media technologies. Accessibility is "making equivalent possibilities for a user with a disability" or "ensuring equivalent access to information and interfaces for all users regardless of their individual abilities." Equivalence lifts any expectation of direct correspondence and pushes forward a notion of equity as the determining factor. Furthermore, it may be seen as measured not in terms of content itself but in terms of functionality; content is not to be equivalent, access experiences are.

A screenshot of http://www.whitehouse.gov on December 27, 1996, as archived by the Internet Archive's Wayback Machine and accessed in 2014. The gray background and simple layout of text and (missing) images are typical of the era.

Perhaps unavoidably, arguments for equivalent access to media content (as for access to public spaces, government services, education, and so on) have a tendency to lead to the creation of a separate, secondary, and often inferior system for those who require assistive measures. Though not comparable to explicit separate-but-equal educational policies that enforced racial hierarchies, the creation of separate and equivalent means of digital media access has nonetheless reified notions of disability access as different, difficult, and poorly designed.[76] The limitations of a separate-but-equivalent approach to content accessibility reverberate through the history of accessible digital media. In the very early days of web content accessibility, WCAG 1.0 suggested that creating a separate, text-only HTML page could satisfy accessibility needs. Such a page would be easily operated via existing assistive technology in the 1990s and would be comprehensible even in Lynx, a text-only browser popular with many users with disabilities (particularly visual impairments) at the time. A text-only version of a webpage from the 1990s is not difficult to imagine. For instance, the screenshot of http://www.whitehouse.gov shown in figure 4.2 was taken from the Internet Archive and represents the state of this web page on December 27, 1996. Images are no longer available, resulting in the empty rectangles seen at the top and bottom of the page. However, upon encountering this page, a screenreader at the time could have either read the images' alternative text or skipped over them.[77] The web form and textual content could then be machine-read and understood aurally fairly easily.

It is conceivable that the text-only version of this page was equivalent in its meanings, offering the same possibilities for interpretation and cutting out only a few stylistic elements. Many accessibility offerings during the 1990s were simply text-only versions of a page, usually accessed through a link placed at the top of the page, that offered a streamlined, graphics-free version of the content. However, developers and accessibility advocates moved away from the text-only option around the turn of the century. The reasons for this were threefold: First, maintaining a separate page was time-consuming, and the "accessible" text-only page often languished, un-updated, becoming a clearly inferior experience or source of information; second, as the web evolved beyond HTML to incorporate new document formats and additional scripting languages, the appearance and function of sites were not easily converted into a text-only experience; third, Web 2.0 and user-generated content disrupted the process of creating static content "for" an audience, leading to the mass production of multimedia-heavy content without any textual equivalent. This last point is particularly salient, as it also entails movement away from an ideology of ability in which disability access is separated from (and considered less important than) mainstream access. As one accessibility advocate stated in a recent W3C email exchange, "However, nobody today is going to build two separate versions. And the whole idea of 'here's a separate site for "the disabled"' has long been abandoned in favour [sic] of inclusive single-site solutions."[78] The use of scare quotes around *the disabled* aptly demonstrates the ways in which separation of access led to hierarchies of content, access, and users among online cultures at large.

A text-only version of a contemporary website is difficult to conceive of; shopping, booking travel, automatically refreshing social networking streams, and other common features depend upon dynamic content, often created using JavaScript. Even http://www.whitehouse.gov now offers complex features, as seen in figure 4.3: dynamic menus, copious links, an embedded video, a search functionality, a topical organizational option, and dynamically updated feeds of White House news and Twitter content. Rendering this page in a separate, static, text-only

A screenshot of http://www.whitehouse.gov, taken
from the author's web browser in July 2014, shows
dynamically generated news content, streaming video,
Twitter feeds, and interactive features with which
users can navigate and interact with the site's content.

format would be nearly impossible. With so many options, functions,
and possible interactions, more sophisticated tools are necessary to provide equivalent access to content. Along these lines, in the same email,
a developer explained that text-only solutions were untenable because
"approaches needed to make modern web applications (sites that are
not merely static content/documents, but actual systems) accessible are
increasingly complex, but that's because these sites themselves are increasingly complex."[79]

The complexity of digital media content comes along with the growing sophistication of computer-mediated culture, in which algorithms,
databases, and robots increasingly determine importance, recommend
content to users, and dynamically deliver hyper-targeted advertisements.[80] Cultural studies of technology scholar Ted Striphas writes that
"[C]omputers, running complex mathematical formulae, engage in
what's often considered to be the traditional work of culture: the sort-
ing, classifying, and hierarchizing of people, places, objects, and ideas."[81]
In this "algorithmic culture," automation appears to be the goal, with
human labor shifted from these cultural processes to the derivation of
more sophisticated algorithms or to the service labor of (perhaps unwit-
tingly) providing data to drive this automation.

Such a shift is particularly risky in the case of accessibility for users with disabilities, as "accessibility labor" has been a form of not merely informational but *cultural* labor of translation.[82] Scholar of geography, technology, and communication Greg Downey has demonstrated the longstanding invisibility of the closed captioning industry, pointing to current trends that might lead to its being "entirely extracted from human minds and hands existing as automated algorithmic labor."[83] Such automation ignores the deep contextual skills involved in captioning as a form of cultural labor. Downey understands this accessibility labor as a form of translation that allows information to be accessed and circulated, and he notes that doing so requires speedy decisions to make the captions match onscreen activity.[84] Similarly, a captioning executive explains:

> If you have a college football game, there's a hundred players on each team. Before you even get out there to caption you have to make sure you can spell and pronounce every single one of those [players' names]. If you're sitting in a control room you'll see a captioner sitting there with their steno keyboard and a monitor in front of her and she'll have taped all over the room the names of every player and the phonetic keystrokes she needs to stroke to get that player's name spelled right. . . . It's amazing.[85]

The processes described here indicate that there is a cultural awareness inherent to captioning, as captioners must make moment-by-moment decisions and produce a final product that is different from but similar (or equivalent?) to the original. Not only the spelling of names, but also the action of the football game, or the trajectory of the television narrative, is important to creating a quality form of accessible content. The choices made by captioners effectively alter content to make it accessible, resulting in what translation scholars Zoe De Linde and Neil Kay call the "dilemma of accuracy"; captioners must find a balance between fidelity to the spoken components and its stylistic or larger function within a context of restricted space and limited time in which viewers could read content synced with the video.[86] Given the level of technical skill and cultural literacy involved, it seems that automation of captioning is part of a larger de-skilling of labor. That these workers are largely women, not understood as content creators, often located in non-urban areas, and doing work that is related to content (not to technological forms) is neither coincidental nor unimportant. Automation appears as a rationalization of access to content via captions, even as it dilutes the quality of this method of access and devalues the nuanced cultural work involved in producing these translations. Of course, if captions are simultaneously (or primarily) serving as text for algorithmic manipulation, the accuracy and cultural relevancy of each statement may not be as high a priority as the creation of vast corpuses of data.[87]

A final point regarding content access as necessarily different from, and ideally equivalent to, mainstream content lies in the semiotic and phenomenological domains. As all texts may have multiple readings, as discussed above, texts accessed via accessible or assistive media technologies may produce drastically different user positions and resultant readings. For instance, there may be multiple interpretive communities stemming from different conditions of access, just as interpretive communities may differ by ideology or geography. In the case of captions, De Linde and Kay argue that image and caption inform each other's meanings: "[W]hen oral dialogue is substituted by textual discourse (i.e. subtitles) the overall structure of the film narrative is changed. Verbal and visual information can no longer be processed simultaneously; instead, they have to be processed in succession."[88] In this context, the meanings, interpretations, and authorship of media are all opened up into new directions. They are best examined, perhaps, through divergent experiences of digital media access, as will be explored in the next chapter.

Conclusion

At the beginning of this chapter, I indicated that content is a particularly fraught analytic lens. Few concrete conclusions are possible, particularly when using cultural studies to understand content accessibility. Instead, what has emerged is a particular conjuncture in which media texts and technologies are differently valued, differently regulated, and differently made available to specific audiences. This conjuncture has two dominant tensions.

First, studying the site of content reveals a persistent politics of pleasure regarding types of content and types of audiences in U.S. policies, industries, and popular media. Digital media accessibility has grown out of what was initially understood as "web content accessibility," a process by which forms were altered to enable equivalent access to content. However, such a formulation relied upon a minimal and functionalist understanding of content that largely divorced it from the cultural processes of meaning-making and downplayed the semiotic significance of nontextual elements such as color, design, audio, and dynamic content. Consequently, accessibility has often fallen back upon a conception of "content" as "information," prioritizing particular forms of content and disparaging or ignoring others. Most notably, entertaining content and diverting uses of media have been figured as optional, unimportant, or otherwise lesser; this has reinforced ideologies of disability as deficit and further entrenched the moral policing of the disadvantaged by figuring pleasure as the proper domain of the privileged. As a result, the efforts to make video games accessible—via activism, representation, or production opportunities—ought to be seen as a political intervention into both the hierarchization of content in policy and an ideology of disability as deficit.

Second, the site of content reveals that distinctions regarding copyright, sameness, and transformation are unstable at best. Content is often altered in the process of making it accessible for people with disabilities, but such alterations are usually not understood to be transformative (as in the sense of copyright) or culturally valuable (as in the case of captioners' choices). What is accessible, then, is often not the same as the "original" content. Yet accessible media has enjoyed a copyright exemption as it is explicitly understood not to be a transformative use. As the possible metamorphoses of digital media increasingly draw together accessibility measures with desirable options for able-bodied populations (as in the case of the Kindle 2), these distinctions are called into question. Oddly absent in these discourses, however, are the voices of people with disabilities concerning the *quality* of accessible media content. Thus, automation has emerged as a possible solution, despite obvious limitations, because the cultural labor of making content accessible remains invisible to most users, industries, and policymakers, as does the experience of using accessible content.

I conclude with a provocation. If content is *what* is being accessed, is encouraging access to digital media for people with disabilities simply enabling them to be brought more fully into a neoliberal system of consumer choice, de-skilled labor, and individual de-politicized forms of identity? Currently, neoliberal subjectivity in the United States involves managing the self, as if a corporation or a celebrity, evaluating "risk, reward, and responsibility."[89] As discussed in earlier chapters, neoliberal subjects also are expected to advocate for their own interests on an individual, rather than a collective, basis. A neoliberal sense of self as citizen, furthermore, may be based upon "semiotic self-determination,"[90] in which markers of identity and participation in a larger group or public are gleaned from cultural representation. Though such "DIY citizenship" may enable people with disabilities to take up identities within this system,[91] it seems to work against the importance of collectivism in various disability rights movements and the utility of the public or state in disability reformations.[92] Access, in fact, may be a form of incorporation into the dominant power structure and its politics of individualism and consumerism.

In order to consider the implications of such an assertion, in the next chapter I move more directly to the level of the individual and the extraordinarily varied experiences of digital media access. Although this chapter has attempted to separate content from its form and resultant experiences for the sake of analysis, that study returned us to their articulations and the circulations of power among these components of our "access kit." The final analytic interrogatory—experience—considers the individualization of access conditions, needs, and cultural experiences alongside the potential means of forming collectivities, making political alliances, and engaging in participatory forms of what I describe as "cultural accessibility."

5

The Net Experience

Intersectional Identities and Cultural Accessibility

"I don't know why I'm doing this!" Tommy Edison exclaims as he holds a smartphone horizontally in front of his eyes. Edison, a blind man, is making a YouTube video demonstrating how he uses Instagram, a mobile photo editing and sharing service. Though he cannot see through the phone's viewfinder, he enacts the normative processes of taking a photograph. By holding his phone up, Edison communicates that he is taking a picture and alerts those who may be caught in the frame. After taking a photo—in this case, a picture of the crew that is filming him—Edison browses photo filters on Instagram, his phone reading their names aloud, then selects one and posts to the social networking site.[1] Though superficially similar to how a sighted user might use Instagram, this experience has different meanings. Edison admits to having little creative investment in his photographs. Instead, he enjoys the subsequent social experience, when his Instagram followers tell him what the picture looks like or otherwise comment on it. He is interested in the sharing and social components, while the artistic or expressive elements are less important. For Edison, the taking of a photo is less an expression of self or of technological mastery than it is the beginning of a social interaction. Edison's experience is both different from and similar to that of other users, as he produces user-generated content, shares it with others, and exchanges comments and expressions of approval using a range of mainstream and assistive technologies.

Edison's video, "How a Blind Guy Uses Instagram," and similar clips indicate an awareness that his experience is atypical. Through explanations of his experiences, the connections between use, content, form, and experience—and their resultant influences on the possibilities of meaning-making—are made visible. Notably, they are made visible primarily to a sighted audience, as the videos assume no knowledge of accessible media and have been picked up and shared via *The Huffington Post* and other hubs for the spread of entertaining web content via social media.[2] Even the name of Edison's YouTube channel—*TommyEdisonXP*—indicates awareness of spreading his experience (which he often universalizes as "blind person"), using "xp," which often stands for "experience" in video games and other digital media contexts.

The case of Tommy Edison illustrates how experience binds all pieces of the "access kit"—outlined in the Introduction to this book—together. It is through lived experiences that concerns of regulation, use, form, and content are articulated to one another. These articulations are made, unmade, and remade with each media encounter, rendering them (like digital media accessibility) impossible to define outside of context. Studying access in terms of experience therefore entails deep attention to that context and the ways in which lived, embodied, social, and material factors produce particular relationships between culture, bodies, and technologies.

This chapter begins with an explication of "experience" as a category through which to investigate media access. I then use ethnographic material from a disability blogosphere as the basis for an investigation of the access strategies deployed by people with disabilities to both consume and produce digital media, and the politics of such activities and contexts. Too often, accessibility calls upon a neoliberal subjectivity based upon individual choices and market logics; when people with disabilities engage with accessibility discourses or practices, they may find such forms of identification reinforced and used to perpetuate technological exclusion.

From this point, I explicate an alternate formulation of the experience of access to digital media, "cultural accessibility," arguing that functional access must be a collaborative experience rooted in coalitional identity politics. I draw this term from the language used by many bloggers with disabilities in stating their own definitions of digital media accessibility, which extended well beyond the technical, legal, or professional. This chapter highlights alternative arrangements of access, investigating the ways in which non-normative experiences affect experiences of and ideas about web use. It directly challenges preferred user positions and demonstrates the necessity of richly intersectional understandings of identity, access, and participation. Centering these often-marginalized experiences of digital media enables them to contribute to a more truthful understanding of the relationships of access between bodies, technologies, and culture.

Interrogating Experience

The "access kit" developed in the Introduction to this book grouped research questions into five categories: regulation, use, form, content, and experience. These divisions are analytically useful in teasing apart various dimensions of the variable relationships that constitute media access. They are not perfect descriptors, and in this separation, some of the connections between media forms, regulations, uses, and content may be lost. The fifth and final category, and the focus of this chapter, aims to restore some of those connections between various perspectives. After all, it is in the *experience* of "accessing" digital media that articulations between regulations, uses, form, and content are made, unmade, and remade. As a result, these questions explicitly focus on the articulations of bodies, technologies, and culture within varied contexts:

How is a medium experienced and defined by various groups or individuals, in relation to particular embodied identities, material forms, or social contexts?
What are (some of) the variations in access—to content, via technological form, in regulatory definition, or in terms of use—revealed by experience?
By what processes, and in what contexts, can access be taken advantage of or extended?

These questions offer only a starting point; the dynamic, intersectional, and highly variable dimensions of experience ought inevitably to lead to more specific questions and loci of analysis. My construction of "experience" as a lens for the study of media attempts to look not only at the experience of "having" access, or "accessing" media, but also at the experiences of creating or granting access. It is important to bear in mind that those who produce content to be accessed, or technologies for access, are also relevant in this broad category of "experience."

The notion of "experience" is complicated as a result of its ability to extend analysis beyond material factors to incorporate phenomenology, structures of feeling, intersectional identities and standpoints for knowledge, and the interior, personal dimensions of media use. *Experience* was included as one of cultural studies scholar Raymond Williams's "keywords" in 1976, when he noted the etymological connection between *experience* and *experiment*, writing that

> Experience, in this major tendency, is then the fullest, most open, most active kind of consciousness, and it includes feeling as well as thought. This sense has been very active in aesthetic discussion, following an earlier religious sense, and it can come to be contrasted, over a wide area, with the kinds of consciousness involved in reasoning and conscious experiment.
>
> It is evident that the grounds for reliance on experience past ("lessons") and experience present (full and active "awareness") are radically different, yet there is nevertheless a link between them, in some of the kinds of action and consciousness which they both oppose.[3]

In short, rationalism and objectivity are challenged by notions of experience as one's lived lessons or active awareness. Revisiting Williams's dissection of *experience* from the present day reveals notable similarities both to theories of phenomenology and poststructuralist and feminist conceptions of identity and intersectionality.

Phenomenology, or the knowing of things through sensory experience, offers a philosophy and ontology that is located at the intersection of bodies and the world that surrounds them. It resists any unitary formulation of "the body" and thus speaks to a multiplication of ways of knowing associated with different modes of embodiment. Furthermore, phenomenology suggests that the ability to know things through our senses is extended through the objects that we incorporate into our sense of our embodied selves.[4] Phenomenology can be made particularly useful for the study of disability when understood in connection with poststructuralist theories in which culture exerts productive power upon the formation of bodies and their relationships to space, matter, and other bodies. Media scholar Jason Farman, in *Mobile Interface Theory*, makes a persuasive case for what he calls the sensory inscribed body, in which embodiment is experienced as a culturally specific spatial practice. Farman argues that "We are embodied through our perceptive being in the world and simultaneously through our reading of the world and our place as an inscribed body in the world."[5] He unites the work of French philosophers Maurice Merleau-Ponty and Jacques Derrida, arguing that in an age of mobile and computerized media, theories of embodiment must be updated to incorporate the sensory perception of the material and digital landscape as well as the "sociocultural inscriptions of the body in these emerging spaces."[6]

In bringing together sensory forms of knowledge with cultural practices of inscription, Farman is part of a larger theoretical conversation in which materiality and identity are placed into dynamic relationships with each other. In the field of disability studies, specifically, recent theorizations that move beyond the social model attempt to think about the material realities of lived experiences of disability or impairment as they relate to the hierarchies, representations, and narratives that make disability culturally meaningful. Much of this work involves integrating feminist scholarship in the study of disability, particularly ideas about intersectionality, social constructionism, and the politics of non-normative embodiment.[7] Disability theorist Tobin Siebers explicitly situates the study of disability as part of, and an advancement of, theories of intersectionality, emphasizing that theories of intersectional identity require a grounding in material, embodied realities and that this may challenge the "strong constructionism" of postmodern theories of identity as discursively produced. Such mutual shaping is key to understanding access through a lens of "experience," as bodies, material technologies, and cultural ideologies are brought into particular relationships in particular contexts.

Yet even with its multiple valences, *experience* does not fully convey what I intend by this analytic focus. While *experience* may connote a single event, or a momentary feeling, this site of analysis ought not to be limited by the moment but should also contain dynamic shifts and ongoing states of being and doing. In order to capture these dynamics, the notion of "process" is a helpful addition to my framing of "experience."

"Process" entails temporality in that it captures durations of time, whether ongoing or transitory but, more important, it offers the possibility of thinking in terms of interdependence. Where "experience" is often highly individualized, process suggests the engagement of multiple actors, institutions, and artifacts in a shared pursuit. Cultural anthropologist Gabriella Coleman writes that experience is intersubjective, "rooted in collective and practical activities whose nature is stable, co-herent, and patterned, although constantly, if minutely, in flux."[8] The process of access thus brings together experiences and social connec-tions, activities and collaborations. As disability scholars have argued, the atomistic neoliberal individual is often an unattainable subject posi-tion for people with disabilities; thinking about "process" directs our focus out from the individual's access to what rhetorician and disability scholar Jay Dolmage refers to as a "circuit of interchange borne of inter-dependency."[9] That is to say, access is a phenomenon that arises out of the relationships and actions of people, institutions, and technologies and in doing so challenges universalizing tendencies.

Experiences of access are always highly variable, because, as acces-sibility expert Gregg Vanderheiden explains, "what's accessible to a person, and usable by a person, in the morning may be completely inac-cessible later in the day when they're fatigued, if it's not designed right. And what's accessible to one person who's blind is not accessible to an-other person who's blind, and there is nothing that's accessible to every-body."[10] Individual identities, circumstances, and practices are intrinsic to the experience of access and color its outcomes. It is thus impera-tive to study the variable conditions of any media encounter, ranging from material artifacts and physical positions to the goals, motivations, and interests of the individual. Consideration of access as an experi-ence entails attention not just to forms, regulations, or content but also to the embodied and affective dimensions of those involved and their choices regarding use. It requires conceiving of the user—whether the producer or beneficiary of access—in terms of an intersectional identity that forms a standpoint from which the means and goals of access may (or may not) be understood, produced, or achieved.

For example, sociologist Jenna Burrell observes that in the internet cafés of Ghana, using computer technology was a process of famil-iarization with foreign technologies, social cues, and metaphors. De-spite the "transparency" that technologists may attempt to build into user interfaces (such as the GUI discussed in chapter 3) in an alterna-tive context, meanings and uses were opaque. Burrell writes that "the initial experience of entering the internet café, as recounted by young Ghanaians, drew attention instead to confusing multiplicity and simul-taneity of computer screens' interface elements, software applications, and peripherals (keyboard, mouse, monitor, Webcam)."[11] In the face of this experience, Ghanaians often underwent a process of social knowledge formation in which alternative scripts, explanations, and practices guided them to forms of computer and internet use that differed substantially from those thought by Western developers and users to be normative. The experiences of Burrell's participants remind us that experience is not only embodied and material but must be understood as social and situated.

Though theoretically dense in its explication, experience is in many ways the most intuitive lens for the study of access. It values identity, individuals, processes of both production and reception, embodied and material dimensions, and the articulations between diverse components of an access experience. It seeks the differences in experiences, the unexpected outcomes, and the collaborative potentials in media access. In doing so, it resists universalizing claims and uses the multiple particularities as a source of knowledge from which to gain a broader perspective and deeper analytic capacity regarding the phenomenon of media access.

In order to capture "experience," this chapter relies heavily on ethnographic research. This involved immersion in a "disability blogosphere" for nearly a year between 2011 and 2012. The blogosphere included more than fifty sites, dynamically selected via a snowball sample. I began with three seed sites—*Blind Photographers Disability Studies–Temple University* and *Feminists with Disabilities/Forward* (*FWD/Forward*)—and expanded my sample via blogrolls, links, and authors' other online work. I also conducted open-ended interviews with several particularly active participants to get a better sense of their experiences in blogging and as users of online media. Interview information and a selection of sites studied is available in this book's Appendix, as well as via the online extensions of this text.[12] While I cite specific interviews, web pages, and individuals when that is possible and permission has been granted, I also use quotations without attribution in this chapter in order to indicate sentiments that were commonly expressed. This allows me to preserve some of the colloquial "voices" of research participants without exposing individuals beyond their level of comfort.

Several sites, including *FWD/Forward*, are no longer active; others have undergone significant changes in the succeeding years. The dynamics I describe may persist in current disability blogging or may have migrated to other social media sites or evolved into new forms since I conducted my fieldwork. Nonetheless, the trends observed in this time period, and interviews conducted with bloggers who were active in this space, indicate important avenues of study and analysis for better understanding and learning from the experiences of disability online.

Feeling Frustration

Neither access nor disability is a binary phenomenon. Both, instead, are relational and contextual, formed in connection to other experiences or discursive categories. Experiences of accessing digital media, therefore, are highly contextual and vary dramatically. Nonetheless, one of the consistent features of the experiences of access of people with disabilities involved feelings of frustration with inaccessibility of sites or services. This element of digital media experience highlights people's access to content, or access to consumption, which may seem odd given that my ethnographic research for this chapter focused on bloggers, generally considered online producers. However, the relationships between production and consumption are fluid in online contexts; bloggers routinely repost, comment upon, critique, contextualize, parody, and illustrate others' original content. That is to say, this process of sharing, or spreading, media and embellishing it for niche audiences, according to specific ideologies, or into new contexts, is a form of participation that may not be original production, but it is certainly more active than a reductive notion of passive consumption.[13]

The disability blogosphere I studied depended heavily on the circulation of others' content. Bloggers routinely found, linked to, and commented upon news stories about disability (health care, crimes against people with disabilities, higher education accessibility, discrimination, and so on). Such material not only spread valuable information to those who might be directly affected by it but also contributed to a broader political context in which disability was understood as a matter of identity, rights, and sociocultural meaning. News stories about the Affordable Care Act, and its relationship to existing structures of medical care, for instance, were routinely shared in tones of outrage; bloggers hoped to draw attention to how the legislation might affect disability care. Other commonly shared content included material about representations of disability in popular media, presented in order to advocate for increased or "realistic" representations of people with different disabilities. When news, popular, or social content was technologically inaccessible, this circulation was made impossible (or at least less likely), limiting the scope of what could be engaged with by the disability blogging communities. Such limits could be hypervisible signs of exclusion or could be effectively invisible, as when inaccessible content and technology simply bypassed these communities. Regardless, barriers in the experience of digital media consumption prompted varying feelings of frustration with culture, technology, corporations, individuals, and the phenomenon of access itself.

Frustration ran high in terms of access to digital media, including mainstream hardware, assistive technologies, and financial burdens. Many bloggers experienced the navigation of web pages as a barrier to access, as unclear markup language made it difficult to understand a site's organization or the destination of a given link. This was particularly common among visually impaired individuals, like blogger Mark Willis, who relied on a chosen screenreader and had little patience for sites that did not work with that software.[14] Unsurprisingly, this led to avoidance of sites that were known offenders and constrained the browsing behavior. Such reactions are consistent with research on web usage by blind users, for whom "navigating the Internet using a screen reader was reported to be a frustrating experience due to the lack of feedback received."[15] Empirical studies have suggested that this frustration results in less varied media use, as less experienced users explore pages from top to bottom and rely on a group of known, "blind friendly" sites.[16] In my own usage of screenreaders for the purpose of familiarization, I experienced the same frustrations as many novice users, unsure of how to navigate a single page (let alone multiple pages) and faced with a temporally bounded, linear means of auditory access to content. I attempted to learn navigational strategies but found little support within screenreader programs and encountered a steep learning curve. Again, these frustrating experiences of technology align with existing literature, as the lack of accessible training materials can impede the learning process for assistive technologies,[17] and users who do have accessible reference materials must split their cognitive work between learning the assistive technology, interacting with the web browser, and comprehending the site.[18]

Assistive technologies, particularly material hardware, could also elicit frustration in the experience of using digital media. This was particularly evident in the experiences of bloggers with severe impairments who required assistance in their daily lives. These individuals often felt reluctant to ask for aid with activities, such as digital media use, that might be considered frivolous. Subsequently, they might feel frustrated by feelings of dependency or a lack of autonomy in their use of these media. Additionally, some impairments require significant intervention in order to interface with technology, and assistive devices can be expensive. As one blogger explained, navigating the computer was a struggle because of the expense of hardware; she was eagerly anticipating receiving through a state agency a mouse that could be operated by the chin/tongue. Such assistance is not always forthcoming and presents its own challenges regarding the time and bureaucracy involved in acquiring assistive devices. As a result, many bloggers in this community discussed allowing their assistive technologies to age without replacing them, or sticking with a familiar technology chosen years ago, both of which pose a challenge as digital media develop and change, and assistive technology must be brought up to date in order to be compatible with new media forms.

Other frustrating experiences included particular forms of online content: pop-up windows, multimedia material, and animations. While the frustrations with navigation and screenreaders were largely aimed at the assistive technology (in concert with websites and services), frustrations regarding these elements were squarely aimed at the original formats themselves. Pop-up windows were of special concern for users who used alternative input devices, as the pop-ups might "take control of [the] browser" and force users to spend time and energy navigating out of the window and back to desired content. Animations proved challenging for individuals with a range of conditions that included symptoms of dizziness, migraine, or seizure. Again, avoidance was a common response, as users "don't want to get sick!" The desired accessibility solution in this case would be the opportunity to be warned, to turn off the triggering animation. Absent that, however, people with disabilities were largely resigned to feeling frustration as part of their experiences navigating the web.

Similarly, audiovisual material was a barrier for many individuals with auditory or visual impairments, as neither captions nor video descriptions were necessarily available. Adam Jarachow, a leader of the #CaptionTHIS protest (see chapter 1), explained that "Like everyone else, I enjoy browsing [the] Internet for videos, news, sports and other things (including Facebook and Twitter). It's been getting frustrating for me to enjoy those when I see too many videos without captioning."[19] His experience shifted, then, from pleasure to frustration because of the inaccessibility of these media. No device could solve this problem, no assistive technology could mediate; in this case, frustration was aimed at the videos and their creators.

In both of these brief cases, the feelings of frustration extend from isolated incidents or technologies to a more pervasive frustration with an artificially constrained experience. These barriers essentially render invisible any inaccessible content, leading to a situation in which individuals may know that they are missing something but may not know exactly what it is that they cannot access. Barriers limit the online experience, sometimes severely, and prevent full knowledge or engagement with what may be important or desirable forms of information, entertainment, or communication. Furthermore, this can create an amplified effect, as the frustrations experienced by some users may spread by word of mouth, leading others to avoid a given site or service and further isolating a community of users from a particular digital media experience.[20]

These experiences, however, are quite different from the more personalized frustration experienced when inaccessibility is made hypervisible through the refusal of institutions or individuals to address barriers. Experiences of hypervisible exclusion tended to produce frustration with companies, governments, or individuals, rather than with technologies. In these cases, there was often a sense that someone was responsible for creating access and was actively choosing not to do so. This came up particularly often following requests for accessible features; bloggers whom I interviewed consistently described a "resistance" to the accessible development of digital media. Many active internet users with disabilities have had the experience of notifying a site of an access barrier, only to have their request ignored or met with hostility.

Nearly all bloggers who encountered the rejection of accessibility requests discussed it in terms of "resistance," a word which suggests an underlying, unquestioned belief that the needs of people with disabilities are less important than those of others. As writer s. e. smith said on her personal blog, "Resistance to disabled people makes the world inaccessible for us."[21] More generously, perhaps digital media creators "don't see the problems we [people with disabilities] experience and the frustration."[22] This statement implies that minds can be changed and resistance overcome; by explaining the frustrations of access barriers, individuals can motivate others to better create access.

In attempting to change hearts and minds, users with disabilities must begin from a dual disadvantage. First, they are supplicants, asking those with control over the given media to make changes on their behalf. Second, they are part of a culturally devalued group, associated with a culturally devalued form of technological development. As a result, many users in the disability blogosphere reported consciously attempting to "ask nicely." Such language, and practice, displays a performance of subservience by people with disabilities. Requests are couched politely, deferentially, and as questions rather than as demands. Yet, despite these efforts, "asking nicely" almost never works to break through "resistance"; at best, it produces apologies or explanations for why access was not a priority. Here again, the lesser status of a disabled audience is made evident, and access to content that is not "necessary" is treated as an outrageous request. At worst, resistance turns to hostility, insult, and continued lack of access. An email exchange posted to the Tumblr site *You Fail at Accessibility* (among other sites) is instructive in these dynamics. The exchange began when an individual contacted anonymous sharing site *Six Billion Secrets* (http://www.sixbillionsecrets.com). She said that although she would hate to stop reading the site, its design changes made the site no longer accessible to her, so she would have to cease reading it. The staff member who received her request quickly escalated the situation, accusing the user of making threats. Further communication revealed that the staff member was ignorant of how uses of color can cause problems with particular medical conditions. This indicated a serious lack of awareness of accessibility issues, and the initial overreaction was precisely the kind of experience that makes it frustrating for many users to advocate for digital media accessibility.

To return to the sharing of content that characterized the disability blogosphere, sharing frustrating experiences became a normal means of dealing with the affective dimensions of inaccessibility. Sites such as *You Fail at Accessibility* chronicled moments, online and off, in which access was not prioritized; for instance, a post might include a sign for a handicapped entrance placed at the top of a flight of stairs. The spreading of the *Six Billion Secrets* incident also served this function, as it spread, with various commentary, across numerous sites within my identified blogosphere; links back to the original post came from Tumblrs and Twitter accounts and spawned their own comments, shares, and other forms of engagement. Such spreading of content allowed for experiences of frustration to be transmuted into positive engagement with others who may share, sympathize with, or provide solutions to specific problems. Within the disability blogosphere, shared content acted as "carriers for ideas that are taken up in practice within social networks,"[23] allowing for the spread of particular attitudes, politics, and communities of disability. While these do not always align with a strict social model of disability,[24] such community formation does prioritize the notion of access as a right and provide participants with spaces in which to vent their frustrations and share their solutions.

Feelings of frustration characterize many experiences of people with disabilities in using digital media. These stem from material conditions, hardware or software components, and interactions with others who may have the power to improve access conditions. However, it is no accident that I begin this ethnographic account with an emotion; the ineffability of the category of experience makes the ambiguous site of affect a particularly rich means of understanding connections between the bodily, cultural, and technological elements at play. In what follows, I consider practices observed in the creation of access to blogs and related social media. If requests are most often met with resistance, how is it that access is or is not achieved? And how can frustration be channeled into productive practices and more empowering affective states?

User-Generated Access

Situating this research within a blogosphere revealed the specific experiences that surrounded blogs, social media, and other forms of user-generated content. Instead of highlighting things of concern to a local community, policy concerns for a given group of people, or even material or economic conditions, this sample called attention to how users with disabilities experienced user-generated media in ways that drew upon and reinforced neoliberal models of the self as creator, educator, student, and citizen. As such, accessibility is very much figured as a multidirectional process or interaction; it is a relation between the form, content, use, and embodied users and creators of a given artifact. Not only do developers create access, but they may require it, and bloggers may not only be recipients of access but often learn to create accessible social media, as well.

Social media, and other forms of Web 2.0 services, have proven challenging for advocates of accessibility. This is largely due to the nature of *user*-generated *content*; these technologies and companies are based on their providing a formal structure (blog, content management system, social networking site) to which individuals with minimal technical knowledge can post material (photos, writings, video, etc.) on the web for others to see. As a result of this structure, accessibility regulations are often ineffective. Though services can be made to include accessibility options, users cannot be forced to use them. The example of a PDF is instructive here. Though commonly used in a range of professional, entertainment, and other online contexts, PDF files are often inaccessible to assistive technologies. Most creators do not dig into the software to learn accessibility features, and most users do not require them and thus never notice their absence. Social media operate similarly, as most users do not understand the need for alternative text describing images, or the means by which to create it. Web accessibility may be well understood by professional web developers and implemented by large corporations and government agencies, but it remains far outside the experience of most amateur content creators and casual users of Web 2.0 sites and services.

As user-generated content motivates the use of many Web 2.0 sites and services, with social networking sites in particular relying upon their users to both consume and produce content, adding to the site value that may be monetized through advertising,[25] the inaccessibility of this content may discourage use by people with disabilities. But how can accessibility be increased? If user-generated content is produced by individuals, ought they be responsible for accessibility? Or are the sites and platforms that host this content responsible for ensuring its accessibility? Ought people with disabilities take on the burden of accessibility education or content creation if they want accessible content? Currently a legal, financial, and moral gray area, user-generated content is neither a part of the government nor obviously covered by ADA requirements governing "places of public accommodation." With digital media escaping the confines of traditional gatekeeping institutions, it similarly escapes the grasp of regulation.

Accessibility professionals often understand their task to be enabling accessible development, as in the case of Adobe PDF. In the words of one industry representative, social networking platforms could be expected to "provide [users or content creators] the means to do it. . . . The social media sites have a responsibility, I think, to make the [accessibility] tools available so that people can make their submissions accessible."[26] Curtis Chong, a blind technology user and state accessibility official, similarly argues that enforcement bodies such as Apple's App Store should require accessibility before accepting an app, just as they require functional interfaces and finalized graphics and reject apps that mislead users or misuse users' private information.[27] Thus, gatekeepers could continue to play a role in evaluating and curating content; just as abusive content and malicious software are monitored and removed from spaces such as the App Store or social networking sites, so could inaccessible content be flagged or removed.

Others have argued that accessibility needs to be "easier to do than not to." Blogger and accessibility advocate Glenda Watson Hyatt has elegantly made this point about the incorrect application of alternative text in the WordPress blogging platform. Using a screenshot of the dialog box used to upload an image, she explained that in 2009's version 2.8.4 of WordPress, users were given a space to input a "title" and a "caption." The caption was a visible feature, and the title was metatext. However, there was no space for entering alternative text, and if the user did not seek out that functionality, both the title and alternate text would be automatically populated with the filename of the image (e.g., horses124x300.jpg). Hyatt argued that "WordPress could rectify this issue by simplifying the 'Add an image' dialog box, making it more straightforward for bloggers to use and benefiting blog readers who rely on the correct use of the alt attribute."[28] In fact, it seems likely that a dialog box could promote the accessibility of images by simply asking users to enter a brief description of the image and/or its purpose. End users would not need to know HTML, or accessibility practices, to explain their content. Making accessibility easy in this way avoids the need to impose specialized accessibility training on users and extends the pleasures of creating online content. Yet even with simplifications or rewards, it seems that formal structures, regulations, and industrial decisions can lead users, like horses, to water, but cannot make them drink.

In other words, there is no way to require web users to create accessible content, resulting in an environment in which experiences of inaccessibility and frustration become catalysts for bloggers and other users with disabilities to teach themselves how to advocate for and technologically encode accessibility features in social media. *Feminists with Disabilities/Forward*, a group blog founded by nine writers and run from 2009 to 2011, implemented a large number of accessibility features in order to serve the needs of its readers. Bloggers learned about accessibility "on the job," through research, conversation with users, and asking a larger tech community. Co-founder Chally Kacelnik recalled that the site had a particular incentive to be responsive to accessibility requests: "[G]iven that it was a blog that tried to engage specifically with people with disabilities, with all kinds of needs, accessibility was a big issue. We were self-hosted, and therefore could modify our theme as we pleased, and we tried to fit every kind of option in for readers to modify how they used the site for their own needs: there was a feature that allowed them to change text size, for example."[29] This ability to respond to users' needs is, crucially, linked to the self-hosting and attendant formal flexibility of this blog. Rather than use WordPress or a similar platform that would impose particular structures for creating content, *FWD/Forward* took on the larger task of self-hosting and developing its content in accessible formats.

Here, as elsewhere, accessibility was largely something that bloggers with disabilities learned through practical experience. The process usually begins with conversations with people who had specific access needs, moves to researching accessibility best practices or talking with specialists, and then finally leads to implementing changes. As s. e. smith explains, these include publishing "accessibility policies so people know who to contact about specific accessibility issues."[30] For many bloggers, practical concerns and concrete solutions were the most important components of digital media accessibility. Mark Willis, a legally blind blogger and photographer, explained, "[A]t a practical, existential level, I wouldn't have a job, I wouldn't have a life if I didn't know something about how to make [computer and Internet technologies] accessible for me!"[31] Anna Hamilton, who was part of *FWD/Forward* and continues to maintain other personal sites, also has a working knowledge, focused on specific tasks such as "providing image descriptions for pictures, and transcripts for musical or video material where appropriate."[32]

Such practical knowledge is particularly useful in combination, when users with disabilities pool their experiences, needs, and knowledge in order to create accessibility for themselves and their communities. *Fuck Yeah, Accessibility*, for instance, is a Tumblr dedicated to archiving information about how to make your Tumblr more accessible, offering a central location at which to learn about accessibility from others. A May 2011 post explained that "Essentially, when you upload under the 'picture' option, all you can do is add a caption, not alt text. Then, Tumblr uses the caption as both caption AND alt text. You can get around this by uploading a pic in a 'text' post where you can edit HTML."[33] smith, who was involved in advocating Tumblr accessibility, described such educational work as necessary because "the site doesn't have alt tags and Support [has] repeatedly indicated [it has] no intent[ion] of implementing that feature."[34] Other individuals and groups have shared how-to's regarding media production, as when CripChick, a disabled Korean-American blogger activist, made a video about her changing physical conditions and posted a "skillshare": She wrote, "i made this using my iphone. i recorded my voice with voicememo and used the video camera on the phone to record myself and the ventilator. i pasted the clips together, stripped the audio off the video clips, added the audio off the voicememo, turned the contrast up, and added captions with iMovie, a free program on mac computers. (i did all of this in bed, literally at midnight, by typing with one hand.)"[35]

Sharing accessibility tips and tricks informally via blogs, Tumblrs, and online conversation was a common practice in the blogosphere during my observations. Lifekludger, a site run by David N. Wallace, offers "gadgets, hacks, and kludges for people living with disability."[36] "Kludges" are ways of working around access barriers using available if unconventional materials or techniques. Common in Third World technological contexts, these user-generated solutions are crucial to disability bloggers, who often develop solutions attuned to their individual needs and circumstances. Lifekludger contains posts about a range of digital technologies and physical accessibility devices, as well as instructions for projects such as making one's own touchscreen stylus brush. Wallace explains that the site "grew out of explaining some of the workarounds I use, or could use, to get around barriers in working and doing life with a disability."[37] Blogger Blake Watson described his idea for a similar site that would aggregate individual accessibility solutions: He was interested in using the open source code of UsesThis.com to "[i]nterview people with disabilities, you know, like, what kind of equipment they use, or what do they, how do they access a computer, and if they could have anything, what would—like, if money were no problem, what would they do, and that sort of thing."[38] Though this project has not been completed, Watson and his brother (who both have muscular spinal atrophy, type 2) post reviews and explanations of their uses of assistive technology on the blog *IHateStairs*.

The practice of sharing workarounds and Watson's invocation of open source point to some important similarities between people with disabilities online and what Gabriella Coleman calls a hacker morality. She writes that hackers "are committed to productive freedom. This term designates the institutions, legal devices, and moral codes that hackers have built in order to autonomously improve on their peers' work, refine their technical skills, and extend craftlike engineering traditions."[39] Through this work, Coleman argues, hackers "extend as well as reformulate key liberal ideals such as access, free speech, transparency, equal opportunity, publicity, and meritocracy."[40] Within the disability blogosphere, workarounds and collective knowledge enable users to create their own conditions through which to access and enjoy digital media forms and content. They blur practices of consumption and production, carving out new means of access and enabling others to do the same, and, like hackers, "through this technical production, they also sustain informal social relations and even have built institutions."[41]

In the case of disability blogging, one such institution is *Dreamwidth*, a social networking site similar to *LiveJournal*. *Dreamwidth* has a "Diversity Statement" that reads, in part, "We think accessibility for people with disabilities is a priority, not an afterthought."[42] The site has directly solicited input and aid from users with disabilities, asking about their assistive technologies, "anything from 'JAWS, version 13' [screenreader software] to 'Dragon NaturallySpeaking' [dictation software] to 'NoSquint' [Firefox extension] and anything in between. If you use it to help you make the web more accessible for you, we want to know about it, no matter how minor you may feel it is."[43] With that information, the open source community that maintains *Dreamwidth* works to ensure compatibility and to fix accessibility bugs in a timely fashion. This represents a direct transformation of experience, and colloquial forms of knowledge about accessibility, into a technical knowledge that can improve digital media access for a range of content, users, and uses.

In the face of inaccessible emerging media forms, the experiences within a disability blogosphere have included creativity, community, and accessibility activism. The degree of initiative and skills on display is impressive, and the work conducted by these bloggers is absolutely important. However, although Coleman argues that hacker culture critiques neoliberal structures through its productive freedom, the individually designed kludges of users with disabilities may not exert the same political force. In fact, user-generated access may inadvertently buttress neoliberal models of selfhood and exploitative forms of digital labor.

Self-Help and Neoliberal Identities

The experiences of digital media access described in this chapter are amalgams of barriers, solutions, self-taught skills, and pleasant and less pleasant interactions with individuals and corporations, and they ultimately may enable the use of media for information, entertainment, communication, or self-expression. In many ways, these are experiences that demonstrate the expanded life possibilities offered to people with disabilities by digital media and that further reveal access to be a *process* of attaining, creating, and utilizing relevant technologies, tactics, and talks with others. This process is potentially empowering, allowing users with disability to exert agency and even mastery over their experience of digital media.

Yet, there is also a pernicious element to the individually driven processes of accessibility that are made visible through the study of experience. In accordance with models of the consumer-citizen and the entrepreneurial imperatives of neoliberal selfhood, there is a pervasive shifting of responsibility for access onto the backs of people with disabilities. The need for self-advocacy that may be met with resistance, the need to self-educate about complicated documents such as those that make up the WCAG 2.0 guidelines, and the need to produce solutions for one's self or one's community are all evidence of a niggling narrative of personal responsibility. To the extent that such expectations are perpetuated online (and off), they reduce expectations and responsibilities that ought to pertain when media access is understood as a civil right or public good.

The legal context of accessibility in the United States was discussed in chapter 2, but it bears reiterating that Section 508 violations are enforceable only via complaints from people with disabilities in their capacities as federal employees or members of the public needing to access services. Similarly, the ADA is enforced through a complaint structure, not more proactive means. Although other regulations, such as the Twenty-first Century Communication and Video Accessibility Act (CVAA), use regulation of technology companies to enforce accessibility, there remains an expectation that individuals with disabilities will take an active role in ensuring their own access. For instance, following the CVAA, YouTube initiated a program in which users were asked to "report" videos that ought to have captions but did not.[44] This amounts to a shifting of labor and responsibility from YouTube and content owners (who are legally responsible for captions on covered content) onto those who rely upon captions for access.

Such expectations of self-advocacy are commonplace in commercial contexts. Web developers and corporate spokespeople alike have attempted to excuse inaccessible digital media on the grounds that they do not have any disabled audience or customers;[45] most often, this simply means that people with disabilities have chosen to avoid a site rather than complain and thereby make their presence known. As a result of the ignorance or benign neglect of many commercial enterprises, people with disabilities must take on the role of active "consumer-citizens" and advocate for themselves. In many large corporate contexts, accessibility expert Elle Waters notes, "[I]f more people with disabilities don't complain about the website . . . and I know it's a burden on them to have to be that obnoxious person who calls . . . it's very difficult for someone to argue for budget internally if there's no pressure externally."[46] The provision of access, it seems, is not a priority until customers force the issue.

In these examples of self-advocacy, there is an undercurrent of outsourced labor and neoliberal individualism. The work of identifying (and sometimes correcting) accessibility oversights is pushed onto people with disabilities. They are asked to be not only readers, viewers, players, customers, and citizens but also *de facto* consultants and educators. By waiting for a person with a disability to complain, digital media sites and services take a passive approach to access and absolve themselves of responsibility.

Advocating for accessibility features can easily slide into the provision of extensive free labor, as expectations around self-advocacy may result in assumptions that people with disabilities are experts not only in identifying but also in fixing accessibility problems. Often, people with disabilities are called upon to perform the very labor of making digital media accessible, regardless of their qualifications or their interest in doing so. For instance, one blogger, a woman with a physical impairment who is employed in the web industry, finds that others often assume that she will have accessibility expertise. Similarly, s. e. smith observes:

> People assume I am available as a free accessibility consultant and the burden of access is placed on me as a disabled person, rather than on people creating spaces as creators of spaces. The fact is that accessibility consulting is actually a paid job that involves a lot of comprehensive knowledge, and people seem genuinely shocked when I indicate that I am not available to provide free consulting services and they really need to work with an expert, especially if they are working on something like a major website with high traffic.[47]

This statement succinctly describes how the onus is placed on people with disabilities to educate others, provide expertise, and otherwise help others understand accessibility. The flip side of such expectations would be the sense that accessibility failures are, in fact, failures of people with disabilities to sufficiently advocate for themselves.

These dual expectations reflect an ideology of ability, compatible with the neoliberal models of selfhood, in which successes and failures alike occur at the individual level, masking larger social structures and relations of power that preserve unequal conditions. The ideal neoliberal subject takes on a "particular persona: highly visible, entrepreneurial, and self-configured to be watched and consumed by others."[48] People are exhorted to construct, distribute, and commodify an individualized, actualized, "authentic" self that may be managed "as though the self were a business, entering into alliances metaphorically with other businesses while constantly negotiating the risks and responsibilities of these alliances."[49] These selves are often constructed via consumption and practices of distinction, merging neoliberal and capitalist modes of being. In all of its workings, neoliberal selfhood operates at cross-purposes to the kinds of collectivities, shared identities, and collaborative practices that have often characterized identity-based political movements. In such an environment, action in the public sphere is conceived of as a matter of individual agency and therefore individual risk.[50] This may have an understandably chilling effect, particularly for those such as people with disabilities who may have only a tenuous grasp of socially validated forms of neoliberal citizenship. With limited ability to construct a neoliberal self because of a range of differences and barriers, risking that self in public activism may pose a real threat to the legibility of people with disabilities as consumers, citizens, and contemporary subjects.

Considered in light of such neoliberal models of selfhood, the experiences of creating, taking advantage of, and advocating for digital media access take on a darker tone. It seems that content providers, technology companies, and others involved in digital media can deploy the experiences of people with disabilities against the very cause of collective access. The capacities of people with disabilities to solve accessibility issues, to advocate for themselves, and to educate others may be invoked to excuse the ongoing creation of inaccessible structures and content. Reactive responses to individual complaints work against best practices in accessibility, as companies put out fires after the fact rather than embrace a more inclusive means of conceptualizing and completing their work.

These attitudes, and the accompanying passivity regarding accessible digital media, treat "accommodation" as akin to "tolerance"—it is a mild annoyance, an intrusion into "normal" practices, and a gift offered to those with lesser social status. Suzanna Walters, a scholar of gender, sexuality, and media, argues that "it doesn't make sense to say that we tolerate something unless we think that it's wrong in some way."[51] Similarly, it doesn't make sense to "accommodate" differences unless those differences are understood as non-normative and (nearly always) deficient. Accessibility as discussed throughout this book is a form of accommodation, an alteration made to hardware, software, code, or media in order to enable access by those who might otherwise be excluded. In the context of LGBTQ activism, tolerance assumes a normative majority that graciously offers a minority its acceptance; discourses of tolerance are incompatible with the construction of strong civil rights frameworks and cannot alter hegemonic structures or integrate the specificities of gay experience into the broader culture. In the context of disability access, accommodation suggests a normative technology and user and the need to retrofit or alter this for a specific group understood as lacking access. Furthermore, Walters points out that tolerance privatizes the political by transforming social issues into matters of personal attitude and acceptance.[52] In the case of accommodation, access is privatized in line with neoliberalism, as individuals are called upon to create access for themselves or to beg for the beneficence of others. In both cases, collectivities and political action are watered down, or replaced, by atomistic interactions between individuals. These frameworks preserve hierarchies that mark queerness and disability as lesser markers of identity, even as they call upon individuals to work harder to make themselves nonthreatening, normalized, and thus deserving of concessions from the majority.

Cultural Accessibility

Though the experiences of bloggers with disabilities reveal inaccessible software platforms, unhelpful customer service representatives, and ableist attitudes aplenty, they also contain the seeds for challenging hegemonic arrangements of bodies and technologies. Through the experiences that bloggers (and others) with disabilities have had with digital media, it becomes possible to see a path toward a technocultural future based not upon exclusion and normativity but upon inclusion and variability. I refer to this vision of an accessible future as "cultural accessibility." By expanding discourses of accessibility into cultural—as well as legal, medical, and technological—arenas, I believe that it becomes easier to consider access as a relational phenomenon relevant to a range of bodies, needs, identities, and media practices.

Cultural accessibility entails coalitional, collaborative, and participatory types of media technologies, content, regulation, and use. In the imagined future of cultural accessibility, media are not only technologically accessible to people with disabilities but may be culturally relevant, actively inclusive of difference, and ultimately a co-created process that moves ever toward greater flexibility and lesser restriction. I draw the notion of "cultural accessibility" from a range of observational and interview data, as bloggers with disabilities repeatedly invoked unexpected ideas as related to "accessibility." In the face of exclusions, online disability communities have begun redefining access and working together to create alternative practices and expectations.

In previous chapters, and particularly in policy and professional discourses addressed therein, accessibility has been routinely presented as a technological phenomenon. For instance, one accessibility expert interviewed defined web accessibility as "the adaptation of mainstream technology so that assistive technology will work with it."[53] This definition fits easily into what science and technology studies scholars Alison Adam and David Kreps identified as a "web accessibility" discourse that is invested in standardizing development of the web. They described this discourse as particularly exclusionary, because it can seem dauntingly technical.[54] This may be one reason why, when asked to define accessibility at the conclusion of our interviews, bloggers initially hesitated and nearly always minimized their expertise, perhaps reflecting the sense that accessibility was an exclusive professional concept.

Once they did offer definitions, bloggers' lived experiences resulted in very different understandings of accessibility. Though bloggers' definitions of accessibility incorporated technological elements, they were more attuned to the emotional, cultural, and political dimensions of access to digital media. Many spoke outside of the medical model, casting accessibility in terms of people's needs rather than in terms of medical conditions: "the extent to which someone can access or use something"; "as many people as possible"; "the range of needs a population may have in making use of a particular service, place or thing"; "not a one size fits all kind of thing"; "used by the widest possible audience/consumer." These definitions prioritize individual, varied needs and the *quality* of experiences over any notion of disability as a discrete phenomenon to be ameliorated by accessible practices.

When considering the quality of experiences, people with disabilities were not only interested in accuracy or ease of use, though these were obviously important. Instead, they raised issues of emotional access, or the affective dimensions of digital media use. For example, smith explained that "accessibility is about equal access to all spaces. It's about being safe and comfortable. This includes both physical access, in the sense that people need to be able to physically enter a space and be safe there, and what I call 'emotional access,' that people feel welcomed. A building may be ramped, for example, but if the staff are clearly hostile to disabled visitors, it's not accessible."[55] Such a concept of accessibility could never be codified in policy, or built into a physical or digital environment. It requires a change not only in individual attitudes, as discussed above, but in the very character of a space and those who pass through it. It is a cultural change based upon valuing disability and other variations of human experience.

This understanding of accessibility as a matter of emotional safety in environments that not only tolerate but also welcome differences results in some surprising experiences. Though Tumblr is *technologically* an accessibility disaster, a post on *Fuck Yeah, Accessibility* began as follows: "So tumblr is by far the most accessible site I've ever been on in terms of things like trigger warnings and image descriptions."[56] Trigger warnings, or notifications that a given piece of content might produce psychological triggers in readers with particular experiences of violence or trauma, or in people with particular mental conditions, are increasingly common in fan, feminist, and progressive online communities. They are considered a courtesy, in making online spaces safe for a variety of people. It is therefore unsurprising that although trigger warnings are not a feature of accessibility policies such as Section 508 or WCAG, some people with disabilities considered them crucial to an emotional or cultural accessibility.

Accessibility was further understood to be about the quality of affective experiences. Just as feelings of frustration characterized experiences of inaccessibility and resistance, culturally accessible spaces were understood to be sites of pleasure. As one blogger defined it in our interview, "Accessibility in a web sense means as many people as possible can interact with material, extract key information from it, and enjoy the process."[57] Access was even figured as emotionally restorative, as in the case of a young woman who saw social benefits to participating online and found that "when I'm in pain there's no better cure than some LOLcats and a stupid YouTube video."[58] Emotional or affective access was thus tied to the ability to use digital media for desired, even pleasurable, purposes.

Bloggers also gravitated toward definitions of accessibility based not on accommodation but upon inclusion. One blogger suggested that accessibility meant "a huge spectrum of different accessibilities and possibilities,"[59] while another stated that it meant "making sure that . . . new technologies that are moving forward are inclusive and allow people to participate."[60] These are broad, future-looking definitions which implicitly argue that accessibility ought to be part of the design and development process, rather than something retrofitted after the fact. The following definition, from Kacelnik, revealed this perspective with particular clarity:

> a lot of people who aren't disabled have the unarticulated idea that a given thing, place, or service is "naturally" or by default constituted in a particular way, and accessibility is about making adjustments so that it can be used by people with a narrowly imagined range of disabilities and needs . . . . I think accessibility should be about *radically re- imagining the kinds of people who are welcome to, or might want to, make particular uses of things* or live particular kinds of lives, and making that normative.[61] (author's emphasis)

This statement emphasizes the imaginative, nontechnical components of disability, technology, and accessibility. Kacelnik indicated that unexamined attitudes and patterns of thinking are a barrier in accessibility implementation and suggested that accessibility requires "re-imagining" or otherwise changing those ways of thinking from the ground up. It seems that bloggers viscerally understood and made the same critiques of "accommodation" or "tolerance" outlined above; accommodation did not challenge ableism or serve the interests of people with disabilities.

Though technological fixes have value, and bloggers would surely prefer more WCAG 2.0–compliant websites than the alternative, they appear to have concluded that framings of technological accommodation cut off the possibility of "real and robust integration."[62] Such integration is evident in smith's description of access as "[meaning that] you're welcomed in that space with an inclusive, rather than tolerant, attitude."[63] Here, smith uses *inclusive* in the same sense in which Suzanna Walters proposes "robust integration" as an alternative to tolerance—it "articulates the deeper benefits of full integration for *all* concerned. It's not just that gays [and/or people with disabilities] will be more welcome, less likely to suffer from self-hatred and fear, but that the ground of what is 'normal' will itself begin to shift."[64]

Such is the project of disability arts and the incipient cultures of disability that extend online and off. A culturally accessible environment must incorporate the voices and cultural productions of people with disabilities. One such environment was the community of Blind Photographers.[65] Employing a range of mainstream and assistive technologies, these blind and visually impaired people were able to use photography to move from the object of the artistic gaze or medicalizing stare and turn their gaze back upon the world, expressing artistic vision and alternative perspectives.[66] Looking to the websites and Flickr and Tumblr accounts maintained by visually impaired photographers, one can see these visions emerge, grounded both in creation and distribution of others' photographic content. The loose community of blind photographers, dispersed over Twitter, Tumblr, Flickr, and various blogs, created a culturally accessible space. Within this space, different conversations about art, vision, disability, and creative process can occur than may be had elsewhere, and certainly it is a welcoming participatory cultural space that aims explicitly to be inclusive of disability arts. Sociologists and disability scholars Colin Barnes and Geof Mercer write that disability arts "is potentially educative, transformative, expressive, and participative."[67] Blind Photographers functioned as a network of diverse photographers, representing a range of artistic perspectives, experiences of visual impairment, and connections to amateur, commercial, and art world photography. It was culturally accessible because it is culturally relevant, a collaborative and inclusive community based within what might be called a disability culture.

The concept of disability culture is somewhat controversial, as disability (again, like queerness) is a dispersed identity group that may not easily produce shared signs or rituals. Yet, through shared histories and alliances, a disability culture may emerge, as described by disability scholar and advocate Steven Brown: "People with disabilities have forged a group identity. We share a common history of oppression and a common bond of resilience. We generate art, music, literature, and other expressions of our lives and our culture, infused from our experience of disability. Most [important], we are proud of ourselves as people with disabilities. We claim our disabilities with pride as part of our identity. We are who we are: we are people with disabilities."[68] The notion of claiming disability is expanded by disability studies scholar Simi Linton, who writes that disability culture comes from "finding one another, of identifying and naming disability in a world reluctant to discuss it, and of unearthing historically and culturally significant material that relates to our experience."[69] This, then, is not a static culture but a constantly desired and created phenomenon, a *process*, as disability and performance scholar Petra Kuppers has described.[70] Navigating discrimination and barriers to access are part of what binds the community together, and disability cultures emerge from the kludges, collectivities, and alternative perspectives with which people with disabilities respond to the mainstream culture. Blogger Wheelie Catholic reflected on this for *Disability Studies Quarterly* several years ago, writing "Do I transmit the values of the disability culture in my blog? I like to think that I am a part of that but only in connection with relative to other disability blog writers [sic] and advocates. . . . There is an ever-changing current in the blogosphere, one that is based not only on the fact that there is immediate access to new issues concerning disabilities but also on the interplay of personalities among blog writers."[71] Disability culture, online and off, is a collaborative, inclusive, shifting, and potentially transformative thing.

Cultural accessibility grounds itself in the experiences of people with disabilities and their cultural productions and practices. It moves past accommodation, or tolerance, to integration and calls upon society to include and integrate the different bodies, knowledges, perspectives, and possibilities offered within disability cultures.

Conclusion

Experience as a lens for the study of access offers both the most complex and the most potentially transformational results, as it is impossible to generalize, but it is necessary to consider the conditions of possibility for the people who are at the heart of any question of media access. This chapter has made only limited claims, choosing to focus on those dynamics within the disability blogosphere that spoke to accessibility as a phenomenon, and bloggers' conceptions of themselves as users of digital media.

From this, it appears that many users with disabilities are engaged in practices that oppose normative and exclusionary technological and cultural structures. Their activism is visible not only in hashtag protests but also in the kludges, the Tumblrs, and the photographs they produce and circulate within communities. Cultural accessibility is not, properly, my concept—it belongs, collectively, to those who participated in the spaces that I observed, to those whom I interviewed, and to those whose cultural productions circulated in this community.

Given the threats of neoliberal identity and exploitative labor that haunt digital media access for people with disabilities, this concept and its collectivity are particularly important. Cultural accessibility is individual, but it exists in connections. Unlike neoliberal modes of consumer-citizenship, cultural accessibility offers to meet individuals' needs as they meet those of others. In this way, it values the modes of interdependency advocated by some people with disabilities and scholars of disability studies. It also breaks down distinctions that may emerge between those who "make" accessibility happen and those who "receive" it, between developers and their audience, between experts and amateurs.

Politically, cultural accessibility is aligned with coalitional politics, based not upon singular shared identities but upon the overlapping needs, actions, and interests of a diverse group. At its best, it is intersectional, attuned to differences in power and experience and inclusive of differences of gender, race, sexuality, nation, and class. Legal and critical race scholar Kimberlé Crenshaw's groundbreaking work on intersectionality calls for locating identity politics at the point where categories intersect, avoiding essentialism and reconceptualizing those categories as coalitions of simultaneous similarity and difference.[72] Each of us may be located at a singular point of intersectionality, requiring a particular form of cultural accessibility; in order to have those needs met (whatever they may be, and whatever identities may inform them), we must bring together such "partial, locatable, critical knowledges sustaining the possibility of webs of connections called solidarity in politics and shared conversations in epistemology."[73]

The formation of coalitions and the enacting of intersectional politics within cultural and civic spheres is built upon the alliance of people across differences. Thus, one need not be a person with a disability to advocate cultural accessibility as a possibility rooted in the experiences of people with disabilities that likely offers significant benefit to the mainstream. Instead, one may, in the words of race and disability scholar Sami Schalk, "disidentify." Schalk argues that minoritarian subjects can build coalitions and political solidarity through the recognition of common interests and related experiences borne out of different identity categories.[74] In the context of digital media access, such disidentification could unite people with disabilities with those in the Third World, those who lack access in the United States, the uneducated, the elderly, and those who are politically invested in ameliorating these differences in experience that stem from differences in social power.

In concluding her critique of the "tolerance trap," Walters ponders robust integration, writing that it "always implies an unfinished project or a project always in the making."[75] Inclusion, here as in practices of cultural accessibility, is thus a process, an *experience* that offers to transform normative cultural and material structures. In the words of cultural theorist Paul Gilroy, we must consider how to "go beyond the issue of tolerance into a more active engagement with the irreducible value of diversity within sameness."[76] To do this, the experiences of the marginalized are of utmost importance, and the building of connections among and between those with a stake in the digital arena must be an ongoing process, undertaken through meaningful, participatory forms of interaction and co-construction.

Conclusion

Collaborative Futures

The preceding chapters have oscillated between investigating the historical and material specifics of digital media accessibility for people with disabilities and theoretical concerns with media access, the cultural politics of dis/ability, and methods of media study. There is an unresolved tension in these arguments, as it seems that disability is, unquestionably, productive of important questions and illustrative of social and cultural hierarchies, but many desired outcomes produce benefits for mainstream technologies, cultures, academics, and citizenries. It is with this in mind that I conclude by exploring what it might mean to advance cultural accessibility in ways that do not erase or instrumentalize disability.

Cultural accessibility, as described in chapter 5, is potentially valuable because it moves beyond narrow technocentric notions of accessibility, or accommodation, to address a range of factors relevant to the intersection of technologies, bodies, and cultures. Much like the concept of "cultware," elaborated by Australian media and disability scholars Katie Ellis and Mike Kent,[1] it "describes the digital and analog environment in which the user is embedded and the value and characteristics of that environment," including cultural contexts and social factors.[2] But cultural accessibility aims to go further, considering how contexts affect accessibility and also reimagining what access means, could be, and to whom it may be relevant. In order to do this, any consideration of media access ought to look to the voices and needs of those who experience a lack of access; their conceptions of what access would entail are often markedly different from hegemonic understandings of media access.

There may, of course, be overlap in the kinds of access that serve mainstream and excluded audiences. As argued by disability scholar Tanya Titchkosky, access is relevant to everyone, and disability is one among many potential variations in the ability to access.[3] Projects such as the Global Public Inclusive Infrastructure (GPII), discussed in chapter 3, offer to create flexible, personalized forms of technological accommodation, linking the assistive technologies developed for people with disabilities with the personalization desires of a broader audience. Similarly, Ellis and Kent use "accessibility 2.0" to describe how trends such as mobile access, augmented reality, and voice commands prove that "accessibility is important and adds to optimum functioning" for a majority of digital media users, regardless of dis/ability.[4] This is similar to longstanding arguments for "universal design," in which the constraints of designing for disability lead to gains for all audiences.

However, all of these examples reinforce existing hierarchies in which capitalist, neoliberal modes of being are both normative and abled. In each case, arguing that accessibility produces benefits for the mainstream can reinforce an instrumentalist approach to disability, figuring disability as an origin for innovations that will serve other (ostensibly more important) interests. This line of argument was widely used in the growth of television closed captioning in the United States, as captions were understood to serve children and immigrants learning to read or speak English, rather than as necessary features for d/Deaf and hard-of-hearing Americans.[5] It positions accessibility features as "options," benefits, consumer choices in media technologies; in doing so, arguments about mainstream utility may distance accessibility from civil rights and disability politics or activism. In order to value accessibility, these sentences appear to invoke mainstream benefits and appeal as more important or productive than civil rights framings of disability access. Universal design arguments often do the same. Feminist disability scholar Aimi Hamraie writes that the utility of universal design has been to shore up claims about the social model of disability; if universal access is possible, then disabling conditions are the result of social structures.[6] Yet the risk of universal design is that these conditions (and products made to address them) will lose all connection to disability, particularly through rhetoric that emphasizes utility for abled bodies.[7] Though all of these frameworks may result in innovations that ameliorate conditions of access for people with disabilities, they can also further entrench the invisibility of disability and its attendant devaluation in society at large.

Such erasure of disability must be avoided in pursuit of cultural accessibility, in order to value and preserve the contributions of people with disabilities, disability culture, disability rights movements, and scholars of disability studies to produce nuanced, coalitional, and inclusive modes of cultural and political interaction.[8] People with disabilities and the legacies of disability as a cultural category ought to remain visible in projects of cultural accessibility. This may be best done by pursuing cultural accessibility through participatory collaborations between users, policymakers, industries, nonprofits, and other stakeholders. Too often, attempts to broaden access have focused on powerful institutions such as schools, government, industry, or other top-down service providers. Even in the chartering of the W3C's Web Accessibility Initiative (WAI), which would go on to develop WCAG 1.0 and 2.0, there was an understood need for collaboration between "government, industry, and community leaders," but there was not a mention of including the perspectives of people with disabilities.[9] As argued by Henry Jenkins, Sam Ford, and Joshua Green (and demonstrated in the activities of a disability blogosphere), "[M]any of the most powerful efforts to broaden participation have instead come from communities working together to overcome constraints on their communication capacities."[10] The contributions of people with disabilities are core to the creation of new models of media access, and recognition of this as both an origin and an ongoing source of knowledge is important to any future in which media accessibility is prioritized for a wide variety of human bodies and cultures.

Cultural accessibility, therefore, calls for a kind of participatory, open process that combines the best elements of coalitional politics with the possibilities for collaboration that characterize digital media spaces and technologies. Exercises in crowdsourcing or outsourced labor do not, alone, constitute cultural accessibility (and may be further evidence of the exploitative labor described in chapter 5). Radically inclusive technocultures must simultaneously challenge the capitalist and neoliberal frameworks of digital media services and users, building coalitions on the basis of sameness through difference and creating accessible paths to self-expression, community, and even citizenship. Such activity is evident, to varying degrees, in several current projects aimed at producing more accessible digital media spaces and technologies.

Collaborating with the Crowd, in the Cloud

Several current innovators in digital media accessibility enact these inclusive processes of integrating disability into the expansion of access. In varying ways, online services Amara, EasyChirp, Fix the Web, and Dreamwidth all enact cultural and technological collaborations that include people with disabilities, challenge neoliberal forms of identity, and expand upon the technocratic or bureaucratic understandings of accessibility seen elsewhere. By doing so, these services may not only increase access but can draw attention to the politics of access, the political valences of disability and able-bodiedness, and the possibility of alternatives to normative conceptions of media access and use.

Amara offers cloud-based tools for the simple inputting and syncing of closed captions with video content, allowing users to caption their own materials, or to volunteer to caption content for others. Amara has an ongoing beta test in which some users are tasked with producing content for Netflix, suggesting that this distributed model of accessibility labor is also popular for its cost-saving potential. This is a standard dynamic for crowdsourcing projects, which adopt "a new web-based business model that harnesses the creative solutions of a distributed network of individuals."[11] As a project of the Participatory Culture Foundation, which executive Dean Jansen describes as supporting a "collaboratively built culture" by "making sure that people have the tools to facilitate this free exchange of knowledge," Amara is ideologically invested in open, participatory cultures and forms of production.[12] Some organizations have found Amara's volunteer labor force to be quite useful in providing captions or translations; the Technology, Entertainment, Design (TED) conferences, for instance, used Amara to translate their high-profile talks and thus expand their global reach. Amara was launched as an easier method for captioning but has not yet solved the problem of motivation; captioning is often difficult and tedious, making it an unappealing activity for many would-be participants. Jansen acknowledges that for some organizations "using volunteers can be difficult" because of content that may not be intended for public consumption, or a lack of popular interest in the material.[13] Perhaps in response, Amara now offers "ProServices" that include use of their platform by internal staff at your company, as well as a direct means to order captions with a guaranteed turnaround time. While crowdsourcing is the foundation of the service, a higher price tag will bring a more centralized and controlled result and may, as a consequence, cut out the failures and possibilities of open accessibility by limiting inclusion and participation.

Strategic communication scholar Daren Brabham notes that participation in crowdsourced projects is limited by barriers to access at the levels of hardware and software and is further constrained by a lack of "access to problem-specific skills and technologies."[14] Such barriers run against the very potential of crowdsourcing to draw in a range of individuals and perspectives, allowing for the building of collective knowledge and the combination of multiple standpoints. Brabham warns that if groups of people are excluded from these projects, whether actively or through neglect, crowdsourcing will ultimately serve the interests of the already powerful and replicate their aesthetics, values, and business practices. Though it is possible that Amara attracts people with disabilities to participate in its crowdsourced captioning or that people with disabilities independently use the site to produce captioned content, there is no evidence that this is the case. In short, there may be a disconnect that renders people with disabilities ultimately incidental to the goals and practices of accessible development, even as it is instantiated in crowdsourced formats. Like professional accessibility contexts, Amara may inadvertently foster a division between those who make and those who benefit and preserve charity-based understandings of disability.

A second, and quite different, case is that of EasyChirp (formerly Accessible Twitter). Using the open Twitter API, web developer and accessibility advocate Dennis Lembrée created a fully accessible web-based interface for Twitter in 2009. EasyChirp, which has received wide praise, improves the cultural accessibility of Twitter by enabling users with disabilities to participate in the same way as other users, and without revealing their use of assistive technology or being forced to disclose disability.[15] While Easy Chirp incorporates a number of accessibility features on the user's end, making Twitter more compatible with screenreaders and incorporating audio signals as warnings when users approach the 140-character limit of each tweet, the resulting tweets are indistinguishable from those tweets coming from any other Twitter client. This fosters full inclusion at a technical level, fosters use positions other than the preferred user positions upheld through Twitter's software, and potentially breaks down a range of barriers for people with disabilities. In Lembrée's words, "[I]t allows people to communicate who otherwise may not be able to well due to a physical or mental disability. It also helps break the social barrier with those who may at first be uncomfortable socializing with people with disabilities."[16] Thus, EasyChirp may foster cultural accessibility by allowing for conversation on equal terms and promote not just accommodation but integration, or inclusion, of non-normative users and perspectives in a site of mainstream mediated culture. Given the potential of Twitter to be used for activism, as seen in its utility for grassroots protests such as #CaptionTHIS, this cultural accessibility may further encourage the uptake of civic values and civic identities, enabling greater inclusion of people with disabilities in the local, national, and global bodies politic. Access to cultural spaces may facilitate access to civic cultures, acting as a kind of introduction to the forms of interaction that may be applied to civic engagement.[17] Thus, access to Twitter or social networking in general opens up the possibility of using media for political ends.

EasyChirp, though it fosters culturally accessible modes of interaction via Twitter, is not an open, collaborative project. A more participatory form of accessibility advocacy is a project called Fix the Web. Launched in the U.K. in 2010, Fix the Web asserts that "our solution is to make it super easy for people facing accessibility issues (such as many disabled and older people) to report problems with websites. Volunteers do the work of contacting the website owners and signposting them to support. In doing this work, volunteers will understand more about e-accessibility for themselves, as well as giving crucial information to website owners. Everybody wins!"[18] Gail Bradbrook, who coordinates the project, explains that the ethos of Fix the Web is that "the disabled person's voice should be enabled," meaning that while of course people with disabilities can self-advocate, "they shouldn't be bothered by that unless they want to be."[19] Fix the Web aspires to be a complaints-handling service, which would allow people with a disability (or any others with accessibility needs) to use a simple browser toolbar or a web form (seen in figure 6.1) to signal a problem as they use the internet. The organization then deals with these reports and parcels them out to volunteers, who may either contact the websites in question or offer to implement fixes themselves.

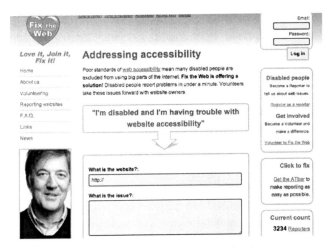

Fix the Web offers a web form that enables people who encounter accessibility problems to report them. Complaints will then be handled by volunteers, sparing people with disabilities the effort and emotional risk of accessibility enforcement.

This model works directly against the more troubling labor implications of asking people with disabilities to advocate for their own media access. This responsibility and the attendant risk of hostile responses is spread out among those willing to take on this work (which may include people with disabilities, accessibility experts, and other users). These volunteers are not necessarily trained in accessible technologies but are competent to make contact with the website owners and discuss problems; thus, the outside complaints that may be so motivating to businesses can occur, without requiring individuals with disabilities to take on this work.

Bradbrook recalls that in conversations with major companies, this feedback is often quite desirable. However, she thinks that volume is crucial to getting the kind of awareness-raising that would be transformative on a large scale. "Crowdsourcing," she said, "hasn't proved itself yet as a really effective solution" in achieving that volume.[20] The open, collaborative volunteer processes of Fix the Web offer an interesting approach to integrating people with disabilities, allies, and experts in the pursuit of web accessibility. Though this inclusion is admirable, it seems to come at the expense of expertise; many volunteers do not have the technical know-how to consult on accessibility practices. Where Easy-Chirp produces reliable technology, Fix the Web offers advocacy. In both, however, there remains a hint of the charity model of disability, in that taking the onus off of people with disabilities could be read as another case of the nondisabled majority's doing things "for" people with disabilities out of pity or self-interest. People with disabilities are generally absent from the Fix the Web site and promotional materials, which seem designed to reach out to content creators and potential complaint handlers, while in the case of EasyChirp, people with disabilities are generally users with little involvement in development. The potential of inclusive, open, participatory forms of cultural accessibility has not been fully realized in these projects.

A final example of the instantiation of cultural accessibility is Dreamwidth, a social networking and journaling service, introduced in chapter 5, that values people with disabilities as users, developers, and critics of its open source platform. Dreamwidth's guiding Diversity Statement and its open source development enable an unusually robust mode of participation in defining, encoding, and taking advantage of cultural accessibility. Deborah Kaplan, currently a co-lead on the accessibility team for Dreamwidth development, recalls that "The diversity statement as a whole, including the accessibility statement, was refined over time with community participation."[21] Such inclusion at the opening stages of development promoted the ongoing inclusion of people with disabilities and an ongoing commitment to access. The diversity statement drew people with disabilities to the #dw Twitter hashtag, where they expressed their needs to developers. A user, and volunteer, remembered when "DW came along . . . and I realized that I matter. I as a user, my needs and wants matter. DW even has a policy that says I matter."[22] This is the kind of emotional access described by bloggers with disabilities— not an attitude of tolerance or accommodation but an active welcome and recognition of disability as a part of life that brings its own valuable perspectives. One volunteer developer recalls that "Their surprise at the warm welcome from #dw in contrast to other less accessible sites and their stories of accessibility_fail were compelling; these people were now my friends, and I was cranky on their behalf."[23] Through such interactions, inclusion of people with disabilities actually worked to educate, build friendships and alliances, and create coalitions of developers and users who could participate in the ongoing creation of the Dreamwidth service and community.

The open source, volunteer development model further fostered meaningful inclusion and cultural accessibility by enabling people to contribute to the best of their abilities. Kaplan observed that she had "never seen such a large percentage of disabled developers in [her] life."[24] This inclusiveness has also resulted in a large percentage of women, particularly unusual in open source projects, further indicating that creating welcoming and inclusive media forms and content can itself facilitate greater access to media use and production. The development community includes first-time contributors and is supportive of the different degrees to which individuals may be willing or able to contribute at different moments. The community is exceptionally supportive and flexible, recognizing that individuals may come and go, participate and then take a break, or otherwise need to manage their efforts. For Kaplan, "the appreciation for the physical, cognitive, emotional limits on the developers, it makes me stay. And it makes me work harder."[25] The labor of people with disabilities in Dreamwidth is not exploitative, or coerced, or subject to the individual imperatives of neoliberal self-advocacy. Instead, it is requested, appreciated, and given support within a larger community. This, it seems, is cultural accessibility being built from the ground up, cultural accessibility at its best.

All of the foregoing cases offer some degree of cultural accessibility through their services, development processes, collaborative emphases, or resulting accessible media. They also would have been inconceivable when web accessibility first gained traction in the 1990s. The ability of individuals to communicate across time and distance and difference, fostered by new media forms, has the potential to be one of the most groundbreaking advances in access for people with disabilities. To squander this potential by hewing to narrow understandings of policies, business models, default users, technological forms, or types of content would be to deprive digital media culture of the insights available from some of the richest and most transformative experiences of access.

Access, Participation, and Collaboration

This book has highlighted the ways in which digital media accessibility for people with disabilities is regulated, used, implemented in form and content, and experienced by users with and without disabilities.

Throughout, it has argued that access is not a simple phenomenon but a conjoining of bodies, technologies, and culture that produces variable relationships to media, to other people, and to society at large. The (abled) preferred user position structures access by requiring particular means of interaction and often simultaneously produces excluded or deficient positions. When one considers the use and design of digital media in this light, it is evident that circumstances of access are variable, dependent, and potentially open to transformation. By wrestling with the margins, and looking to the often-ignored role of disability as identity, social category, and cultural trope, one can call into question the assumptions of access and equivalence. It becomes impossible to conceive of a single media "user," a single experience, a single point of entry to the mediatized environment that is the site of our personal, educational, work, and political lives. Disability offers important challenges to technocultural hegemonies, to the structure of the neoliberal self and society, and to the ways in which cultural participation may be meaningfully extended.

The prismatic nature of access, and the multitude of attendant insights that arise from its consideration, resulted in the construction of an "access kit" that structures this book. As elaborated in the Introduction and carried throughout this text, the proposed kit comprises five analytic categories that offer to elucidate some of the most difficult phenomena associated with (media) access. Each is associated with a series of questions, and attendant possible methodologies, offering a distinct picture of the access experience being studied. Each, alone, can offer important insights into the oft-ignored moment of access as experienced by those understood to lack it. Together, they compose a three-dimensional, nuanced impression of the ideologies, structures, identities, and politics at play in media cultures. Though developed—and deployed—in the study of digital media accessibility, this kit is intended to be moveable, flexible, and available for repurposing and reinterpretation. It coheres only in that it offers a set of tools assembled for a purpose—the granular study of access as an unequal and relational phenomenon that may set the tone for all other moments' cultural exchange.

It now seems clear that access is not a prerequisite to participation—*access and participation depend upon each other.* Just as access enables participation, so does increased participation by diverse people in diverse contexts and practices ultimately make possible expansions of access. Too often, discourses and theories of participation elide access, to their detriment. In turning a lens on access and considering the possibilities of cultural accessibility, I offer not simply a corrective but an impetus for the continued relevance of participation as a theoretical framework through which to understand contemporary media, culture, and politics. It is not just that those who care about cultural and political participation should attend to differences in access, as they may reflect and perpetuate existing power differentials. We must go further, delving into how it is that specific forms of technology, regulations of media, types of content, and uses of digital media challenge existing structures of power and ideologies of identity by revealing what is hidden by mainstream advertising or utopian discourses surrounding new media.

Participatory culture offers an attractive vision of a digitally enabled culture in which increased access to media production, political participation, and social collaboration produces more just, egalitarian forms of culture. It values collaboration, openness, sharing, community-building, and transformative uses of cultural artifacts. From the study of disability and digital media it is clear that those who would support participatory cultures must also come to value and prioritize coalitional politics, inclusive forms of social interaction, and the contributions of often-invisible users. Ethnographer Jenna Burrell writes that invisibility is caused by the lack of accommodation of minority or disempowered groups by those with technological power, but that "invisibility may be conceived of as its own form of power allowing forms of transgressive behavior to go unchecked."[26] The kludges, activist hashtags, video game representations, policy challenges, and ongoing social interactions that characterize experiences of digital media accessibility for people with disabilities are a source of knowledge, inspiration, and alternative imaginings of what digital media culture could be and how access to it might be valued, made possible, and extended in new directions.

Participatory forms of access are possible, but they require the hard work of interdependence and collaboration. At Wis-Con, a feminist science fiction convention held annually in Madison, Wisconsin, accessibility is a core component of creating a positive experience for all attendees. Many of the bloggers with disabilities interviewed in the course of my research attended, or hoped to attend, Wis-Con, and I attended twice when I lived in the area. Though not an online space, this convention models participatory access particularly well: Accessibility is achieved through ongoing conversations about individuals' and groups' needs, and accommodations are available for all (not tied to disability status) and include unusual features such as a "quiet room" as well as interpretive services, wheelchair seating, and other conventional forms of physical and communicative accommodation. Accessibility is used to talk about equalizing access on the basis of disability but is extended to be relevant to class, race, and other differences as well. This is not simply universal design but is *participatory* in that it is collaborative, ongoing, and responsive to a community of people who both need and create accessible conditions. In these processes, "disability becomes less about a single person's experience and more about a collective need to address the public."[27]

Such intensely collaborative modes of generating access can also become models of interdependence. Disability and performance scholar Petra Kuppers writes that "interdependence is a word with resonance in disability culture circles, where the self-reliant individual is often out of reach, and self-reliance's ableist features discernable."[28] The neoliberal individual self is not always attainable by those who require in-home assistance, rely upon others' aid, or otherwise operate in interdependent ways of being. In its inaccessibility, the neoliberal self is sidelined, pushed away to enable alternative ways of being. Interdependent selves are a resource for thinking outside of these constraints and considering how access might be a shared project, a phenomenon of inclusion and collaboration in which users, producers, policymakers, activists, family members, and others may all be equally implicated. It seems that "often access serves as the catalyst for collaborative energies,"[29] and harnessing and extending the values of collaboration and interdependence may enhance the transformative potential of participatory cultures and digital media by fostering a deep, politicized, and affective understanding of what it means to work, and be, together.

Collaboration is the linchpin in the union of access, participation, and the kinds of interdependence valued in disability studies and in coalitional politics more broadly. While digital media, like older media forms, may facilitate the development of do-it-yourself citizenship,[30] enable the development of civic cultures,[31] and foster public values that work in opposition to neoliberal imperatives,[32] it is in the shared spaces, cultures, and ongoing interactions enabled by networked technologies that collaboration emerges as a possible foundation for making possible meaningful forms of cultural and political engagement. Technology and information scholars Matt Ratto and Megan Boler identify such potential in a revitalized form of DIY citizenship, located within communities of people who make things (online and off). They argue that that "DIY ethos and culture provide a compelling and coherent framework for understanding contemporary forms of activism and collective identities."[33] This is a reclaiming of "DIY" through an insistence on togetherness, rather than through the kinds of expressive individuality that easily slide into consumerism. These creative communities collaborate, cooperate, and teach one another, enacting the practices of participatory culture and potentially building civic values. Within fan communities, practices, relationships, and ideas associated with media texts and online interactions can be taken up and repurposed in services of political ends.[34] Technological activism, such as that seen in Dreamwidth, may enact norms of labor and social relations that challenge not only capitalism but the exploitative tendencies of new media labor.[35]

Yet in order for such collaborations to fulfill their progressive potential, they must attend to differences in embodied identity, power structures, and needs. As cautioned by technology scholar Christina Dunbar-Hester, we must "understand the difficult and elusive work of building and maintaining structures of participation, especially egalitarian participation."[36] Participation is not automatically accessible simply because it is available; developing collaborative means of cultural and political interaction requires creating forms of cultural accessibility that value differences in experience and standpoints and not only tolerate but welcome difference.

Can we build collaborative forms of participation that lead to new results, new possibilities, and new structures within which to increase access and enable cultural and civic participation? These are tall orders and complicated processes. Yet it is necessary work. Media access, disability, and participation are endlessly complicated phenomena, but they are exactly the problems through which it becomes possible to, in the words of Tanya Titchkosky, "[insert] into the world alternative ways of being and alternative ways of knowing. In this the possibility of beginning something new arises."[37] To imagine differently, to build more accessible futures, and to welcome the messy differences of bodies, cultures, and technologies—these are the challenges and the rewards of unearthing the variations of ability and access.

APPENDIX: ETHNOGRAPHIC RESEARCH, INTERVIEWS, AND SELECTED BLOGS

The ethnographic work in this project is based upon a nine-month participant observation of a "disability blogosphere"; here, *disability* refers to either a claimed identity, a topic of discussion, a framing theme, or a combination thereof, and *blogosphere* is intended to describe a linked network of blogs that exist in conversation with one another and may share audiences. Thus, although most bloggers involved identify as people with disabilities, not all do.

The blogosphere was established via a snowball sample, beginning with three seed sites: *Blind Photographers*; *Disability Studies–Temple University*; and *Feminists with Disabilities/Forward*. Each site offered a distinct profile for research. *Blind Photographers* is a now-defunct collaborative site written by photographers with a range of visual impairments. It was closely tied to a Flickr group (which still exists). *Disability Studies–Temple University* is a group blog that tends to be academic in content but offers an extensive blogroll (links to other blogs). *Feminists with Disabilities/Forward* was a group blog with a decidedly activist perspective, numerous ties to social networking sites, and a range of topics. Regular posting ceased in early 2011, but as the archives, contact information, and blogroll of the site remained intact, it was retained as a seed site.

This snowball method of constructing my field utilized many of the key characteristics of blogs: links and blogrolls, comments, and authors' other online presences (Twitters, Tumblrs, other blogs, web magazines). Through these connections, I identified spaces of sociality and interaction that could constitute a blogosphere. By the conclusion of fieldwork, this blogosphere as field site included fifty-two blogs, thirty Twitters, twenty-six Flickrs, and eleven Tumblrs.

More than forty interviews were conducted in the research of this book. These included oral history interviews with accessibility professionals from industry, government, and academia as well as open-ended interviews with bloggers and web users/developers. The former were used to contextualize archival and industrial sources regarding web and digital media accessibility, and the latter were used to delve more deeply into the dynamics observed in the field. All interviews were done under the auspices of Institutional Research Boards at the University of Wisconsin–Madison and Indiana University–Bloomington. Most interviewees were willing to be referred to by name; those who were not were referred to only by group characteristics in the text (and as "participants" below), and those who wished to speak only on background are not referenced specifically.

INTERVIEWS

Rather than include interview information in the bibliography, I have listed here the details regarding the interviews I conducted. This list includes only those participants whose interviews were directly incorporated into the text, though all interviews were used for background and crucially informed this research. Many thanks to all interview participants.

Abou-Zahra, Shadi. Skype, April 15, 2013.
Bailey, Bruce. Telephone, May 13, 2011.
Bradbrook, Gail. Skype, June 6, 2013.
Chong, Curtis. Telephone, May 6, 2011.
Christina, Marissa. Skype, October 1, 2011.
Clark, Joe. Telephone, April 19, 2011.
Dardarian, Linda. Face to face, March 1, 2013.
Feingold, Lainey. Face to face, March 1, 2013.
Goldberg, Larry. Telephone, April 11, 2013.
Hamilton, Anna. Email, December 3, 2011.
Henry, Liz. Email. March 3, 2012.
Jansen, Dean. Email. April 24, 2013.
Jarashow, Adam. Email, April 20, 2013.
Kacelnik, Chally. Email, November 3, 2011.
Kaplan, Deborah. Skype, April 16, 2013.
Kirkpatrick, Andrew. Face to face, March 1, 2013.
Lembrée, Dennis. Email, April 1, 2012.
———. Face to face, March 1, 2013.

May, Matt. Face to face, March 1, 2013.

Participant 4. Telephone, May 17, 2011.

Participant 8. Telephone, October 19, 2011.

Participant 17. Skype, April 27, 2011.

Participant 18. Telephone, March 6, 2012.

Participant 38. Face to face, March 1, 2013.

Participant 40. Telephone, June 18, 2013.

Participant 44. Skype, December 8, 2013.

smith, s. e. Email, December 19, 2011.

Vanderheiden, Gregg C. Telephone, December 10, 2008.

———. Telephone, May 14, 2011.

Wakefield, Doug. Telephone, December 8, 2008.

Waters, Elle. Skype, November 5, 2012.

Watson, Blake. Skype, October 21, 2011.

Willis, Mark. Skype, December 20, 2011.

SELECTED BLOGS

A small selection of the sites studied is provided here. These are more public sites, rather than personal blogs intended for a limited audience; though I am grateful for the participation of a range of bloggers who produced a range of content, I do not wish to create unnecessary individual exposure. Not all of these sites are currently active, but those listed here have old content that is still publicly available. Many of these sites are, themselves, interesting and excellent resources for further information about disability and digital media.

Accessibility Fail—http://accessibility-fail.dreamwidth.org

Amara—https://amara.org

BBC Ouch!—http://www.bbc.com/news/blogs/ouch

Beauty Ability—http://beautyability.com

Bitch Magazine Blogs—www.bitchmagazine.org/blogs

Blind Flaneur—http://blindflaneur.com

Blind Photographers (Flickr group)—http://www.flickr.com/groups/
blind_photographers

But You Don't Look Sick—http://www.butyoudontlooksick.com

Disability Studies–Temple University—http://www.disstud.blogspot.com

Dreamwidth—http://www.dreamwidth.org

EasyChirp—http://www.easychirp.com
Feminists with Disabilities/Forward—www.disabledfeminists.com
Fix the Web—http://www.fixtheweb.net
Fuck Yeah, Accessibility—http://fuckyeahaccessibility.tumblr.com
Life Kludger—http://www.lifekludger.com

NOTES

INTRODUCTION

1 McLaughlin and Neal, "CAPTION FAIL: Lady Gaga Putt-Putt Rally."

2 Jenkins et al., *Confronting the Challenges of Participatory Culture*, 5.

3 Like few others working in web video, McLaughlin and Neal have translated their online success into a multimedia career. Short-form comedy has been a productive means of breaking from web media into the mainstream media industries, as discussed by Marx, "'The Missing Link Moment'"; Christian, "Fandom as Industrial Response"; Warner, "Where Do We Go from Here."

4 Rhett James McLaughlin and Charles Lincoln "Link" Neal, "CAPTION FAIL: Lady Gaga Putt-Putt Rally," 2011, http://www.youtube.com/watch?v=hVNrkXM3TTI.

5 The distinction between *deaf* and *Deaf* is often used to differentiate deafness as medical condition from Deaf language, culture, and communities in the United States (see Lane, "Construction of Deafness"). Like many others, I often use *d/Deaf* in an attempt to address both those who do and do not identify with Deaf culture, particularly when discussing physical impairments and accessibility needs. However, as suggested by Brueggemann in *Deaf Subjects*, in the linking of these terms the distinction may be undermined and made less useful. Thus, in cases where I have knowledge of the cultural affiliations of those under discussion, I use either *deaf* or *Deaf*.

6 YouTube, "Innovation in Accessibility."

7 Google, *Automatic Captions in YouTube Demo*, 2009, http://www.youtube.com/watch?v=kTvHIDKLFqc.

8 Wendell, *The Rejected Body*, 14.

9 White, "Where Do You Want to Sit Today?"

10 Fox, *Americans Living with Disability and Their Technology Profile*.

11 The Union of the Physically Impaired Against Segregation and The Disability Alliance, *Fundamental Principles of Disability*.

12 Fraser, "Rethinking the Public Sphere."

13 See, for instance, Bruns, *Blogs, Wikipedia, Second Life, and Beyond*; Burgess and Green, *YouTube*; Jenkins et al., *Confronting the Challenges of Participatory Culture*; Jenkins, *Convergence Culture*; Jenkins, Ford, and Green, *Spreadable Media*; Tapscott and Williams, *Wikinomics*.

14 Burgess and Green, *YouTube*, 108.

15 Meikle, "Social Media, Visibility, and Activism."

16 Carpentier, *Media and Participation.*

17 Dahlgren, "Television, the Public Sphere and Civic Cultures"; Giroux, "The Crisis of Public Values in the Age of the New Media"; Hinck, "Theorizing a Public Engagement Keystone."

18 McRuer, *Crip Theory*, 30.

19 Hall, Massey, and Rustin, "After Neoliberalism?" 19.

20 Goggin and Newell, *Digital Disability*, 54.

21 Hall, Massey, and Rustin, "After Neoliberalism?" 19.

22 Lievrouw, "The Information Environment and Universal Service," 157.

23 Kirkpatrick, "'A Blessed Boon.'"

24 Dolmage, "Mapping Composition—Inviting Disability in the Front Door."

25 Price, *Mad at School.*

26 Titchkosky, *The Question of Access*, 13.

27 Kafer, *Feminist, Queer, Crip.*

28 Hall, "On Postmodernism and Articulation," 141.

29 These language choices are, of course, fraught. Many scholars and activists with disabilities in the English-speaking world have embraced the language of *disabled* as it more clearly signals one's status as disabled *by society* rather than suggests that disability is an individual attribute. Additionally, the language of *crip* has been reclaimed by numerous scholars, artists, and activists. Finally, the language of able-bodiedness has been criticized for an overemphasis on physical disability to the exclusion of sensory, mental, or intellectual disabilities; some scholars have begun using the term *mindbodies* to signal this breadth in discussing ability and disability. Because I hope for this text to be accessible to people who are new to disability studies, and because I routinely engage with policy languages, and for the sake of consistency, I will use person-first language and understand it to encompass the variety of experiences and identities indicated within these debates.

30 The Americans with Disabilities Act (1990) defines *disability* as "(A) a physical or mental impairment that substantially limits one or more major life activities of such individual; (B) a record of such an impairment; or (C) being regarded as having such an impairment" (42 U.S.C. § 12102).

31 Although much research for this book has focused on web content accessibility, I predominantly use the phrase *digital media accessibility* because it is both broader than *web content accessibility* and dependent upon it. It is broader, as mobile phones and similar devices, video game consoles, desktop computer programs, e-readers, and even classroom technologies fit within its confines. It is dependent upon *web content accessibility*, however, because this is the form of digital media accessibility with the longest history of standardization, and because the recommendations of web content accessibility are increasingly being used as the basis for other accessibility policies and innovations. Prioritizing *digital media accessibility* also forces my analysis to move beyond the specific technologies of the web

to consider the ways in which media convergence has fostered an increasingly integrated media environment.

32 HTML is HyperText Markup Language; CSS refers to Cascading Style Sheets. Both are standards developed by the World Wide Web Consortium.

33 Foucault, *The Archaeology of Knowledge & The Discourse on Language*, 229.

34 Ankerson, "Writing Web Histories with an Eye on the Analog Past."

35 For more on this approach to studying policy, see Streeter, *Selling the Air*.

36 Havens, Lotz, and Tinic, "Critical Media Industry Studies."

37 Rosemarie Garland-Thomson theorizes the "normate" subject position to refer to a privileged body, without stigma, that functions as a universal type in a given society (*Extraordinary Bodies*).

38 Coleman, "Ethnographic Approaches to Digital Media," 489.

39 Schneider and Foot, "Web Sphere Analysis."

40 Kuppers, *Disability Culture and Community Performance*, 5.

41 Online extensions of this book are available at http://scalar.usc.edu/works/restricted-access/index.

42 D'Acci, "Cultural Studies, Television Studies, and the Crisis in the Humanities"; Du Gay, *Doing Cultural Studies*; Johnson, "What Is Cultural Studies Anyway?" Circuit models are admirable in their attention to mutually influential processes and complex relationships; D'Acci's model is particularly useful in its mapping of cultural studies *research* rather than of cultural artifacts. However, these models are often based firmly in a broadcast model of media culture and have not wrestled with what might be different in the contexts of digital, networked, or participatory media cultures.

43 Bucy and Newhagen, eds., *Media Access*; van Dijk, *The Deepening Divide*; Warschauer, *Technology and Social Inclusion*. The major drawback of digital divide and related ICT literature for my purposes was that by abstracting real-world phenomena these models offered extremely linear frameworks in which access is positioned as a finite, achievable goal (rather than a variable set of relations).

44 Bolter and Grusin, *Remediation*; Chun, *Programmed Visions*; Galloway, *Protocol*; Lessig, *Remix*; Manovich, *The Language of New Media*.

45 Manovich, *The Language of New Media*, 37.

46 Etymologically, *kit* comes first through a Middle Dutch word for a jug or wooden container and was popularly used in English by the eighteenth century to refer to a soldier's personal effects. Subsequent centuries expanded the use of *kit* to refer to a set of workman's tools and then to describe an "article to be assembled by the buyer." See Harper, "'Kit' n1."

47 Grossberg, *Cultural Studies in the Future Tense*, 27.

48 Cousineau, *The Painted Word*.

49 O'Toole, "Disclosing Our Relationships to Disabilities."

50 Schalk, "Coming to Claim Crip."

51 Herndon, "Disparate but Disabled," 258.

CHAPTER 1. REGULATING DIGITAL MEDIA ACCESSIBILITY

1 Numbers and Twitter quotations are culled from my personal archiving of this hashtag, spanning June 6–12, 2012. After June 10, there was a lower volume of tweets and more obvious uses of the hashtag that were not related to the protest. Jarashow now regrets the specific choice of hashtag, as #captionthis has been used by others to solicit and spread memes involving captioning a specific photo.

2 Jarashow, Personal Interview.

3 Classen, *Watching Jim Crow*; Perlman, "Feminists in the Wasteland."

4 Jarashow, Personal Interview.

5 Tryon, *On-Demand Culture.*

6 Foucault, *The Birth of Biopolitics.*

7 Gill, "'Life Is a Pitch.'"

8 Ellcessor, "<ALT='Textbooks'>"; Kennedy, *Net Work.*

9 Kirkpatrick, "Bringing Blue Skies Down to Earth."

10 Ibid., 310.

11 Goggin and Newell, "The Business of Digital Disability."

12 Winner, "Do Artifacts Have 'Politics'?" 28.

13 Much of this analysis is made possible through close readings of primary texts, including the emails, phone call minutes, and in-person minutes of the Web Accessibility Initiative Guidelines Working Group (WAI GL WG), available through the W3C website; the text of laws and announcements published in the *Federal Register*; draft guidelines and standards documents; documentation on the Trace Research & Development Center from the University of Wisconsin–Madison Archives; and materials shared by interviewees, including personal emails, internal documents, and copies of public comments received on the Section 508 standards Notice of Proposed Rulemaking in 2000.

14 29 USC Sec. 794d (a)(1)(A)(i) and (a)(1)(A)(ii). 1998.

15 To develop these standards, the Access Board assembled the Electronic and Information Technology Access Advisory Committee, comprising a range of industry, academic, and nonprofit representatives. The committee, and Access Board, anticipated looking to the standards already written for implementation of section 255 of the Telecommunications Act of 1996, those written in relation to the ADA, the guidelines for accessible hardware and software developed by the GSA and the Department of Education, and accessible web guidelines that had been "created by several entities," presumably including the then-in-progress WCAG 1.0. The EITAC Advisory Committee released its first report in May 1999, after which the Access Board worked to produce a set of standards that addressed accessibility in terms of procurement, web materials, and other technologies used within the federal government.

16 29 USC Sec. 794d. 36 CFR 1194.22 notes. 2000. Most provisions were drawn from WCAG 1.0's Priority 1 Checkpoints, those guidelines deemed most important for

achieving a degree of accessibility because of their effects and/or ease of enactment (vs. Priority 2 and 3 checkpoints, which were more difficult to achieve or which would affect smaller populations).

17 Ellcessor, "Bridging Disability Divides."

18 Downey, *Closed Captioning*; Ellcessor, "Captions On, Off, on TV, Online"; Strauss, *A New Civil Right.*

19 Telecommunications and Electronic and Information Technology Advisory Committee, *TEITAC Report*. Sec. 2.3.

20 Access Board, "Board Proposes Updated ICT Accessibility Requirements," Government, *United States Access Board* (February 18, 2015), http://www.access-board. gov/guidelines-and-standards/communications-and-it/about-the-ict-refresh/ news-release; "Proposed Information and Communication Technology (ICT) Standards and Guidelines," *Federal Register*, February 27, 2015 (80 FR 10880), 36 CFR Parts 1193 and 1194.

21 Kennedy, *Net Work*, 129.

22 Matt May, Personal Interview.

23 Participant 38, Personal Interview.

24 The W3C is a membership organization, meaning that interested parties may join for a fee and be involved in all processes. Member organizations include industry leaders such as Microsoft, IBM, Intel, and AT&T; state organizations like the British Broadcasting Corporation and the Chinese Academy of Sciences; activist organizations such as the Electronic Frontier Foundation; and numerous universities around the world. Additionally, through an "invited expert" structure, representatives of nonmember organizations may participate; this has been a popular choice for employees of the U.S. federal government, for accessibility consultants, and for representatives of disability awareness or activist organizations, many of whom cannot afford membership fees.

25 Busch, *Standards*, 13.

26 Ibid., 26.

27 "World Wide Web Consortium (W3C) Launches International Web Accessibility Initiative."

The formation of WAI was endorsed by the White House under President Bill Clinton and slightly predated the 1998 amendments to Section 508 of the Rehabilitation Act of 1973. Though separated analytically, these processes featured significant overlap in personnel and in their goals.

28 Participant 4, Personal Interview.

29 "WAI Markup Guidelines Working Group Charter."

30 WCAG 1.0 was published along with a Techniques document; the former were normative and fixed, while the latter was published as "notes" so that they could be updated over time in accordance with technological developments.

31 Participant 4, Personal Interview.

32 "Web Content Accessibility Guidelines Working Group (WCAG WG) Charter."

33 Easton, "The Web Content Accessibility Guidelines 2.0."

34 Adam and Kreps, "Disability and Discourses of Web Accessibility"; Brys and Vanderbauwhede, "Communication Challenges in the W3C's Web Content Accessibility Guidelines"; Easton, "The Web Content Accessibility Guidelines 2.0"; Farrelly, "Practitioner Barriers to Diffusion and Implementation of Web Accessibility."

35 Gregg C. Vanderheiden, Personal Interview, May 14, 2011.

36 Ben Caldwell et al., "Web Content Accessibility Guidelines (WCAG) 2.0," *World Wide Web Consortium*, December 11, 2008, http://www.w3.org/TR/WCAG20/.

37 Web Accessibility Initiative, "WAI Page Author Guideline Conference Call—July."

38 Ellcessor, "<ALT='Textbooks'>."

39 Caldwell et al., "Web Content Accessibility Guidelines (WCAG) 2.0."

40 Digital Entertainment Merchants Association, "DigitalEMA," *DigitalEMA*, 2013, www.digitalema.org.

41 Statement of Interest of the United States of America in Opposition to Defendant's Motion for Judgment on the Pleadings, National Association of the Deaf, Western Massacusetts Association of the Deaf and Hearing Impaired, and *Lee Nettles v. Netflix, Inc.*, No. 03–11-cv-30168 (United States District Court, District of Massachusetts, Springfield Division, May 5, 2012).

   Brief of Petitioner-Appellant at 48, *United States v. Ali Saleh Kahlah Al-Marri*, No. 03–3674.

42 Kate Johnston, "Netflix Reaches Deal to End Lawsuit over Closed Captioning of Streamed Movies, TV Shows," *Boston.com*, October 11, 2012, http://www.boston.com/businessupdates/2012/10/10/netflix-reaches-deal-end-lawsuit-over-closed-captioning-streamed-movies-shows/JkVQPbvy8uuL79zFVeFRNK/story.html.

43 Associated Press, "By the Numbers: Netflix Subscribers," *Yahoo! News*, May 24, 2013, http://news.yahoo.com/numbers-netflix-subscribers-205626746.html.

44 Memorandum. Donald Cullen, on behalf of himself and all others similarly situated, v. Netflix, Inc., No. 13–15092 (United States Court of Appeals for the Ninth Circuit, March 13, 2015). http://cdn.ca9.uscourts.gov/datastore/memoranda/2015/04/01/13-15092.pdf.

   For analysis of the hearing that led to this statement, see the following legal blog post: Christina F. Jackson, Kristina M. Launey, and Minh N. Vu, "Ninth Circuit Hears Arguments: Are Web-Only Businesses 'Places of Public Accommodation' Subject to Title III?," *ADA Title III News & Insights: Seyfarth Shaw, LLC*, March 20, 2015, http://www.adatitleiii.com/2015/03/ninth-circuit-hears-arguments-are-web-only-businesses-places-of-public-accommodation-subject-to-title-iii/.

45 Goldberg, Personal Interview.

46 Digital Entertainment Merchants Association, "EMA's Best Practices for Closed Captioning of Internet Protocol–Delivered Video Programming [Draft—June 12, 2013]" (Digital Entertainment Merchants Association, June 12, 2013), 2–3, www.digitalema.org.

47 Participant 40, Personal Interview.

48 Ibid.

49 Digital Entertainment Merchants Association, "EMA's Best Practices," 4.

50 Vaidhyanathan, *The Googlization of Everything*.

51 Ibid.

52 Ellcessor, "Captions On, Off, on TV, Online."

53 Kennedy, *Net Work*, 129.

54 Web Accessibility Initiative, "Developing a Web Accessibility Business Case for Your Organization: Overview," *World Wide Web Consortium*, September 7, 2012, http://www.w3.org/WAI/bcase/Overview.html.

55 Karl Groves, "Chasing the Accessibility Business Case—Conclusion," *Karl Groves*, January 27, 2012, http://www.karlgroves.com/2012/01/27/chasing-the-accessibility-business-case-conclusion/.

56 Web Accessibility Initiative, "Developing a Web Accessibility Business Case for Your Organization: Overview."

57 Waters, Personal Interview.

58 Ibid.

59 Dardarian, Personal Interview.

60 As quoted in Kennedy, *Net Work*, 102.

61 Ibid., 85.

62 Gill, "'Life Is a Pitch.'"

63 Havens, *Black Television Travels*.

64 Ellcessor, "<ALT='Textbooks'>."

65 Ibid.; Kennedy, *Net Work*.

66 Dennis Lembrée, Personal Interview, March 1, 2013.

67 Waters, Personal Interview.

68 Karl Groves, "How Dare You Try to Infiltrate Our Special Club?," *Karl Groves*, February 7, 2013, http://www.karlgroves.com/2013/02/07/how-dare-you-try-to-infiltrate-our-special-club/.

69 Kennedy, *Net Work*.

70 Christina, Personal Interview.

71 Ibid.

72 Jeffrey Zeldman, *The Big Web Show*, MP3, n.d., http://5by5.tv/bigwebshow/55.

73 Watson, Personal Interview.

74 Kennedy, *Net Work*, 79.

75 Ensmenger, "The 'Question of Professionalism' in the Computer Fields."

76 Ibid., 61.

77 May, Personal Interview.

78 Ibid.

79 Kirkpatrick, Personal Interview.

80 "About IAAP," *International Association of Accessibility Professionals*, accessed April 9, 2015, http://www.accessibilityassociation.org/content.asp?contentid=1.

81 Busch, *Standards*, 33.

82 Kirkpatrick, Personal Interview.

83 Ellcessor, "<ALT='Textbooks'>"; Gill, "'Life Is a Pitch'"; Alice Marwick, "Internet Famous," Talk presented at ROFLCON 2008, *Tiara.org: A Feminist Technology Blog*, (April 29, 2008), http://www.tiara.org/papers/roflcon_talk.txt.

84 Shawn Lawton Henry, "Understanding Web Accessibility," in *Web Accessibility: Web Standards and Regulatory Compliance*, by Richard Rutter et al., 1st ed. (friendsofED, 2006), 42.

85 Chong, Personal Interview.

86 *Landmark Precedent in NAD vs. Netflix* (National Association of the Deaf, June 19, 2012), http://nad.org/news/2012/6/landmark-precedent-nad-vs-netflix.

87 Goggin and Newell, *Digital Disability*, 139.

88 Ellis and Kent, *Disability and New Media*; Goggin and Noonan, "Blogging Disabilty"; Haller, *Representing Disability in an Ableist World*; Thoreau, "Ouch! An Examination of the Self-representation of Disabled People on the Internet."

89 Frank Mounts, "Comment on FR Doc #2010–18334," Public Submission (July 29, 2010), http://www.regulations.gov/#!documentDetail;D=DOJ-CRT-2010–0005–0026.

90 Busch, *Standards*, 43.

91 May, Personal Interview.

CHAPTER 2. YOU ALREADY KNOW HOW TO USE IT

1 Apple, "What Is iPad? Advertisement," 2010, http://www.youtube.com/watch?v=easogl2DT34.

2 Ellis and Kent, *Disability and New Media*, 66–67.

3 Mitchell and Snyder, "Narrative Prosthesis and the Materiality of Metaphor."

4 Jenkins, Ford, and Green, *Spreadable Media*, 193.

5 Livingstone, "Media Literacy and the Challenge of New Information and Communication Technologies," 8.

6 Friedman, *Electric Dreams*.

7 Streeter, *The Net Effect*, 133.

8 National Telecommunications and Information Administration, *Falling Through the Net: A Survey of the "Have Nots" in Rural and Urban Americal* (Washington: U.S. Department of Commerce, July 1995), www.ntia.doc.gov/ntiahome/fallingthru.html.

9 Kafer, *Feminist, Queer, Crip*, 20.

10 Nakamura, *Cybertypes*, 87.

11 "You Will." Advertisement. 1993. http://www.adsavvy.org/how-accurate-were-atts-you-will-ads-from-1993/.

12 "Anthem." Advertisement. 1997. http://vimeo.com/2445340.

13 Nakamura, *Cybertypes*, 88.

14 Norden, *The Cinema of Isolation*; Haller, *Representing Disability in an Ableist World*.

15 Kafer, *Feminist, Queer, Crip*, 3.

16 Ankerson, "Dot-Com Design."

17   Tim O'Reilly, "What Is Web 2.0: Design Patterns and Business Models for the Next Generation of Software," *O'Reilly*, September 30, 2005, http://www.oreillynet.com/lpt/a/6228.

18   Schudson, *Advertising, the Uneasy Persuasion*.

19   Andrejevic, "The Work of Being Watched"; Van Dijck, *The Culture of Connectivity*.

20   "YouTube—Yahoo! 'It's You' TV Commercial," 2009. October 13, 2010. http://www.youtube.com/watch?v=VhtUloGIyVw.

21   Van Dijck, *The Culture of Connectivity*.

22   Chun, *Control and Freedom*, 13. *Produser* is a reference to the concept of a hybrid producer-user explained in Axel Bruns, *Blogs, Wikipedia, Second Life, and Beyond: From Production to Produsage* (New York: Peter Lang, 2008).

23   White, *The Body and the Screen*.

24   Van Dijck, "Users Like You?"

25   Streeter, *The Net Effect*, 11.

26   Chun, *Control and Freedom*; Chun, *Programmed Visions*; Fuller, ed., *Software Studies*; Galloway, *Protocol*; Gillespie, "The Stories Digital Tools Tell"; Manovich, *The Language of New Media*; Manovich, *Software Takes Command*; Montfort and Bogost, *Racing the Beam*; Montfort, ed., *10 PRINT CHR$(205.5+RND(1));: GOTO 10*.

27   Chun, *Programmed Visions*.

28   Hall, "Encoding/Decoding."

29   Friedman, *Electric Dreams*; Johnson, *Interface Culture*; Nakamura, *Cybertypes*.

30   Deuze, "Participation, Remediation, Bricolage"; Hine, *Virtual Ethnography*; White, "Where Do You Want to Sit Today?"

31   Morley, *Media, Modernity, Technology: The Geography of the New*, 251.

32   Kathryn Balint, "An Equal Voice: For Those with Disabilities, Computing Is a 'Lifeline,'" *The San Diego Union-Tribune*, February 29, 2000, sec. Computer Link; Mindy Blodgett, "Blind Users Stymied by New Internet Graphics," *Computerworld*, September 30, 1996, sec. News.

33   Blodgett, "Blind Users Stymied by New Internet Graphics."

34   Debra Nussbaum, "Bringing the Visual World of the Web to the Blind," *The New York Times*, March 26, 1998.

35   Sreenath Sreenivasan, "Blind Users Add Access on the Web," *The New York Times*, December 2, 1996.

36   Netivation.com, "Netivation.com Acquires Disability Mall," *PR Newswire*, March 28, sec. Financial News.

37   Balint, "An Equal Voice."

38   K. Oanh Ha, "Internet Becomes Lifeline for the Disabled," *San Jose Mercury News*, August 7, 1999.

39   Carl R. Augusto, "Technology Gap," *New York Times*, April 3, 1996, sec. Editorial Desk.

40   Robyn E. Blumner, "Blind Group's Suit against AOL a Good Cause but a Bad Idea," *St. Petersburg Times*, November 14, 1999, sec. Perspective.

41 "Shopping Goes Online," *Consumer Reports*, November 1998.

42 Sreenivasan, "Blind Users Add Access on the Web."

43 Ha, "Internet Becomes Lifeline for the Disabled."

44 For a discussion of how technology encourages normative user positions, see Valentine and Skelton, "'An Umbilical Cord to the World.'"

45 Goggin and Newell, *Digital Disability*.

46 Lamont Wood, "Blind Users Still Struggle with 'Maddening' Computing Obstacles—Computerworld," *Computerworld*, April 16, 2008, http://www.computerworld.com/s/article/9077118/Blind_users_still_struggle_with_maddening_computing_obstacles?nlid=1&source=NLT_AM.

47 AFP, "Internet an Equalizer for People with Disabilities—Yahoo!Xtra News," *Yahoo!Xtra News*, September 6, 2010, http://nz.news.yahoo.com/a/-/technology/7887329/internet-an-equalizer-for-people-with-disabilities/; Kim Hart, "Access Denied," *The Washington Post*, August 26, 2010, http://www.washingtonpost.com/wp-dyn/content/article/2008/06/18/AR2008061803080.html?hpid=artslot.

48 "Giz Explains: How Blind People See the Internet," August 25, 2010, http://gizmodo.com/5620079/giz-explains-how-blind-people-see-the-internet.

49 Moser, "Disability and the Promises of Technology."

50 The Blind Photographer Flickr group (http://www.flickr.com/groups/blind_photographers) was used as a seed site for constructing the field of ethnographic analysis. The immediately associated sites and social media accounts were www.twitter.com/BlindPhotogs; www.blindphotographers.com; and www.blog.blindphotographers.org.

51 Murray, "Digital Images, Photo-Sharing, and Our Shifting Notions of Everyday Aesthetics."

52 Krauss, "Reinventing the Medium."

53 "YouTube—McCain Can't Type, but YES WE CAN!," 2008, http://www.youtube.com/watch?v=ggIjrTM23Uw.

54 Boehlert, *Bloggers on the Bus*.

55 Produced in 2007 by satire site BarelyPolitical.com, it featured a young woman in a bikini singing about her new-found love of Barack Obama (D-Ill.); the producers affirmed that the Obama campaign was not involved and stated that the video was made in fun, not as an endorsement.

56 Toby Harnden, "John McCain 'Technology Illiterate,' Doesn't Email or Use Internet," *Telegraph.co.uk*, July 13, 2008, http://www.telegraph.co.uk/news/newstopics/uselection2008/johnmccain/2403704/John-McCain-technology-illiterate-doesnt-email-or-use-internet.html.

57 Alper et al., "Reimagining the Good Life with Disability."

CHAPTER 3. TRANSFORMERS

1 Matt May, "Wanted: Mobile Dev with 40 Years Experience" (South by Southwest Interactive, Austin, TX, March 12, 2013), http://www.sxswparties.com/audio/2013/wanted-mobile-dev-40-years-experience-sxsw-interactive-2013.

2 Gregg Vanderheiden, "A Brief History of the Trace R&D Center's Origins in the Department of Electrical and Computer Engineering," August 17, 1995, Record Group #8, University Archive, University of Wisconsin–Madison.

3 "Trace Center Overview: College of Engineering, University of Wisconsin–Madison" (Trace Center, October 22, 1999), Record Group #8, University Archive, University of Wisconsin–Madison.

4 Gregg C. Vanderheiden, Personal Interview, 2008.

5 Zeynep Tufekci, "It's a Man's Phone—Technology and Society," *Medium*, accessed July 15, 2014, https://medium.com/technology-and-society/its-a-mans-phone-a26c6bee1b69.

6 Vanderheiden and Chisholm, "Design of HTML Pages to Increase Their Accessibility to Users with Disabilities."

7 Gregg C. Vanderheiden, Wendy Chisholm, Neal Ewers, and Shannon M. Dunphy, "Unified Web Site Accessibility Guidelines 1.0," March 1997. Email message to author from Vanderheiden, October 28, 2008.

8 Manovich, *The Language of New Media*, 64.

9 Galloway, *Protocol*, 52.

10 Ibid.

11 Winner, "Do Artifacts Have 'Politics'?" 30.

12 Norman, *The Design of Everyday Things*, 162.

13 Winner, "Do Artifacts Have 'Politics'?" 28.

14 Curtis Chong, Personal Interview; Norman Coombs, "Liberation Technology"; Joseph J. Lazzaro, "Windows of Vulnerability," *BYTE Magazine*, June 1991, 416.

15 Chong, Personal Interview.

16 Lazzaro, "Windows of Vulnerability."

17 Richard S. Schwerdtfeger, "Making the GUI Talk: New Technology Holds Promise for Blind and Learning-Disabled People Who Live in a GUI-Oriented World," *BYTE Magazine*, December 1991, 118–130.

18 Lawrence H. Boyd, Wesley L. Boyd, and Gregg C. Vanderheiden, *The Graphical User Interface Crisis: Danger and Opportunity*, National Institute on Disability and Rehabiiltation Research (ED/CSERS) (Madison: Trace Center, University of Wisconsin–Madison, September 1990), 1, Wisconsin Historical Society.

19 Ibid., 8.

20 Schwerdtfeger, "Making the GUI Talk," 128.

21 *Trace Research and Development Center; Report of Progress, 1987–1994*, National Institute of Handicapped Research (Madison, WI: Trace Center, University of Wisconsin–Madison, 1994).

22 Johnson, *Interface Culture*, 50.

23 Balsamo, *Designing Culture*.

24 See Ellis and Kent, *Disability and New Media*; Goggin and Newell, *Digital Disability*.

25 Chun, *Control and Freedom*.

26 See http://www.csszengarden.com.

27 See Galloway, *Protocol*, on "seamlessness" as a formal component of the web.

28 Chisholm et al., "Web Content Accessibility Guidelines 1.0."

29 Ankerson, "Dot-Com Design," 312.

30 Ellcessor, "<ALT='Textbooks'>."

31 Jim Heid, "A Call to Action: Making Flash Accessible," *Heidsite*, September 22, http://www.heidsite.com/archives/flashaccess.html.

32 Joe Clark, "Flash MX: Clarifying the Concept," *A List Apart*, April 26, 2002, http://www.alistapart.com/articles/flashmxclarifying/; Andrew Kirkpatrick, "Flash MX: Moving Toward Accessible Rich Media," *A List Apart*, April 26, 2002, http://www.alistapart.com/articles/flashmxmoving/.

33 Kirkpatrick, "Flash MX."

34 Clark, "Flash MX."

35 Andrew Kirkpatrick, Personal Interview, 2013.

36 Bruce Bailey, Personal Interview; Participant 8, Personal Interview; Participant 17, Personal Interview; Gregg C. Vanderheiden, Personal Interview, 2011.

37 Berners-Lee, *Weaving the Web*.

38 Participant 38, Personal Interview.

39 Kirkpatrick, Personal Interview.

40 Pullin, *Design Meets Disability*.

41 Ibid., 3.

42 Goggin, "Adapting the Mobile Phone."

43 Jo Rabin and Charles McCathieNevile, "Mobile Web Best Practices 1.0," *World Wide Web Consortium*, July 29, 2008, http://www.w3.org/TR/mobile-bp/. Section 1.5.

44 Ibid., Section 8.

45 Alan Chuter, "Relationship between Mobile Web Best Practices 1.0 and Web Content Accessibility Guidelines 1.0, Version of," *World Wide Web Consortium: W3C Editor's Draft*, November 25, 2007, http://www.w3.org/2005/MWI/BPWG/Group/TaskForces/Accessibility/drafts/ED-mwbp-wcag-20071125.

46 Connors and Sullivan, "Mobile Web Application Best Practices: W3C Recommendation."

47 Ibid.

48 Alan Chuter to MWI BPWG Public, "Relationship to Other WCAG in BP2 Draft," February 18, 2008, http://lists.w3.org/Archives/Public/public-bpwg/2008Feb/0078.html.

49 Alan Chuter, Yeliz Yesilada, and Shawn Lawton Henry, "Shared Web Experiences: Barriers Common to Mobile Device Users and People with Disabilities," *World Wide Web Consortium: Web Accessibility Initiative*, January 22, 2013, http://www.w3.org/WAI/mobile/experiences.

50 Tom Worthington to MWI BPWG Public, "Re: Updated Mobile-Accessibility Documents," October 28, 2008, http://lists.w3.org/Archives/Public/public-bpwg/2008Oct/0060.html.

51 Shawn Lawton Henry and Justin Thorp, "Web Content Accessibility and Mobile Web: Making a Website Accessible Both for People with Disabilities and for Mo-

bile Devices," *World Wide Web Consortium: Web Accessibility Initiative*, January 22, 2013, http://www.w3.org/WAI/mobile/overlap.html.

52 Rabin and McCathieNevile, "Mobile Web Best Practices 1.0," 3.1.

53 Ibid., 2.6.

54 Ibid., 3.2.

55 Emily B. Hager, "IPad a Therapeutic Marvel for Disabled People," *The New York Times*, October 29, 2010, sec. N.Y. / Region, http://www.nytimes.com/2010/10/31/nyregion/31owen.html.

56 Hamilton, Personal Interview.

57 Watson, Personal Interview.

58 Howard Hill, "My iPhone Has Revolutionised My Reading," *The Guardian*, April 6, 2010, http://www.theguardian.com/education/2010/apr/06/iphone-makes-reading-books-easier.

59 Emily B. Hager, "IPad a Therapeutic Marvel for Disabled People," *The New York Times*, October 29, 2010, sec. N.Y. / Region, http://www.nytimes.com/2010/10/31/nyregion/31owen.html; Supraja Seshadri, "iPad Gives Voice to Kids with Autism," *CNN*, accessed July 17, 2013, http://www.cnn.com/2012/05/14/tech/gaming-gadgets/ipad-autism/index.html; "Apps for Autism: Communicating on the iPad," *60 Minutes* (CBS, October 23, 2011), http://www.cbsnews.com/8301-18560_162-20124225/apps-for-autism-communicating-on-the-ipad/.

60 "Mobile Accessibility Survey," *Paciello Group*, n.d., http://www.paciellogroup.com/mobile/.

61 Chong, Personal Interview.

62 Hager, "IPad a Therapeutic Marvel for Disabled People."

63 See the Appendix for more information about ethnographic research on this disability blogosphere.

64 Zittrain, *The Future of the Internet and How to Stop It*.

65 Rosemarie Garland-Thomson, "Siri and Me," *Huffington Post*, September 10, 2013, http://www.huffingtonpost.com/rosemarie-garlandthomson/siri-and--me_b_3896939.html.

66 Paul Walsh to MWI BPWG Public, "RE: Best Practices Document—Not Best Practices," July 22, 2005, http://lists.w3.org/Archives/Public/public-bpwg/2005Jul/0013.html.

67 Kevin Holley to MWI BPWG Public, "RE: Best Practices Document—Not Best Practices," July 22, 2005, http://lists.w3.org/Archives/Public/public-bpwg/2005Jul/0013.html.

68 Vanderheiden, Personal Interview, 2008.

69 Mace et al., *Accessible Environments*, 30.

70 Cynthia Waddell, "Applying the ADA to the Internet," *International Center for Disability Resources on the Internet*, June 17, 1998, http://www.icdri.org/CynthiaW/applying_the_ada_to_the_internet.htm.

71 Gregg C. Vanderheiden and Charles C. Lee, *Guidelines for the Design of Computers and Information Processing Systems to Increase Their Access by Persons with*

Disabilities. Version 2.0., National Institute of Handicapped Research Grants G0083C0020; G008300045, Guidelines Task Force of the Government–Industry Intitiative on Access to Computer Systems by Disabled Persons (Madison: Trace Center, University of Wisconsin–Madison, April 1986).

72 May, Personal Interview.

73 Wendy Chisholm and Matt May, *Universal Design for Web Applications: Web Applications That Reach Everyone.* (Sebastapol, Calif.: O'Reilly Media, 2008).

74 Jakob Nielsen, *Designing Web Usability.* Second edition (Indianapolis: New Riders Publishing, 2000).

75 Jakob Nielsen and Hoa Loranger, *Prioritizing Web Usability.* First edition (Indianapolis: New Riders, 2006), xix.

76 "Usability Evaluation Basics," October 8, 2013, http://www.usability.gov/what-and-why/usability-evaluation.html.

77 Wakefield, Personal Interview.

78 Abou-Zahra, Personal Interview.

79 Lembrée, Personal Interview (2013).

80 Shneiderman, "Preface," ix.

81 Vanderheiden, "Fundamental Principles and Priority Setting for Universal Usability."

82 "Designing for Inclusion," *World Wide Web Consortium: Web Accessibility Initiative,* August 31, 2012, http://www.w3.org/WAI/users/.

83 Davis, *Bending Over Backwards,* 32.

84 Hamraie, "Universal Design Research as a New Materialist Practice."

85 Dolmage, "Mapping Composition—Inviting Disability in the Front Door."

86 Raising the Floor, "GPII," *Global Public Inclusive Infrastructure,* 2011, gpii.net.

87 Gregg Vanderheiden and Jutta Treviranus, "Creating a Global Public Inclusive Infrastructure," in *Universal Access in Human-Computer Interaction. Design for All and eInclusion,* ed. Constantine Stephanidis, Lecture Notes in Computer Science 6765 (Springer Berlin Heidelberg, 2011), 517–26, http://link.springer.com/chapter/10.1007/978-3-642-21672-5_57.

88 Raising the Floor, "GPII."

89 Raising the Floor, "Benefits to Consumers," *Global Public Inclusive Infrastructure,* 2011, http://gpii.net/ConsumerBenefits.

90 Ibid.

91 Jim Tobias et al., "Making Progress on Global Inclusion (GPII)" (CSUN Annual International Technology & Persons with Disabilities Conference, San Diego, CA, February 28, 2013), www.csun.edu/cod/conference. Current sources of funding include major grants in Europe, Canada, and the United States as well as private contributions. Cloud4All is a large-scale project focused on the cloud computing elements of the GPII, funded by the European Commission. The Canadian government also provides matching funds for Cloud4All. The U.S. Department of Education is funding this project through several grants, including those awarded to Edcloud, and National Institute on Disability and Rehabilitation Research (NIDRR) grants made to the Trace Center, and Raising the Floor (the latter grant

also funded the Institute for the Study of Knowledge Management in Education, Inclusive Design Research Center, IBM, Inclusive Technologies, and WGBH's National Center for Accessible Media).

92 Raising the Floor, "Get Involved," *Global Public Inclusive Infrastructure*, 2011, http://gpii.net/content/get-involved.

93 Kelly et al., "Accessibility 2.0"; Ellis and Kent, *Disability and New Media*.

94 Kelly et al., "Accessibility 2.0."

95 Ellis and Kent, *Disability and New Media*, 59.

96 Raising the Floor, "GPII."

97 Zittrain, *The Future of the Internet and How to Stop It*.

98 See Meryl Alper's work for discussion of augmentive and alternative communication devices and apps. Alper, "Augmentative, Alternative, and Assistive"; Alper et al., "Reimagining the Good Life with Disability."

99 Apple, "Where There's a Need, There's an App," *Apple*, 2013, http://www.apple.com/accessibility/third-party/.

100 "Mobile Accessibility Survey."

101 Apple, "Accessibility Programming Guide for iOS," *iOS Developer Library*, 2012, https://developer.apple.com/library/ios/documentation/UserExperience/Conceptual/iPhoneAccessibility/Introduction/Introduction.html; "Accessibility Developer Checklist," *Android Developers*, 2013, http://developer.android.com/guide/topics/ui/accessibility/checklist.html.

102 Goggin, *Cell Phone Culture*, 207.

103 Galloway, *Protocol*, 172.

CHAPTER 4. CONTENT WARNINGS

1 Dardarian, Personal Interview; Feingold, Personal Interview.

2 "MLB Accessible Website Agreement," *Law Office of Lainey Feingold*, accessed July 30, 2014, http://lflegal.com/2010/02/mlb-agreement/.

3 Jason Woods, "Blind Sox Fan Gets MLB to Even Game Boston.com By Jason Woods, Globe Correspondent Like Any True Red Sox Fan, Brian Charlson Attends as Many Games as Possible," *Boston.com*, February 12, 2010, http://www.boston.com/yourtown/news/newton/2010/02/blind_sox_fan_gets_mlb_to_even.html.

4 "Entertainment Apps for the Blind and Visually Impaired: iPad/iPhone Apps AppList," *AppAdvice*, accessed November 18, 2013, http://appadvice.com/applists/show/fun-apps-for-blind-and-visually-impaired.

5 Meyrowitz, "Multiple Media Literacies."

6 Bucy and Newhagen, eds., *Media Access*.

7 Manovich, *The Language of New Media*.

8 Ibid.; Montfort and Bogost, *Racing the Beam*; Galloway, *Protocol*; Kirschenbaum, *Mechanisms*.

9 Chun, *Programmed Visions*, 1.

10 Sterne, *MP3*.

11 Shawn Lawton Henry, "Essential Components of Web Accessibility," *W3C Web Accessibility Initiative*, August 2005, http://www.w3.org/WAI/intro/components.php.

12 Manu Joseph, "Let the Poor Have Fun," *The New York Times*, September 16, 2013, sec. Opinion, http://www.nytimes.com/2013/09/17/opinion/let-the-poor-have-fun.html.

13 Warschauer, *Technology and Social Inclusion*, 90.

14 Lazar et al., "Improving Web Accessibility"; Lilly and Van Fleet, "Wired But Not Connected," 5; Ellison, "Assessing the Accessibility of Fifty United States Government Web Pages"; Farrelly, "Practitioner Barriers to Diffusion and Implementation of Web Accessibility."

15 Compaine and Weinraub, "Universal Access to Online Services," 150.

16 Ibid., 172.

17 Telecommunications Act of 1996, Pub. L. 104–104, 110 Stat. 56 (1996). § 3(a)(2)(48).

18 Telecommunications Act of 1996, Pub. L. 104–104, 110 Stat. 56 (1996). § 3(a)(2)(41).

19 Megan Totka, "Social Media, Disabilities and You | Disability.Blog," November 6, 2013, http://usodep.blogs.govdelivery.com/2013/11/06/social-media-disabilities-and-you/#more-7579.

20 Ibid.

21 Miguel Helft, "Google to Caption YouTube Videos—NYTimes.com," *The New York Times*, November 19, 2009.

22 Hilmes, *Radio Voices*; Hoynes, *Public Television for Sale*; Ouellette, *Viewers Like You?*

23 Ouellette, *Viewers Like You?*, 211.

24 Gunkel, "Second Thoughts," 507.

25 DiMaggio et al., "Digital Inequality"; Hargittai, "Digital Na(t)ives? Variation in Internet Skills and Uses among Members of the 'Net Generation'"; Ito et al., *Hanging Out, Messing Around, and Geeking Out*; Tripp, "'The Computer Is Not for You to Be Looking Around, It Is for Schoolwork'"; van Dijk, *The Deepening Divide*.

26 Hartley, *Uses of Television*, 159.

27 Jacka, "'Democracy as Defeat'"; Marwick, *Status Update*; Ratto and Boler, eds., *DIY Citizenship*.

28 Ratto and Boler, *DIY Citizenship*.

29 Goggin and Newell, *Digital Disability*.

30 Oliver, "The Social Model in Context"; Siebers, *Disability Theory*, Corporealities.

31 Fiske, *Understanding Popular Culture*, 75.

32 Nakamura, "Interrogating the Digital Divide."

33 Long, "Introducing the New and Improved Americans with Disabilities Act," 217.

34 McRuer and Mollow, *Sex and Disability*.

35 Disability is also largely invisible in industrial systems of media production. Lack of awareness in the gaming industries often means that even basic accessibility features are left out, and people with disabilities are rarely considered as a target audience, or even as part of a mainstream audience. Furthermore, the dearth of visible people with disabilities within game development further exacerbates many of these problems, as in the case of any underrepresented group in media production.

36 "AbleGamers Holiday Gift Guide for Gamers with Disabilities | The AbleGamers Charity," accessed July 31, 2014, http://www.ablegamers.com/ablegamers-news/ ablegamers-2013-holiday-gift-guide. AbleGamers. 2014. http://www.ablegamers. com/ablegamers-news/ablegamers-holiday-gift-guide-for-gamers-with-disabilities.

37 Ibid.

38 Mark C. Barlet and Steve D. Spohn, *Includification: A Practical Guide to Game Accessibility* (The AbleGamers Foundation, 2012), 9.

39 Cassandra Khaw, "Ablegamers Foundation Introduces Includification—The Next Step in Bringing Gaming to Everyone," *G4tv.com*, September 12, 2012, http:// www.g4tv.com/thefeed/blog/post/727870/ablegamers-foundation-introduces- includification-the-next-step-in-bringing-gaming-to-everyone/.

40 Barlet and Spohn, *Includification*, 3.

41 Ibid., 1.

42 Participant 44, Personal Interview.

43 "Characters," *Katawa Shoujo*, accessed June 15, 2014, http://www.katawa-shoujo. com/characters.php.

44 McRuer and Mollow, *Sex and Disability*.

45 Samuels, "Critical Divides."

46 McRuer, *Crip Theory*.

47 Kafer, "Amputated Desire, Resistant Desire."

48 Siebers, "A Sexual Culture for Disabled People."

49 Ibid., 39.

50 Shuttleworth and Mona, "Introduction."

51 Shuttleworth, "Bridging Theory and Experience," 61.

52 Long, "Introducing the New and Improved Americans with Disabilities Act."

53 Fiske, *Reading the Popular*, 80.

54 Goldberg, Personal Interview.

55 Clark, Personal Interview.

56 Goldberg, Personal Interview.

57 Ellcessor, "Captions On, Off, on TV, Online."

58 Ellcessor, "Bridging Disability Divides."

59 Pub.L. 111–274.

60 Participant 4, Personal Interview.

61 Participant 17, Personal Interview.

62 Ellcessor, "<ALT='Textbooks'>."

63 As explained by Linda Dardarian, an attorney who works with Lainey Feingold, LLC, and was involved in representing the plaintiffs in this case, California's Unruh Civil Rights Act and Disabled Persons Act (California Civil Code, Sections 51 and 54, respectively), operate in the same spirit as the ADA but are broader in scope, making them more useful in this particular case.

64 Dardarian, Personal Interview. See also full decision, *Greater Los Angeles Agency on Deafness, Inc.; Daniel Jacob; Edward Kelly; Jennifer Olson, on behalf of them- selves and all others similarly situated v. Cable News Network, Inc., incorrectly sued*

as Time Warner Inc., No. 12–14807, Opinion Filed 2/5/14, written by Judge M. Margaret McKeown.

65 "Amazon's Kindle 2 Pits Authors Versus the Blind | Gadget Lab," *WIRED*, April 7, 2009, http://www.wired.com/2009/04/visually-challe/.

66 Roy Blount Jr., "The Kindle Swindle?," *The New York Times*, February 25, 2009, sec. Opinion, http://www.nytimes.com/2009/02/25/opinion/25blount.html.

67 Ibid.

68 "NFB Kindle 2009," n.d., https://nfb.org/node/1184.

69 "No Text to Speech in Amazon's New Paperwhite Kindles: Why? To Push Us toward Fire Tablets and Boost Amazon-Owned Audible? | LibraryCity," accessed May 29, 2014, http://librarycity.org/?p=5583.

70 "Neil Gaiman's Journal: Quick Argument Summary," accessed May 29, 2014, http://journal.neilgaiman.com/2009/02/quick-argument-summary.html.

71 Barthes, *Image-Music-Text*; Derrida, *Positions*; Fish, *Is There a Text in This Class?*; Hall, "Encoding/Decoding"; Foucault, "What Is an Author?"

72 Fiske, *Understanding Popular Culture.*

73 Hackett and Parmanto, "A Longitudinal Evaluation of Accessibility"; Murphy et al., "An Empirical Investigation into the Difficulties Experienced by Visually Impaired Internet Users."

74 Ibid.

75 Murphy et al., "An Empirical Investigation into the Difficulties Experienced by Visually Impaired Internet Users," 6.

76 Ellcessor, "<ALT='Textbooks'>."

77 Alternative text is an accessibility feature in which the HTML carries a textual description of an image or its function, to be read when the technology encounters the image in the markup.

78 Patrick H. Lauke, "Re: Undoubtedly, an Oversimplification . . . ," May 2, 2014, http://lists.w3.org/Archives/Public/w3c-wai-ig/2014AprJun/0129.html.

79 Ibid.

80 Chun, *Programmed Visions*; Galloway, *Protocol*; Gillespie, Boczkowski, and Foot, *Media Technologies.*

81 Ted Striphas, "Algorithmic Culture. 'Culture Now Has Two Audiences: People and Machines': A Conversation with Ted Striphas," April 30, 2014, https://medium.com/futurists-views/2bdaa404f643.

82 Downey, "Making Media Work."

83 Downey, *Closed Captioning*; Downey, "Making Media Work," 145.

84 Downey, "Making Media Work," 158.

85 Participant 40, Personal Interview.

86 De Linde and Kay, *The Semiotics of Subtitling.*

87 Ellcessor, "Captions On, Off, on TV, Online."

88 De Linde and Kay, *The Semiotics of Subtitling*, 17.

89 Gershon, "Publish and Be Damned"; Gill, "'Life Is a Pitch'"; Marwick, *Status Update*; Neff, *Venture Labor.*

90 Hartley, *Uses of Television*, 161.

91 Goggin and Newell, *Digital Disability*.

92 Charlton, *Nothing About Us Without Us*; Linton, *Claiming Disability*.

CHAPTER 5. THE NET EXPERIENCE

1 Tommy Edison, *How Blind People Use Instagram*, YouTube, 2012, https://www.youtube.com/watch?feature=player_embedded&v=P1e7ZCKQfMA#!.

2 Recall similar media artifacts about accessibility for an able-bodied audience described in chapter 2. As in those cases, this illustrates the non-normativity of Edison's user position; equally, however, as a first-person account of using digital media, it is communicative of his experience in a way that many of those examples were not.

3 Williams, *Keywords*, 127.

4 Merleau-Ponty, *Phenomenology of Perception*.

5 Farman, *Mobile Interface Theory*, 33.

6 Ibid., 13.

7 Garland-Thomson, "Feminist Disability Studies"; Kafer, *Feminist, Queer, Crip*; Siebers, *Disability Theory*.

8 Coleman, *Coding Freedom*, Kindle loc 977–79.

9 Jay Dolmage, "Mapping Composition," 14.

10 Vanderheiden, Personal Interview (2011).

11 Burrell, *Invisible Users*, 20.

12 Online extensions of this book are available at http://scalar.usc.edu/works/restricted-access/index. This site includes links and clips of media texts discussed in the book, additional information about ethnographic and interview research, and links to accessibility resources.

13 Burgess, "All Your Chocoloate Rain Are Belong to Us"; Jenkins, Ford, and Green, *Spreadable Media*.

14 Willis, Personal Interview.

15 Murphy et al., "An Empirical Investigation into the Difficulties Experienced by Visually Impaired Internet Users."

16 Dobransky and Hargittai, "The Disability Divide in Internet Access and Use"; Murphy et al., "An Empirical Investigation into the Difficulties Experienced by Visually Impaired Internet Users."

17 Gerber, "The Benefits of and Barriers to Computer Use for Individuals Who Are Visually Impaired," 545.

18 Theofanos and Redish, "Bridging the Gap."

19 Jarashow, Personal Interview.

20 Dobransky and Hargittai, "The Disability Divide in Internet Access and Use," 7.

21 s. e. smith, "Access Is a Twofold Issue," *This Ain't Livin'*, May 3, 2011, http://meloukhia.net/2011/05/access_is_a_twofold_issue/.

The lowercase spelling is used consistently by s. e. smith in writing across the web and other publications and thus is used in this book, as well.

22 Farrelly, "Access Denied," 30.

23 Burgess, "All Your Chocolate Rain Are Belong to Us?," 8.

24 Thoreau, "Ouch! An Examination of the Self-representation of Disabled People on the Internet."

25 Van Dijck, *The Culture of Connectivity*.

26 Participant 17, Personal Interview.

27 Apple. "Common App Rejections." Apple Developer Program. 2015. https://developer.apple.com/app-store/review/rejections/

28 Glenda Watson Hyatt, "WordPress Misses the #1 Accessibility Tip," *Do It Myself Blog—Glenda Watson Hyatt*, September 28, 2009, http://www.doitmyselfblog.com/2009/wordpress-misses-the-1-accessibility-tip/.

29 Kacelnik, Personal Interview.

30 smith, Personal Interview.

31 Willis, Personal Interview.

32 Hamilton, Personal Interview.

33 paristhroughthewindow, "Tumblr Accessibility Annoyance #1," *Fuck Yeah, Accessibility*, May 10, 2011, http://fuckyeahaccessibility.tumblr.com/post/5361428092/tumblr-accessibility-annoyance-1.

34 smith, Personal Interview.

35 Stacey Milburn, *CripChick*, accessed June 4, 2011, http://blog.cripchick.com/archives/9092.

36 David N. Wallace, "Lifekludger—Disability: Technology: Life," *Lifekludger: Gadgets, Hacks Kludges for People Living with Disability*, accessed July 18, 2014, http://lifekludger.com/.

37 David N. Wallace, "About Lifekludger," *Lifekludger: Gadgets, Hacks Kludges for People Living with Disability*, accessed July 18, 2014, http://lifekludger.net/about/.

38 Watson, Personal Interview.

39 Coleman, *Coding Freedom*, Kindle loc 250–51.

40 Coleman, *Coding Freedom*, Kindle loc 258–60.

41 Ibid., Kindle loc 497–505.

42 "Diversity Statement," *Dreamwidth Studios*, May 22, 2011, http://www.dreamwidth.org/legal/diversity.

43 Denise Paolucci, "Assistive Tech (semi-) Poll," *Dreamwidth Accessibility*, May 11, 2012, http://dw-accessibility.dreamwidth.org/21053.html?thread=192061.

44 "YouTube Wants You to Tell on Publishers without Closed Captions," *GigaOM*, October 8, 2012, http://gigaom.com/2012/10/08/youtube-fcc-closed-captions/.

45 Ellcessor, "<ALT='Textbooks'>."

46 Waters, Personal Interview.

47 smith, Personal Interview.

48 Marwick, *Status Update*, 13.

49 Gershon, "Publish and Be Damned," 72.

50 Ibid., 73.

51 Walters, *The Tolerance Trap*, 2.

52 Ibid., 11.
53 Participant 18, Personal Interview.
54 Adam and Kreps, "Disability and Discourses of Web Accessibility. "
55 smith, Personal Interview.
56 "Sound Transcriptions and Accessability," *Fuck Yeah, Accessibility*, 2011, http://fuckyeahaccessibility.tumblr.com/post/5314469269.
57 smith, Personal Interview.
58 "The Internet & Disability: Tales of a Special 'Special Needs' Person," *Crippie's Corner*, May 1, 2011, http://crippiescorner.blogspot.com/2011/05/internet-disability.html.
59 Henry, Personal Interview.
60 Christina, Personal Interview.
61 Kacelnik, Personal Interview.
62 Walters, *The Tolerance Trap*, 259.
63 smith, Personal Interview.
64 Walters, *The Tolerance Trap*, 262.
65 As of 2014, the Blind Photographers blog is no longer online. The Flickr group and individual pages, however, remain active.
66 Garland-Thomson, "Staring at the Other"; Mirzoeff, "Blindness and Art."
67 Barnes and Mercer, *Exploring Disability*, 15.
68 Brown, "What Is Disability Culture?"
69 Linton, *Claiming Disability*, 5.
70 Kuppers, *Disability Culture and Community Performance*.
71 Harrigan, "Wheelie Catholic."
72 Crenshaw, "Mapping the Margins."
73 Haraway, "Situated Knowledges."
74 Schalk, "Coming to Claim Crip."
75 Walters, *The Tolerance Trap*, 261.
76 Gilroy, *After Empire*, 67.

CONCLUSION
1 Ellis and Kent, *Disability and New Media*.
2 Ibid., 66–67.
3 Titchkosky, *The Question of Access*.
4 Ellis and Kent, *Disability and New Media*, 142.
5 Downey, *Closed Captioning*; Strauss, *A New Civil Right*.
6 Hamraie, "Universal Design Research as a New Materialist Practice."
7 Williamson, "Getting a Grip."
8 Erevelles, "Thinking with Disability Studies."
9 "WAI Markup Guidelines Working Group Charter," August 1997, http://www.w3.org/WAI/GL/charter.html.
10 Jenkins, Ford, and Green, *Spreadable Media*, 190.
11 Brabham, "Crowdsourcing as a Model for Problem Solving."
12 Jansen, Personal Interview.

13 Ibid.

14 Brabham, "Crowdsourcing as a Model for Problem Solving," 88.

15 Gill Valentine and Tracey Skelton, "'An Umbilical Cord to the World': The Role of the Internet in D/deaf People's Information and Communication Practices."

16 Lembrée, Personal Interview (2012).

17 Dahlgren, "The Internet, Public Spheres, and Political Communication"; Hinck, "Theorizing a Public Engagement Keystone."

18 "About | Fix the Web," August 11, 2011, http://fixtheweb.net/about.

19 Bradbrook, Personal Interview.

20 Ibid.

21 Kaplan, Personal Interview.

22 Ricky Buchanan, "Did You Catch Accessibility Too?," Dreamwidth Accessibility, April 25, 2013, http://dw-accessibility.dreamwidth.org/23872.html.

23 Ibid.

24 Kaplan, Personal Interview.

25 Ibid.

26 Burrell, Invisible Users, 9.

27 Wagner and Lothian, "Access and Fandom."

28 Kuppers, Disability Culture and Community Performance, 231.

29 Jarman and Kafer, "Guest Editors' Introduction."

30 Hartley, Uses of Television.

31 Dahlgren, "The Internet, Public Spheres, and Political Communication."

32 Giroux, "The Crisis of Public Values in the Age of the New Media."

33 Ratto and Boler, eds., DIY Citizenship, 23.

34 Hinck, "Theorizing a Public Engagement Keystone."

35 Dunbar-Hester, "Radical Inclusion?"; Milberry, "(Re)making the Internet."

36 Dunbar-Hester, "Radical Inclusion?," 85–86.

37 Titchkosky, The Question of Access, 231.

BIBLIOGRAPHY

Adam, Alison, and David Kreps. "Disability and Discourses of Web Accessibility." *Information, Communication & Society* 12, no. 7 (October 2009): 1041–58. doi:10.1080/13691180802552940.

Ali-Hasan, Noor F., and Lada A. Adamic. "Expressing Social Relationships on the Blog through Links and Comments." ICWSM Conference. Boulder, Colo., 2007.

Alper, Meryl. "Augmentative, Alternative, and Assistive: Reimagining the History of Mobile Computing and Disability." *IEEE Annals of the History of Computing* 37, no. 1 (January 2015): 93–96. doi:10.1109/MAHC.2015.3.

Alper, Meryl, Elizabeth Ellcessor, Katie Ellis, and Gerard Goggin. "Reimagining the Good Life with Disability: Communication, New Technology, and Humane Connections." In *Communication and the Good Life*, ed. H. Wang. ICA Annual Conference Theme Book Series. New York: Peter Lang, 2015.

Andrejevic, Mark. "The Work of Being Watched: Interactive Media and the Exploitation of Self-Disclosure." *Critical Studies in Media Communication* 19, no. 2 (June 2002): 230–48.

Ankerson, Megan Sapnar. "Dot-Com Design: Cultural Production of the Commercial Web in the Internet Bubble (1993–2003)." Diss., University of Wisconsin–Madison, 2010.

———. "Writing Web Histories with an Eye on the Analog Past." *New Media & Society* 14, no. 3 (2012). doi:10.1177/1461444811414834.

Balsamo, Anne. *Designing Culture: The Technological Imagination at Work*. Durham, N.C.: Duke University Press, 2011.

Barnes, Colin, and Geof Mercer. *Exploring Disability*. Second edition. Cambridge, UK; Malden, Mass.: Polity Press, 2010.

Barthes, Roland. *Image-Music-Text*. Trans. Stephen Heath. New York: Hill and Wang, 1978.

Berners-Lee, Tim, with Mark Fischetti. *Weaving the Web: The Original Design and Ultimate Destiny of the World Wide Web*. First edition. San Francisco: HarperOne, 1999.

Boehlert, Eric. *Bloggers on the Bus: How the Internet Changed Politics and the Press*. New York: Free Press, 2010.

Bolter, Jay David, and Richard Grusin. *Remediation: Understanding New Media*. First edition. Cambridge, Mass.: MIT Press, 2000.

Brabham, Daren C. "Crowdsourcing as a Model for Problem Solving: An Introduction and Cases." *Convergence: The International Journal of Research into New Media Technologies* 14, no. 1 (February 1, 2008): 75–90. doi:10.1177/1354856507084420.

Brown, Steven E. "What Is Disability Culture?" *Disability Studies Quarterly* 22, no. 2 (April 15, 2002). http://dsq-sds.org/article/view/343.

Brueggemann, Brenda Jo. *Deaf Subjects: Between Identities and Places.* New York: New York University Press, 2009.

Bruns, Axel. *Blogs, Wikipedia, Second Life, and Beyond: From Production to Produsage.* Digital Formations. New York: Peter Lang, 2008.

Brys, Catherine M., and Wim Vanderbauwhede. "Communication Challenges in the W3C's Web Content Accessibility Guidelines." *Technical Communication* 53, no. 1 (2006): 60–78.

Bucy, Erik P., and John E. Newhagen, eds. *Media Access: Social and Psychological Dimensions of New Technology Use.* Mahwah, N.J.: Lawrence Erlbaum Associates, 2004.

Burgess, Jean. "All Your Chocolate Rain Are Belong to Us?" In *Video Vortex Reader: Responses to YouTube*, ed. Geert Lovink and Sabine Niederer, 101–10. Institute of Network Cultures 4. Amsterdam: Institute of Network Cultures, 2008.

Burgess, Jean, and Joshua Green. *YouTube.* New York: Polity Press, 2009.

Burrell, Jenna. *Invisible Users: Youth in the Internet Cafés of Urban Ghana.* Cambridge, Mass.: MIT Press, 2012.

Busch, Lawrence. *Standards: Recipes for Reality.* Cambridge, Mass.: MIT Press, 2011.

Carpentier, Nico. *Media and Participation.* New York: Intellect Ltd., 2011.

Charlton, James I. *Nothing About Us Without Us: Disability Oppression and Empowerment.* First edition. Berkeley: University of California Press, 2000.

Chisholm, Wendy, Gregg Vanderheiden, and Ian Jacobs. "Web Content Accessibility Guidelines 1.0." *Interactions* 8, no. 4 (July 2001): 35–54.

Christian, Aymar Jean. "Fandom as Industrial Response: Producing Identity in an Independent Web Series." *Transformative Works and Cultures* 8 (2011). http://journal.transformativeworks.org/index.php/twc/article/view/250/237.

Chun, Wendy Hui Kyong. *Control and Freedom: Power and Paranoia in the Age of Fiber Optics.* Cambridge, Mass.: MIT Press, 2008.

——. *Programmed Visions: Software and Memory.* Reprint edition. Cambridge, Mass.: MIT Press, 2013.

Classen, Steven D. *Watching Jim Crow: The Struggles over Mississippi TV, 1955–1969.* Durham, N.C.: Duke University Press, 2004.

Coleman, E. Gabriella. *Coding Freedom: The Ethics and Aesthetics of Hacking.* Princeton, N.J.: Princeton University Press, 2012.

——. "Ethnographic Approaches to Digital Media." *Annual Review of Anthropology* 39 (October 2010): 487–505.

Compaine, Benjamin M., and Mitchell J. Weinraub. "Universal Access to Online Services: An Examination of the Issue." In *The Digital Divide*, ed. Benjamin M. Compaine, 147–77. Cambridge, Mass.: MIT Press, 2001.

Connors, Adam, and Bryan Sullivan, eds. "Mobile Web Application Best Practices: W3C Recommendation." World Wide Web Consortium, December 14, 2010. http://www.w3.org/TR/mwabp/.

Coombs, Norman. "Liberation Technology: Equal Access via Computer Communication." *EDU Magazine*, Spring 1992. http://people.rit.edu/easi/lib/oppo1.htm.

Cousineau, Phil. *The Painted Word: A Treasure Chest of Remarkable Words and Their Origins*. Berkeley, Calif.: Viva Editions, 2012.

Crenshaw, Kimberlé. "Mapping the Margins: Intersectionality, Identity Politics, and Violence Against Women of Color." *Stanford Law Review* 43 (1991): 1241–99.

D'Acci, Julie. "Cultural Studies, Television Studies, and the Crisis in the Humanities." In *Television After TV: Essays on a Medium in Transition*, ed. Lynn Spigel and Jan Olsson, 418–45. Console-Ing Passions. Durham, N.C.: Duke University Press, 2004.

Dahlgren, Peter. "The Internet, Public Spheres, and Political Communication: Dispersion and Deliberation." *Political Communication* 22, no. 2 (April 2005): 147–62. doi:10.1080/10584600590933160.

———. "Television, the Public Sphere and Civic Cultures." In *A Companion to Television*, ed. Janet Wasko. Hoboken, N.J.: Wiley, 2010.

Davis, Lennard J. *Bending Over Backwards: Essays on Disability and the Body*. New York: New York University Press, 2002.

De Linde, Zoé, and Neil Kay. *The Semiotics of Subtitling*. New York: Routledge, 1999.

Derrida, Jacques, and Alan Bass. *Positions*. First edition. Chicago: University of Chicago Press, 1982.

Deuze, Mark. "Participation, Remediation, Bricolage: Considering Principal Components of a Digital Culture." *The Information Society* 22, no. 2 (2006): 63–75.

DiMaggio, Paul, Eszter Hargittai, Coral Celeste, and Steven Shafer. "Digital Inequality: From Unequal Access to Differentiated Use." In *Social Inequality*, ed. Kathryn M. Neckerman, 355–400. New York: Sage, 2004.

Dobransky, Kerry, and Eszter Hargittai. "The Disability Divide in Internet Access and Use." *Information, Communication & Society* 9, no. 3 (2006): 313–34.

Dolmage, Jay. "Mapping Composition—Inviting Disability in the Front Door." In *Disability and the Teaching of Writing: A Critical Sourcebook*, ed. Cynthia Lewiecki-Wilson and Brenda Jo Brueggemann, 14–27. Boston: Bedford/St. Martin's, 2008.

Downey, Gregory John. *Closed Captioning: Subtitling, Stenography, and the Digital Convergence of Text with Television*. Baltimore: Johns Hopkins University Press, 2008.

———. "Making Media Work: Time, Space, Identity, and Labor in the Analysis of Information and Communication Infrastructures." In *Media Technologies: Essays on Communication, Materiality, and Society*, ed. Tarleton Gillespie, Pablo J. Boczkowski, and Kirsten A. Foot, 141–66. Cambridge, Mass.: MIT Press, 2014.

Du Gay, Paul. *Doing Cultural Studies: The Story of the Sony Walkman*. Thousand Oaks, Calif.: Sage, 1997.

Dunbar-Hester, Christina. "Radical Inclusion? Locating Accountability in Technical DIY." In *DIY Citizenship: Critical Making and Social Media*, ed. Matt Ratto and Megan Boler, 75–88. Cambridge, Mass.: MIT Press, 2014.

Easton, Catherine. "The Web Content Accessibility Guidelines 2.0: An Analysis of Industry Self-Regulation." *International Journal of Law and Information Technology* 19, no. 1 (March 20, 2011): 74–93. doi:10.1093/ijlit/eaq015.

Ellcessor, Elizabeth. "<ALT='Textbooks'>: Web Accessibility Myths as Negotiated Industrial Lore." *Critical Studies in Media Communication* 31, no. 5 (2014): 448–63. doi:10.1080/15295036.2014.919660.

———. "Bridging Disability Divides." *Information, Communication & Society* 13, no. 3 (April 2010): 289–308. doi:10.1080/13691180903456546.

———. "Captions On, Off, on TV, Online: Accessibility and Search Engine Optimization in Online Closed Captioning." *Television & New Media* 13, no. 4 (July 1, 2012): 329–52. doi:10.1177/1527476411425251.

Ellis, Kate, and Mike Kent. *Disability and New Media*. New York: Routledge, 2010. http://www.routledge.com/books/details/9780415871358/.

Ellison, Jim. "Assessing the Accessibility of Fifty United States Government Web Pages." *First Monday* (2004). http://www.firstmonday.org/issues/issue9_7/ellison/index.html.

Ensmenger, N. L. "The 'Question of Professionalism' in the Computer Fields." *IEEE Annals of the History of Computing* 23, no. 4 (December 2001): 56–74. doi:10.1109/85.969964.

Erevelles, Nirmala. "Thinking with Disability Studies." *Disability Studies Quarterly* 34, no. 2 (March 18, 2014). http://dsq-sds.org/article/view/4248.

Farman, Jason. *Mobile Interface Theory: Embodied Space and Locative Media*. New York: Routledge, 2012.

Farrelly, Glen. "Access Denied: Overcoming Barriers to Adoption and Implementation of Web Accessibility." M.A., Royal Roads University (Canada), 2010.

———. "Practitioner Barriers to Diffusion and Implementation of Web Accessibility." *Technology & Disability* 23, no. 4 (November 2011): 223–32.

Fish, Stanley Eugene. *Is There a Text in This Class?* Cambridge, Mass.: Harvard University Press, 1980.

Fiske, John. *Reading the Popular*. New York: Routledge, 1989.

———. *Understanding Popular Culture*. Boston: Unwin Hyman, 1989.

Foucault, Michel. *The Archaeology of Knowledge & The Discourse on Language*. Reprint edition. New York: Vintage, 1982.

———. *The Birth of Biopolitics: Lectures at the Collège de France, 1978-1979*. First edition. New York: Palgrave Macmillan, 2008.

———. "What Is an Author?" *Partisan Review* 4 (1975): 603–14.

Fox, Susannah. *Americans Living with Disability and Their Technology Profile*. Washington: Pew Internet & American Life Project, January 21, 2011. http://www.pewinternet.org/Reports/2011/Disability.aspx.

Fraser, Nancy. "Rethinking the Public Sphere: A Contribution to the Critique of Actually Existing Democracy." *Social Text*, no. 25/26 (January 1, 1990): 56–80. doi:10.2307/466240.

Friedman, Ted. *Electric Dreams: Computers in American Culture*. New York: New York University Press, 2005.

Fuller, Matthew, ed. *Software Studies: A Lexicon*. Cambridge, Mass.: MIT Press, 2008.

Galloway, Alexander R. *Protocol: How Control Exists After Decentralization*. Cambridge, Mass.: MIT Press, 2004.

Garland-Thomson, Rosemarie. *Extraordinary Bodies: Figuring Physical Disability in American Culture and Literature*. New York: Columbia University Press, 1997.

———. "Feminist Disability Studies." *Signs: Journal of Women in Culture & Society* 30, no. 2 (2005): 1557–87.

———. "Staring at the Other." *Disability Studies Quarterly* 25, no. 4 (October 15, 2005). http://www.dsq-sds.org/article/view/610/787.

Gerber, E. "The Benefits of and Barriers to Computer Use for Individuals Who Are Visually Impaired." *Journal of Visual Impairment & Blindness* 97, no. 9 (2003): 536–50.

Gershon, Ilana. "Publish and Be Damned: New Media Publics and Neoliberal Risk." *Ethnography* 15, no. 1 (March 1, 2014): 70–87. doi:10.1177/1466138113502514.

Gill, Rosalind. "'Life Is a Pitch': Managing the Self in New Media Work." In *Managing Media Work*, ed. Mark Deuze, 249–62. London: Sage, 2010.

Gillespie, Tarleton. "The Stories Digital Tools Tell." In *New Media: Theories and Practices of Digitextuality*, ed. Anna Everett and John Thornton Caldwell, 107–26. AFI Film Readers. New York: Routledge, 2003.

Gillespie, Tarleton, Pablo J. Boczkowski, and Kirsten A. Foot. *Media Technologies: Essays on Communication, Materiality, and Society*. Cambridge, Mass.: MIT Press, 2014.

Gilroy, Paul. *After Empire: Melancholia or Convivial Culture? Multiculture or Postcolonial Melancholia*. First edition. London: Routledge, 2004.

Giroux, Henry A. "The Crisis of Public Values in the Age of the New Media." *Critical Studies in Media Communication* 28, no. 1 (2011): 8–29.

Goggin, Gerard. "Adapting the Mobile Phone: The iPhone and Its Consumption." *Continuum* 23, no. 2 (2009): 231–44. doi:10.1080/10304310802710546.

———. *Cell Phone Culture: Mobile Technology in Everyday Life*. New edition. Routledge, 2006.

Goggin, Gerard, and Christopher Newell. "The Business of Digital Disability." In *Foucault and the Government of Disability*, ed. Shelley Tremain, 261–77. Ann Arbor: University of Michigan Press, 2005. http://site.ebrary.com/id/10373071.

———. *Digital Disability: The Social Construction of Disability in New Media*. Critical Media Studies. Lanham, Md.: Rowman & Littlefield, 2003.

Goggin, Gerard, and Tim Noonan. "Blogging Disabilty: The Interface between New Cultural Movements and Internet Technology." In *The Uses of Blogs*, ed. Axel Bruns and Joanne Jacobs, 161–72. New York: Peter Lang, 2006.

Google, *Automatic Captions in YouTube Demo*, 2009, http://www.youtube.com/watch?v=kTvHIDKLFqc.

Grossberg, Lawrence. *Cultural Studies in the Future Tense*. Durham, N.C.: Duke University Press, 2010.

Gunkel, David J. "Second Thoughts: Toward a Critique of the Digital Divide." *New Media & Society* 5, no. 4 (December 1, 2003): 499–522. doi:10.1177/146144480354003.

Hackett, Stephanie, and Bambang Parmanto. "A Longitudinal Evaluation of Accessibility: Higher Education Web Sites." *Internet Research* 15, no. 3 (2005): 281–94.

Hall, Stuart. "Encoding/Decoding." In *Media and Cultural Studies: Keyworks*, ed. Meenakshi Gigi Durham and Douglas Kellner, 166–76. Malden, Mass.: Blackwell, 2001.

———. On Postmodernism and Articulation." In *Stuart Hall: Critical Dialogues in Cultural Studies*, ed. David Morley and Kuan-Hsing Chen, 131–50. London: Routledge, 1996.

Hall, Stuart, Doreen Massey, and Michael Rustin. "After Neoliberalism? The Kilburn Manifesto." *Soundings*, April 29, 2013. http://www.lwbooks.co.uk/journals/soundings/pdfs/manifestoframingstatement.pdf.

Haller, Beth. *Representing Disability in an Ableist World: Essays on Mass Media*. Louisville, Ky.: Avocado Press, 2010.

Hamraie, Aimi. "Universal Design Research as a New Materialist Practice." *Disability Studies Quarterly* 32, no. 4 (2012). http://dsq-sds.org/article/view/3246/3185.

Haraway, Donna. "Situated Knowledges: The Science Question in Feminism and the Privilege of Partial Perspective." *Feminist Studies* 14, no. 3 (October 1, 1988): 575–99. doi:10.2307/3178066.

Hargittai, Eszter. "Digital Na(t)ives? Variation in Internet Skills and Uses among Members of the 'Net Generation'*." *Sociological Inquiry* 80, no. 1 (2010): 92–113.

Harper, Douglas. "'Kit' n1," *Online Etymology Dictionary*, n.d., http://www.etymonline.com/.

Harrigan, Ruth. "Wheelie Catholic." *Disability Studies Quarterly* 27, no. 1/2 (March 15, 2007). http://dsq-sds.org/article/view/3.

Hartley, John. *Uses of Television*. London: Routledge, 1999.

Havens, Timothy. *Black Television Travels: African American Media Around the Globe*. New York: New York University Press, 2013.

Havens, Timothy, Amanda D. Lotz, and Serra Tinic. "Critical Media Industry Studies: A Research Approach." *Communication, Culture & Critique* 2, no. 2 (2009): 234–53. doi:10.1111/j.1753-9137.2009.01037.x.

Herndon, April. "Disparate but Disabled: Fat Embodiment and Disability Studies." In *Feminist Disability Studies*, ed. Kim Q. Hall, 245–62. Bloomington: Indiana University Press, 2011.

Hilmes, Michele. *Radio Voices: American Broadcasting, 1922–1952*. First edition. Minneapolis: Minnesota University Press, 1997.

Hinck, Ashley. "Theorizing a Public Engagement Keystone: Seeing Fandom's Integral Connection to Civic Engagement through the Case of the Harry Potter Alliance." *Transformative Works and Cultures* 10 (2012). doi:10.3983/twc.v10i0.311.

Hine, Christine. *Virtual Ethnography*. Thousand Oaks, Calif.: Sage, 2000.

Hoynes, William. *Public Television for Sale: Media, the Market, and the Public Sphere*. Boulder, Colo.: Westview Press, 1994.

Ito, Mizuko, Heather A. Horst, Judd Antin, et al. *Hanging Out, Messing Around, and Geeking Out: Kids Living and Learning with New Media*. Cambridge, Mass.: MIT Press, 2013.

Jacka, Elizabeth. "'Democracy as Defeat': The Impotence of Arguments for Public Service Broadcasting." *Television & New Media* 4, no. 2 (May 1, 2003): 177–91. doi:10.1177/1527476402250675.

Jarman, Michelle, and Alison Kafer. "Guest Editors' Introduction. Growing Disability Studies: Politics of Access, Politics of Collaboration." *Disability Studies Quarterly* 34, no. 2 (March 27, 2014). http://dsq-sds.org/article/view/4286.

Jenkins, Henry. *Convergence Culture: Where Old and New Media Collide.* New York: New York University Press, 2006.

Jenkins, Henry, Sam Ford, and Joshua Green. *Spreadable Media: Creating Value and Meaning in a Networked Culture.* Postmillennial Pop. New York: New York University Press, 2013.

Jenkins, Henry, Ravi Purushotma, Katherine Clinton, et al. *Confronting the Challenges of Participatory Culture: Media Education for the 21st Century.* Building the Field of Digital Media and Learning. The John D. and Catherine T. MacArthur Foundation, 2005. http://www.newmedialiteracies.org/files/working/NMLWhitePaper.pdf.

Johnson, Richard. "What Is Cultural Studies Anyway?" *Social Text*, no. 16 (December 1, 1986): 38–80. doi:10.2307/466285.

Johnson, Steven A. *Interface Culture.* New York: Basic Books, 1999.

Kafer, Alison. "Amputated Desire, Resistant Desire: Female Amputees in the Devotee Community." Chicago, 2000. http://www.disabilityworld.org/June-July2000/Women/SDS.htm.

———. *Feminist, Queer, Crip.* Bloomington: Indiana University Press, 2013.

Kelly, Brian, David Sloan, Stephen Brown, et al. "Accessibility 2.0: Next Steps for Web Accessibility." *Journal of Access Services* 6, no. 1–2 (2009): 265–94. doi:10.1080/15367960802301028.

Kennedy, Helen. *Net Work: Ethics and Values in Web Design.* New York: Palgrave Macmillan, 2011.

Kirkpatrick, Bill. "'A Blessed Boon': Radio, Disability, Governmentality, and the Discourse of the 'Shut-In,' 1920–1930." *Critical Studies in Media Communication* 29, no. 3 (2012): 165–84. doi:10.1080/15295036.2011.631554.

———. "Bringing Blue Skies Down to Earth: Citizen Policymaking in Negotiations for Cable Television, 1965–1975." *Television & New Media* 13, no. 4 (2012): 307–28. doi:10.1177/1527476411412604.

Kirschenbaum, Matthew G. *Mechanisms: New Media and the Forensic Imagination.* Cambridge, Mass.: MIT Press, 2008.

Krauss, Rosalind E. "Reinventing the Medium." *Critical Inquiry* 25, no. 2 (Winter 1999): 289–305.

Kuppers, Petra. *Disability Culture and Community Performance: Find a Strange and Twisted Shape.* New York: Palgrave Macmillan, 2011.

Lane, Harlan. "Construction of Deafness." In *The Disability Studies Reader*, ed. Lennard J. Davis. Second edition, 79–92. New York: Routledge, 2006.

Lazar, Jonathan, Alfreda Dudley-Sponaugle, and Kisha-Dawn Greenidge. "Improving Web Accessibility: A Study of Webmaster Perceptions." *Computers in Human Behavior* 20, no. 2 (March 2004): 269–88. doi:10.1016/j.chb.2003.10.018.

Lessig, Lawrence. *Remix: Making Art and Commerce Thrive in the Hybrid Economy.* New York: Penguin Press, 2008.

Lievrouw, Leah A. "The Information Environment and Universal Service." *The Information Society* 16, no. 2 (2000): 155–59.

Lilly, Erica B., and Connie Van Fleet. "Wired But Not Connected: Accessibility of Academic Library Home Pages." *Reference Librarian* 67/68 (1999): 5.

Linton, Simi. *Claiming Disability: Knowledge and Identity.* New York: New York University Press, 1998.

Livingstone, Sonia. "Media Literacy and the Challenge of New Information and Communication Technologies." *Communication Review* 7, no. 1 (2004): 3–14.

Long, Alex B. "Introducing the New and Improved Americans with Disabilities Act: Assessing the ADA Amendments Act of 2008." *SSRN eLibrary* 103 (2008): 217.

Mace, Ronald L., Graeme John Hardie, and Jaine P. Place. *Accessible Environments: Toward Universal Design.* Center for Universal Design, North Carolina State University, 1990.

Manovich, Lev. *The Language of New Media.* Cambridge, Mass.: MIT Press, 2001.

———. *Software Takes Command.* INT edition. New York and London: Bloomsbury Academic, 2013.

Marwick, Alice Emily. *Status Update: Celebrity, Publicity, and Branding in the Social Media Age.* New Haven, Conn.: Yale University Press, 2013.

Marx, Nick. "'The Missing Link Moment': Web Comedy in New Media Industries." *The Velvet Light Trap* 68 (Fall 2011): 14–23.

McLaughlin, Rhett James, and Charles Lincoln "Link" Neal, "CAPTION FAIL: Lady Gaga Putt-Putt Rally," 2011, http://www.youtube.com/watch?v=hVNrkXM3TTI.

McRuer, Robert. *Crip Theory: Cultural Signs of Queerness and Disability.* New York: New York University Press, 2006.

McRuer, Robert, and Anna Mollow. *Sex and Disability.* Durham, N.C.: Duke University Press, 2012.

Meikle, Graham. "Social Media, Visibility, and Activism: The Kony 2012 Campaign." In *DIY Citizenship: Critical Making and Social Media,* ed. Matt Ratto and Megan Boler, 373–84. Cambridge, Mass.: MIT Press, 2014.

Merleau-Ponty, Maurice. *Phenomenology of Perception.* Revised edition. London: Routledge, 1981.

Meyrowitz, Joshua. "Multiple Media Literacies." *Journal of Communication* 48, no. 1 (1998): 96–108.

Milberry, Kate. "(Re)making the Internet: Free Software and the Social Factory Hack." In *DIY Citizenship: Critical Making and Social Media,* ed. Matt Ratto and Megan Boler, 53–64. Cambridge, Mass.: MIT Press, 2014.

Mirzoeff, Nicholas. "Blindness and Art." In *The Disability Studies Reader,* ed. Lennard J. Davis. Second edition, 379–90. New York: Routledge, 2006.

Mitchell, David, and Sharon Snyder. "Narrative Prosthesis and the Materiality of Metaphor." In *The Disability Studies Reader,* ed. Lennard J. Davis. Second edition, 205–16. New York: Routledge, 2006.

Montfort, Nick, ed. *10 PRINT CHR$(205.5+RND(1));: GOTO 10*. Cambridge, Mass.: MIT Press, 2012.

Montfort, Nick, and Ian Bogost. *Racing the Beam: The Atari Video Game System*. Platform Studies Series 1. Cambridge, Mass.: MIT Press, 2008.

Morley, David. *Media, Modernity, Technology: The Geography of the New*. New York: Routledge, 2006.

Moser, Ingunn. "Disability and the Promises of Technology: Technology, Subjectivity and Embodiment within an Order of the Normal." *Information, Communication & Society* 9, no. 3 (2006): 373–95. doi:10.1080/13691180600751348.

Murphy, Emma, Ravi Kuber, Graham McAllister, et al. "An Empirical Investigation into the Difficulties Experienced by Visually Impaired Internet Users." *Universal Access in the Information Society* 7, no. 1 (April 1, 2008): 79–91. doi:10.1007/s10209-007-0098-4.

Murray, Susan. "Digital Images, Photo-Sharing, and Our Shifting Notions of Everyday Aesthetics." *Journal of Visual Culture* 7 (2008): 147–64.

Nakamura, Lisa. *Cybertypes: Race, Ethnicity, and Identity on the Internet*. New York: Routledge, 2002.

———. "Interrogating the Digital Divide: The Political Economy of Race and Commerce in New Media." In *Society Online: The Internet in Context*, ed. Philip N. Howard and Steve Jones, 71–85. Thousand Oaks, Calif.: Sage, 2004.

National Telecommunications and Information Administration. *Falling Through the Net: A Survey of the "Have Nots" in Rural and Urban America*. Washington: U.S. Department of Commerce, July 1995. www.ntia.doc.gov/ntiahome/fallingthru.html.

Neff, Gina. *Venture Labor: Work and the Burden of Risk in Innovative Industries*. Cambridge, Mass.: MIT Press, 2012.

Norden, Martin F. *The Cinema of Isolation: A History of Physical Disability in the Movies*. New Brunswick, N.J.: Rutgers University Press, 1994.

Norman, Donald A. *The Design of Everyday Things*. New York: Basic Books, 2002.

Oliver, Michael. "The Social Model in Context." In *Rethinking Normalcy: A Disability Studies Reader*, ed. Tanya Titchkosky and Rod Michalko, 19–30. Toronto: Canadian Scholars Press, 2009.

O'Toole, Corbett Joan. "Disclosing Our Relationships to Disabilities: An Invitation for Disability Studies Scholars." *Disability Studies Quarterly* 33, no. 2 (2013). http://dsq-sds.org/article/view/3708/3226.

Ouellette, Laurie. *Viewers Like You? How Public TV Failed the People*. New York: Columbia University Press, 2002.

Perlman, Allison. "Feminists in the Wasteland—The National Organization for Women and Television Reform." *Feminist Media Studies* 7, no. 4 (2007): 413. doi:10.1080/14680770701631612.

Price, Margaret. *Mad at School: Rhetorics of Mental Disability and Academic Life*. Ann Arbor: University of Michigan Press, 2011.

Pullin, Graham. *Design Meets Disability*. Cambridge, Mass.: MIT Press, 2009.

Ratto, Matt, and Megan Boler, eds. *DIY Citizenship: Critical Making and Social Media.* Cambridge, Mass.: MIT Press, 2014.

Samuels, Ellen. "Critical Divides: Judith Butler's Body Theory and the Question of Disability." *NWSA Journal* 14, no. 3 (Fall 2002): 58.

Schalk, Sami. "Coming to Claim Crip: Disidentification with/in Disability Studies." *Disability Studies Quarterly* 33, no. 2 (2013). http://dsq-sds.org/article/view/3705.

Schneider, Steven M., and Kirsten A. Foot. "Web Sphere Analysis: An Approach to Studying Online Action." In *Virtual Methods: Issues in Social Research on the Internet*, ed. Christine Hine, 157–70. Oxford: Berg, 2005.

Schudson, Michael. *Advertising, the Uneasy Persuasion.* New York: Basic Books, 1986.

Shneiderman, Ben. "Preface." In *Universal Usability: Designing Computer Interfaces for Diverse User Populations*, ed. Jonathan Lazar. First edition, ix–xvi. Hoboken, N.J.: Wiley, 2007.

Shuttleworth, Russell. "Bridging Theory and Experience: A Critical-Interpretive Ethnography of Sexuality and Disability." In *Sex and Disability*, ed. Robert McRuer and Anna Mollow, 54–68. Durham, N.C.: Duke University Press, 2012.

Shuttleworth, Russell, and Linda Mona. "Introduction to the Symposium." *Disability Studies Quarterly* 22, no. 4 (October 15, 2002). http://dsq-sds.org/article/view/368.

Siebers, Tobin. "A Sexual Culture for Disabled People." In *Sex and Disability*, ed. Robert McRuer and Anna Mollow, 37–53. Durham, N.C.: Duke University Press, 2012.

———. *Disability Theory.* Corporealities. Ann Arbor: University of Michigan Press, 2008.

Sterne, Jonathan. *MP3: The Meaning of a Format.* Durham, N.C.: Duke University Press, 2012.

Strauss, Karen Peltz. *A New Civil Right: Telecommunications Equality for Deaf and Hard of Hearing Americans.* First edition. Washington: Gallaudet University Press, 2006.

Streeter, Thomas. *The Net Effect: Romanticism, Capitalism, and the Internet.* New York: New York University Press, 2010.

———. *Selling the Air: A Critique of the Policy of Commercial Broadcasting in the United States.* Chicago: University of Chicago Press, 1996.

Tapscott, Don, and Anthony D. Williams. *Wikinomics: How Mass Collaboration Changes Everything.* Expanded edition. New York: Portfolio Hardcover, 2008.

Theofanos, Mary Frances, and Janice (Ginny) Redish. "Bridging the Gap: Between Accessibility and Usability." *Interactions* 10, no. 6 (November 2003): 36–51. doi:10.1145/947226.947227.

Thoreau, Estelle. "Ouch! An Examination of the Self-Representation of Disabled People on the Internet." *Journal of Computer Mediated Communication* 11, no. 2 (2006): 442–68.

Titchkosky, Tanya. *The Question of Access: Disability, Space, Meaning.* Toronto: University of Toronto Press, 2011.

Tripp, Lisa M. "'The Computer Is Not for You to Be Looking Around, It Is for School-work': Challenges for Digital Inclusion as Latino Immigrant Families Negotiate Children's Access to the Internet." *New Media & Society* 13, no. 4 (June 1, 2011): 552–67. doi:10.1177/1461444810375293.

Tryon, Chuck. *On-Demand Culture: Digital Delivery and the Future of Movies*. New Brunswick, N.J.: Rutgers University Press, 2013.

The Union of the Physically Impaired Against Segregation and The Disability Alliance. *Fundamental Principles of Disability*. London: 1975. http://www.leeds.ac.uk/disability-studies/archiveuk/UPIAS/fundamental%20principles.pdf.

Vaidhyanathan, Siva. *The Googlization of Everything: (And Why We Should Worry)*. First edition. Berkeley: University of California Press, 2011.

Valentine, Gill, and Tracey Skelton. "'An Umbilical Cord to the World': The Role of the Internet in D/deaf People's Information and Communication Practices." *Information, Communication & Society* 12, no. 1 (February 2009): 44–65.

Van Dijck, José. *The Culture of Connectivity: A Critical History of Social Media*. New York: Oxford University Press, 2013.

———. "Users Like You? Theorizing Agency in User-Generated Content." *Media, Culture & Society* 31, no. 1 (January 2009): 41–58.

Van Dijk, Jan A. G. M. *The Deepening Divide*. Thousand Oaks, Calif.: Sage, 2005.

Vanderheiden, Gregg C. "Fundamental Principles and Priority Setting for Universal Usability." In *ACM Conference on Universal Usability: Proceedings on the 2000 Conference on Universal Usability, 16–17 Nov. 2000*, 32–37. Association for Computing Machinery, 2000.

Vanderheiden, Gregg C., and Wendy A. Chisholm. "Design of HTML Pages to Increase Their Accessibility to Users with Disabilities: Strategies for Today and Tomorrow." *SIGWEB Newsl.* 5, no. 1 (1996): 9–20. doi:10.1145/232782.232786.

Wagner, Kathryn, and Alexis Lothian. "Access and Fandom: Disability Studies from a Feminist Science Fiction Perspective." *Disability Studies Quarterly* 34, no. 2 (March 27, 2014). http://dsq-sds.org/article/view/4284.

"WAI Markup Guidelines Working Group Charter," August 1997, http://www.w3.org/WAI/GL/charter.html.

Walters, Suzanna Danuta. *The Tolerance Trap: How God, Genes, and Good Intentions Are Sabotaging Gay Equality*. New York: New York University Press, 2014.

Warner, Kristen. "Where Do We Go from Here: Musings on Issa Rae and Black Content Producers." *In Media Res | Media Commons*, May 3, 2013. http://mediacommons.futureofthebook.org/imr/2013/05/03/where-do-we-go-here-musings-issa-rae-and-black-content-producers.

Warschauer, Mark. *Technology and Social Inclusion: Rethinking the Digital Divide*. Cambridge, Mass.: MIT Press, 2003.

Web Accessibility Initiative, "WAI Page Author Guideline Conference Call—July" (World Wide Web Consortium, July 8, 1999), http://www.w3.org/WAI/ GL/8July99.html.

"Web Content Accessibility Guidelines Working Group (WCAG WG) Charter," *World Wide Web Consortium: Web Accessibility Initiative*, July 7, 2010, http://www.w3.org/2004/04/wcag-charter.

Wendell, Susan. *The Rejected Body: Feminist Philosophical Reflections on Disability*. New York: Routledge, 1996.

White, Michele. *The Body and the Screen: Theories of Internet Spectatorship*. Cambridge, Mass.: MIT Press, 2006.

————. "Where Do You Want to Sit Today? Computer Programmers' Static Bodies and Disability." *Information, Communication & Society* 9, no. 3 (2006): 396–416. doi:10.1080/13691180600751363.

Williams, Raymond. *Keywords: A Vocabulary of Culture and Society*. Revised edition. New York: Oxford University Press, 1985.

Williamson, Bess. "Getting a Grip: Disability in American Industrial Design of the Late Twentieth Century." *Winterthur Portfolio* 46, no. 4 (Winter 2012): 213–36.

Winner, Langdon. "Do Artifacts Have 'Politics'?" In *The Social Shaping of Technology: How the Refrigerator Got Its Hum*, ed. Donald MacKenzie and Judy Wajcman, 26–38. Philadelphia: Open University Press, 1985.

"World Wide Web Consortium (W3C) Launches International Web Accessibility Initiative" (World Wide Web Consortium, April 7, 1997), 10/24/08, http://www.w3.org/Press/WAI-Launch.html.

Zittrain, Jonathan. *The Future of the Internet and How to Stop It*. New Haven, Conn.: Yale University Press, 2008.

INDEX

Bold page numbers refer to figures.

ABOUT THE AUTHOR

Elizabeth Ellcessor is Assistant Professor of Cinema and Media Studies in the Media School at Indiana University–Bloomington. Her research focuses on disability, digital media, and access as they relate to public politics, cultural engagement, and participation. In a previous life, she was a web developer for a nonprofit organization.